A

MW01503659

The Importance of the Dissertation in Practice (DiP):

A Resource Guide for EdD Students, Their Committee Members and Advisors, and Departmental and University Leaders Involved with EdD Programs

"As we consider the future and relevance of our education organizations, our leaders must be prepared to understand systems, identify problems of practice, work to remove barriers, and create solutions that are equitable and look to the future. The process and approach of the dissertation in practice sets this course. The chapters in this book are informative and essential for any practitioner-scholar doctoral program that truly wants to build organizational human capital and activate principled change."

Carole G. Basile, Dean
Arizona State University
Mary Lou Fulton Teachers College

"The Dissertation in Practice (DiP) is a vital bridge between research and praxis in academia, demanding nuanced insights to effectively navigate it. This book, The Importance of the Dissertation in Practice (DiP): A Resource Guide for EdD Students, Their Committee Members and Advisors, and Departmental and University Leaders Involved with EdD Programs, provides an indispensable set of perspectives, strategies, and foundational knowledge that are essential for understanding DiP's methods, context, and structures. Offering expert insights and covering diverse themes, questions, and information, this book serves as an invaluable resource for EdD programs, faculty, scholarly-practitioners, and anyone keen on exploring, understanding, and supporting the dissertation in practice with thoughtful rigor and innovation."

Danah Henriksen, PhD (she/her)
Associate Professor of Leadership & Innovation;
Mary Lou Fulton Teachers College
Affiliate Faculty; Herberger Institute for Design and the Arts
Arizona State University

"Dr. Everson and her colleagues offer a book that helps address a compelling problem of practice for education doctoral programs: how do we provide faculty and students with the foundational knowledge to understand the origins, purpose, and structure of an applied, contextualized research capstone for aspiring scholar practitioners? The authors of The Importance of the Dissertation in Practice offer a multitude of valuable perspectives that help Ed.D. program directors, faculty, and students effectively transition to more powerful and relevant capstone experiences."

Gary Houchens, PhD
Director, Educational Leadership Doctoral Program
Western Kentucky University

"My DiP was a reflective study that brought theory and practice together to better serve my students, college, and community. I used my voice to bring about change in my classroom and encouraged my students to use their agency as they grow and develop while maintaining an awareness of the world around them. "The Importance of the Dissertation in Practice (DiP): A Resource Guide for EdD Students, Their Committee Members and Advisors, and Departmental and University Leaders Involved with EdD Programs" encompasses the plans and process developed in EdD programs that made my experience possible. I encourage reading this book for all to see the planning and devotion by those involved in creating an enlightened experience for all EdD students.

Sherisse G. Jackson, EdD Graduate,
University of South Carolina and DiP of the Year Award Winner

The Importance of the Dissertation in Practice (DiP)

The mission of **The Coming of Age of the Education Doctorate** series is to present volumes of research and work focused on the improvement of the Education Doctorate (EdD) and, over the course of the past 14 years, the efforts that faculty and schools of education around the US and the world have made to professionalize this degree for the advanced preparation of educational practitioners. Specifically, this series will highlight efforts to improve the purpose, curriculum, and milestone experiences of the degree, in addition to highlighting the work of those who have graduated from redesigned EdD programs. The series will consist of print books, e-books, and fractional digital content for faculty, pre-service teachers, practitioners, and libraries.

Dr. Jill Alexa Perry is the Executive Director of the Carnegie Project on the Educational Doctorate (CPED) and an Associate Professor of Practice in the Educational Foundations, Organizations, and Policy at the University of Pittsburgh. Her research focuses on professional doctorate preparation in education, organizational change in higher education, and faculty leadership roles. Currently she is researching the ways EdD programs teach practitioners to utilize research evidence. She teaches and coaches how to teach Improvement Science in EdD programs. Her books include *The Improvement Science Dissertation in Practice, The EdD and the Scholarly Practitioner*, and *In Their Own Words: A Journey to the Stewardship of the Practice in Education*. Dr. Perry is a graduate of the University of Maryland, where she received her PhD in International Education Policy. She holds an MA in Higher Education Administration and a BA in Spanish and International Studies from Boston College. She has over 25 years of experience in leadership and program development in education and teaching experience at the elementary, secondary, undergraduate, and graduate levels in the United States and abroad. She is a Fulbright Scholar (Germany) and a returned Peace Corps Volunteer (Paraguay).

The Importance of the Dissertation in Practice (DiP)

A Resource Guide for EdD Students, Their Committee Members and Advisors, and Departmental and University Leaders Involved with EdD Programs

EDITED BY Kimberlee K. C. Everson,
Lynn Hemmer, Kelly M. Torres, and Suha R. Tamim

Myers Education Press

Gorham, Maine

Copyright © 2024| Myers Education Press, LLC

Published by Myers Education Press, LLC
P.O. Box 424
Gorham, ME 04038

Myers Education Press is an academic publisher specializing in books, e-books, and digital content in the field of education. All of our books are subjected to a rigorous peer review process and produced in compliance with the standards of the Council on Library and Information Resources.

Library of Congress Cataloging-in-Publication Data available from Library of Congress.

13-digit ISBN 978-1-9755-0557-8 (paperback)
13-digit ISBN 978-1-9755-0558-5 (library networkable e-edition)
13-digit ISBN 978-1-9755-0559-2 (consumer e-edition)

Printed in the United States of America.

All first editions printed on acid-free paper that meets the American National Standards Institute Z39-48 standard.

Books published by Myers Education Press may be purchased at special quantity discount rates for groups, workshops, training organizations, and classroom usage. Please call our customer service department at 1-800-232-0223 for details.

Cover design by Teresa Lagrange

Visit us on the web at **www.myersedpress.com** to browse our complete list of titles.

CONTENTS

Section 3: Some DiP Approaches and Formats

Section 4: Concerns and Issues

CHAPTER 1

Introduction

KIMBERLEE K. C. EVERSON, PHD

The Dissertation in Practice (DiP) is an emerging and innovative form of the dissertation that addresses complex problems of practice in various fields and contexts. Unlike traditional research-based dissertations that aim to produce new knowledge and contribute to academic disciplines, the DiP aims to produce context-dependent solutions and contribute to professional practice. The DiP is ideal for scholar-practitioners who want to advance their knowledge, skills, and leadership in their fields of practice, while also making a positive difference in the world.

The DiP has several distinctive features and characteristics that set it apart from other types of doctoral dissertations. First, the DiP focuses on the practitioner-scholar, who is both a consumer and a producer of knowledge, and who integrates theory and practice in a reflective and critical way. Second, the DiP uses innovative approaches which are collaborative and often iterative, and context-sensitive approaches to inquiry and intervention that aim to improve practice and generate learning. Third, the DiP emphasizes impact and change, which are the ultimate goals and outcomes of the student's doctoral work, and which are measured and communicated to various stakeholders. Lastly, the DiP offers a diversity of formats and structures, which allow for flexibility and customization according to the needs and preferences of students, faculty, institutions, and fields of practice.

The DiP has many benefits and challenges for students, faculty, institutions, and society. For students, the DiP provides an opportunity to pursue a doctoral degree that is relevant to their practice, that enhances their professional development and career prospects, and that allows them to make meaningful contributions to their organizations, communities, or society. For faculty, the DiP requires a shift in their roles and responsibilities from being experts and supervisors to being mentors and facilitators, as well as a shift in their epistemological and pedagogical assumptions from often being positivist and transmission-oriented to becoming constructivist and transformation-oriented. For institutions, the DiP demands a change in their policies and procedures from being rigid and standardized to being flexible and adaptive, as well as a change in their cultures and values from being competitive and exclusive to being collaborative and inclusive. For society, the DiP promises a potential impact on social problems and issues that are complex and urgent, as well as a potential contribution to social justice and equity.

However, acceptable best practices surrounding the DiP face many gaps and needs in the current literature and practice. There is a lack of consensus on the definition, purpose, scope, criteria, and quality of the DiP among scholars, practitioners, policymakers, accrediting bodies, and employers. There is a lack of evidence on the effectiveness, outcomes, and impact of the DiP on students, faculty, institutions, fields of practice, and society. There is a lack of guidance on the design, delivery, assessment, evaluation, dissemination, and improvement of the DiP for students, faculty, institutions, fields of practice, and society.

This book aims to address these gaps and needs by exploring the DiP from multiple perspectives and dimensions. It draws on the experiences and insights of leading scholars and practitioners who have been involved in developing, implementing, teaching, mentoring, researching, evaluating, or graduating students from various EdD programs in the United States. It covers a range of topics that are relevant and important for understanding and advancing the DiP as a form of doctoral dissertation that responds to the changing needs and demands of professional practice in the 21st century.

The following is an overview of the sections and chapters of this book.

Section 1: Background to Understanding the DiP

- Chapter 2: The history and evolution of the DiP and how it differs from other types of doctoral dissertations. In this chapter, the origins and development of the DiP within EdD programs are traced, and its features and characteristics are compared with other forms of doctoral dissertations.

- Chapter 3: The roles and competencies of the practitioner-scholar and how they can be developed and assessed in the DiP and described. In this chapter, authors discuss the value of the DiP and the EdD, and the identity and function of the practitioner-scholar within those frameworks.

Section 2: Evaluation and Important Traits of the DiP

- Chapter 4: The evaluation of the DiP in terms of quality, rigor, relevance, and impact. In this chapter, the authors discuss the process that the Carnegie Project for the Educational Doctorate (CPED) DiP award committee followed to develop a rubric for DiPs over a number of years.

- Chapter 5: The problem of practice (PoP) as the central focus and driver of the DiP. In this chapter, the author explores the concept and nature of the PoP, which is a complex and urgent issue or challenge that practitioners face in their fields or contexts. They also examine how PoP issues surround the selection of a PoP.

- Chapter 6: The context and conditions of the PoP as factors that influence the DiP process and outcome. In this chapter, the authors investigate the role and influence of the context and conditions of the PoP on the DiP. They provide several examples of context and conditions within student DiPs.

- Chapter 7: The integration and application of different types of knowledge in the DiP. In this chapter, authors explore how various forms and sources of knowledge can be combined and utilized in the DiP, using the example of Indigenous knowledge in Hawaii.

- Chapter 8: The identification and implementation of focal patterns of action in the DiP. In this chapter, the author investigates how specific actions or interventions can be designed and executed in the DiP to address the PoP. She also describes how focal patterns of action can be planned, monitored, adapted, and sustained in the DiP.

- Chapter 9: The methods and designs for conducting inquiry and intervention in the DiP. In this chapter, authors discuss the methodological and design choices and challenges that face the practitioner-scholar in the DiP. They also review the strengths and limitations of quantitative, qualitative, and mixed methods approaches with examples.

- Chapter 10: The impact of the DiP on practice, practitioner, programs, and society. In this chapter, authors examine the potential impacts of the DiP on various stakeholders, programs, members of the community, and the researcher.

Section 3: Some DiP Approaches and Formats

- Chapter 11: The role and contribution of improvement science to the DiP. In this chapter, the author discusses his university's use of the disquisition as a DiP capstone that uses improvement science. He introduces improvement science as a systematic approach to improving practice through inquiry and intervention.

- Chapter 12: The support and enrichment of the DiP by action research. The author discusses the history, goals, and various forms of action research including: participatory action research (PAR), youth participatory action research (YPAR), and collaborative inquiry.

- Chapter 13: The advantages and disadvantages of the group dissertation, or participatory teams, in the DiP. In this chapter, authors examine the concept and practice of the group dissertation, which is a collective product from a team of students who work on a common PoP. The authors also analyze the benefits and challenges of the group dissertation.

- Chapter 14: The alternative formats and models for organizing and presenting the DiP. In this chapter, authors explore the large diversity and flexibility of the formats, genres, and locales for the change or intervention.

Section 4: Concerns and Issues

- Chapter 15: The mentoring and support of students throughout the DiP process. In this chapter, the author discusses the definition of and various theories surrounding mentoring students; she describes how mentoring might be used particularly within professional EdD programs.

- Chapter 16: The process issues and dilemmas that arise in the DiP and how they can be resolved or managed. In this chapter, authors identify some common issues and dilemmas that students, faculty, institutions, fields of practice, and society may encounter in the DiP process. They also suggest some possible solutions or strategies for resolving or managing these issues and dilemmas in constructive and ethical ways.

- Chapter 17: Issues surrounding public access to regenerative artificial intelligence (AI). In this chapter, the author describes the risks of students using AI to cheat, the benefits of allowing students some use of AI as part of their DiPs, and some of the ways in which AI might best be used as part of the DiP project and writing.

- Chapter 18: The emerging trends and future directions for the

DiP. In this chapter, authors look ahead and anticipate some possible trends and directions for the DiP in the future. They also propose some recommendations and implications for the development, implementation, research, evaluation, and improvement of the DiP as a form of doctoral education that responds to the changing needs and demands of professional practice in the 21st century.

We hope that this book will be useful and informative for a wide range of readers who are interested in or involved in the DiP as a form of doctoral dissertation that addresses complex problems of practice in various fields and contexts. Our intended audience includes students, faculty, administrators, policymakers, practitioners, researchers, evaluators, and employers who are engaged in developing, implementing, teaching, mentoring, researching, evaluating, or graduating from various EdD programs. Our aims are to provide a comprehensive and critical overview of the DiP, to share the experiences and insights of leading scholars and practitioners who have been involved in the DiP, to address the gaps and needs in the current literature and practice of the DiP, and to offer recommendations and implications for the future of the DiP. We hope to enhance the understanding and appreciation of the DiP as an emerging and innovative form of doctoral dissertation that responds to the changing needs and demands of professional practice in the 21st century, and to contribute to the improvement and advancement of the DiP as a valuable and impactful mode of inquiry and intervention that makes a positive difference in the world.

We invite feedback and dialogue from our readers on the themes and questions that we have explored in this book. We welcome your comments, suggestions, critiques, examples, stories, or questions that can enrich our collective knowledge and practice. We also encourage you to share your own experiences and insights on the DiP with us and with others who may benefit from them. We look forward to hearing from you and engaging with you in constructive and collaborative conversations about the DiP.

SECTION 1:

Background to Understanding the DiP

CHAPTER 2

The History of the DiP:

Dissertation in What??

JILL ALEXA PERRY, PHD

*"The era of the dissertation as a single-authored piece of
'original' scholarship is nearing its end."* –Barton, 2005, p. 5.

D r. Barton made this statement in 2005 as part of his own dissertation entitled, *Dissertations: Past, Present, and Future.*
Dr. Barton's field is English. His work focused on the relevance of
the dissertation in the humanities. What Dr. Barton may not have
known, however, is that similar conversations about the dissertation
in education doctorates, both PhD and EdD, had been taking place
throughout the 20th century. In 2005, the Carnegie Project on the
Education Doctorate (CPED) had not yet begun, but Dr. Barton's
words were a foreshadowing of CPED discussions about the purpose, format, and relevance of the EdD dissertation as distinct from
a PhD dissertation. He posed questions such as: *should it be original scholarship? should it be single-authored?* which were central
to CPED discussions about what a dissertation experience for a professional practice doctorate should be and how it should differ from
a traditional PhD dissertation experience. In fact, understanding
the dissertation in the EdD was the hardest question that CPED
members faced early on and often continue to face.

After almost 17 years in existence, CPED members have come
to some understanding of the culminating experience of EdD programs, albeit not a perfect nor clear one. This book endeavors to
improve our understanding by unpacking the perennial questions

that surround the distinction of the CPED design-concept, a *Dissertation in Practice* (DiP), as compared to a traditional 5-chapter dissertation. In support of this effort, I offer a history of the DiP as it was developed by CPED, as well as a discussion of why it is encouraged as the culminating product of the EdD degree. First, I discuss the history of the dissertation in general—how it came to be and the main purpose of this exercise. Next, I provide background on CPED and how the network of member institutions and their faculty settled on the idea of a Dissertation in Practice. Finally, I describe some of what the CPED network has learned by employing the DiP in their EdD programs.

Why Do We Have a Dissertation in Education?

I frequently ask faculty and students this question. To my surprise, only once or twice has anyone been able to answer. My initial reaction to the lack of response is shock that this product has been given such high status in the world of education, yet few know exactly why we require it of our students. The dissertation exists in education for two reasons. First, education is both a discipline and a field (Richardson, 2006). As a discipline, education offers the PhD, which has traditionally been governed by the arts and sciences and which requires an independent body of research as a culminating product (see more information below). As a field, education is a profession. However, because education does not have a licensure body of any kind like other professions such as law and medicine (Wergin, 2011; Perry, in press), to confer a doctoral degree requires some form of evaluation or assessment that demonstrates the student has gained skills, knowledge, and dispositions of their field of study. Traditionally, the dissertation has served the purpose of the final examination in fields that do not have such licensure bodies (Colwill, 2018).

What, then, is so special about a dissertation that it has been given the status of final assessment to conferring a degree? The Royal Literary Fund (RLF) notes that the word dissertation was first used in 1651, where it was described as "an extended written treatment of a subject" (n.d.). In fields such as English, history, or political science, the dissertation provides evidence that the student has become an expert in their field through extensive study and an extensive written piece that both situates this student in the broader literature, as well as provides new knowledge to support further learning in such fields. The RLF also notes that the Latin origins of the word "dissertatre" means to debate (n.d.), which furthers the purpose of the dissertation to mean the building of an argument about a selected topic of study. The exercise of debate often culminates in a defense of the work among other experts in the field of study.

The birth of this exercise in a university setting comes from German universities, which began to require the dissertation in the late 18th century. At first an exercise in demonstrating extensive study of a subject, by the 19th century, German universities introduced the notion of *research* into academic study (McClelland, 1980). This merging of teaching and learning with research resulted in the modern model of the research university, which had a great impact on shaping the modern dissertation. The German model of a dissertation emulated scientific experiments asking students to include methodology, results and findings, and an analysis and interpretation of their findings (McClelland, 1980). Because many early U.S. college administrators were educated in Germany, the German model of a research university and the research dissertation were brought into the U.S. university system.

Therefore, the dissertation has become the demonstration of an extensive research study that builds new knowledge for a discipline of study. In PhD disciplines, this model makes sense as those who study this degree seek to become content knowledge or area experts. In education, the dissertation is a bit more complicated and comes with much confusion and lack of clarity of purpose and format. This confusion stems from the century-long debate about the difference between the PhD in Education and the Education Doctorate (EdD). The history of this debate can be read elsewhere (Perry 2012, Foster et al., 2023), but it is important to understand the purpose for each degree which then trickles into the purpose of the dissertation for each degree. Historically, the education doctorate was meant to serve practitioners seeking higher degrees in the leadership of K-12 school systems that were rapidly flourishing in the early 1900s. However, when the degree was created and designed by Henry Holmes at the newly minted Graduate School of Education at Harvard College (now Harvard University), practitioner needs were not accounted for. Rather, the German model of a research doctorate was adopted, and the number of courses and requirements were altered to "lessen" the amount of work needed for the degree (Perry, 2012). In terms of the dissertation, early studies indicate that the EdD dissertation tended to be more focused on practical issues and the application of existing knowledge to practice (Carter, 1956; Freeman, 1931). Despite these aspects that seemed geared towards preparing practitioners, the doctorate remained confused as some institutions used it to prepare researchers while others used it to prepare practitioners. The dissertation continued to be a "tough and controversial aspect of doctoral study," wrote education historian Lawrence Cremin in 1978 (p. 21-22). Cremin (1978) himself was inclined "to abolish it ... as it is too much a mimicking of the PhD" (p. 21-22).

CPED and the Dissertation in Practice (DiP)

In the few years before the birth of CPED, as the EdD vs. PhD debate was reaching a climax in the U.S., Andrews and Grogan (2005) appealed to colleagues in Educational Leadership EdD programs to "remove the EdD dissertation from the PhD straight jacket" (p. 13); citing that the PhD "concept" greatly hindered the EdD in developing an exercise that better suited the purpose of the degree to prepare Scholarly Practitioners. The authors argued, "the PhD format has done more to hinder than to help the EdD provide practitioners with the knowledge, skills, behaviors and dispositions needed for effective leadership in educational settings" (Andrews & Grogan, 2005, p. 10). All too often, the focus on practical issues and application of existing knowledge to practice meant a watering down of the dissertation experience, which earned the EdD the title of "PhD-lite" (Shulman et al., 2006). It was clear that tackling the dissertation was and is key to distinguishing the EdD as a professional practice doctorate.

CPED and its effort to make the dissertation front and center to the distinction conversation has made strong efforts to respond to Andrews and Grogan's appeal. As a network of education faculty, administrators, and students, working at a grassroots level (Perry, 2013), CPED members collaborated to provide a framework that would allow EdD programs to be distinguished as professional practice doctorates. At the 2010 June convening, just three years after CPED began, faculty members developed a name and definition for the goals and purpose of a CPED-influenced EdD program, the Scholarly Practitioner, or one who:

- blends practical wisdom with professional skills and knowledge to name, frame, and solve problems of practice;

- uses practical research and applied theories as tools for change;

- understands the importance of equity and social justice;

- disseminates their work in multiple ways; and

- resolves problems of practice by collaborating with key stakeholders, including the university, the educational institution, the community, and individuals (CPED, 2010).

This definition is meant to highlight the fact that practitioners "are boundary spanners ... [who] have one foot in the world of the academy and one in the world of practice" (Colwill, 2018, p. 17). The definition further highlights the strong role of applied research as a means for impacting and changing practice.

Defining the EdD dissertation required CPED members to think about the experience with The Scholarly Practitioner definition in mind. After nearly three days of discussion about the goals and purpose of this culminating exercise (and several hours of wordsmithing), the members settled on the title, Dissertation in Practice (DiP), and the definition, "a scholarly endeavor that impacts a complex problem of practice" (CPED, 2010). The fact that the title of "Dissertation in Practice" is not a major diversion from "dissertation" is intentional and serves two purposes. First, many universities classify their EdD programs as "research doctorates," which requires that the work be held to the rules and regulations that govern the traditional research doctorate, the PhD, such as issues of purpose, format, length, etc. These universities are not allowed to change the name of the experience. The title of Dissertation in Practice, supports these institutions by keeping the word dissertation in the title of the experience while also offering other institutions that can be more flexible a title that is distinct. Second, keeping dissertation in the title connotates the importance of research in the experience. Adding "in practice" extends the purpose of the experience to focus on the role of doing research in, for, and with, practice.

The DiP definition supports this purpose. CPED members have been adamant that research and inquiry are extremely important to improving practice. Therefore, the definition highlights a "scholarly endeavor" or research experience that might include, but also go beyond, the traditional dissertation purpose of knowledge creation. The word "impact" builds on the idea of going beyond knowledge creation to compel the work to have a clear impact on practice. The focus of the DiP is a "complex problem of practice" which CPED members defined as "a persistent, contextualized, and specific issue embedded in the work of a professional practitioner, the addressing of which has the potential to result in improved understanding, experience, and outcomes" (CPED, 2010). The DiP definition brings together traditional dissertation purposes (demonstration of an extensive research study that builds new knowledge for a field of study) with an early understanding of EdD research (focus on practical issues and application of existing knowledge to practice) to signal the importance of quality, rigorous research as a tool for changing professional practice, and a skill that the Scholarly Practitioner takes with them and continues once they graduate from their program. An EdD student undertaking a DiP is expected to apply scholarship, inquiry, and research to a broad educational problem that they see playing out and face daily in their organization and work.

Further, the DiP is built into EdD programs in that it is something students work towards (Perry, in press). EdD programs are crafted to provide students with the skills to be successful in this culminating experience. Storey and Maughan (2016) noted that the "DiP is not merely an end product, but rather an outcome of the EdD-process [which] emphasizes scholarly practitioner knowledge, experience, and reflection" (p. 11). Further, Kennedy et al. (2018) suggest:

By acknowledging and promoting contextualized, evolving inter-relationships between scholar, knowledge, and application, the dissertation in practice reflects a constructionist epistemology underlying practitioner scholarship. This epistemological founda-tion positions practitioner scholarship to bridge the divide between research, theory, and practice. Practitioner scholars can study complex educational issues that perpetuate social injustices in par-ticular contexts and figure out how to improve them in collabora-tion with relevant stakeholders (p. 6).

These authors stress two important distinctions of EdD pro-grams and the role of the DiP. First, the DiP is something that stu-dents are trained to do, that their carefully crafted EdD program has woven into the program and provides opportunities for the student to develop the skills needed to undertake an EdD. Second, the DiP is a demonstration of the research and inquiry skills that students will continue to use in practice beyond the DiP. To that end, the DiP becomes the replacement for licensure as the evaluation or assess-ment that demonstrates the EdD student has gained the skills, knowledge, and dispositions to become a Scholarly Practitioner.

What Does the DiP Look Like in Practice?

Periodically, CPED gathers data to learn how its members are implementing the Framework for the (re)design of their EdD pro-grams. Learning about the DiP has helped us to understand how progress towards the DiP definition has been made. For instance, in 2013, university members were surveyed about the types of methodologies used in DiPs. We saw a shift towards more applied methodologies, with 25% of membership reporting the use of action research, 25% reporting the use of evaluation methodologies (N=56). The other 50% were still employing more traditional meth-odologies. We also learned that year that DiPs had begun to see an increase in multiple-authored products. Forty-five percent of mem-bers reported co-authored or group dissertations (N=39).

In 2017, 60% of membership (N=53) responded to the CPED survey. We learned that 35% of members implemented the DiP process through the program. In this same study, we learned that 87% of programs allowed students to choose their own problems of practice and 17% chose the problems for students. Additionally, 80% responded that the purpose of the DiP was to teach students an applied research skill. With the increase in membership from 56 (2013) to 101 (2017), we saw a more traditional 5-chapter dissertation format.

In 2020, with 125 members, 90 institutions responded to the CPED survey. We learned that 63% of responding members used the term "dissertation in practice" at their institutions. Sixty-five percent reported that the DiP process began in the first or second year of the program. With this survey, we also learned that dissertation committees were mostly comprised of three members (71% reporting), with 83% allowing practitioners with a doctorate to participate on these committees. With this most recent survey, we also learned that many CPED-influenced EdD programs were making strides in changing the content, purpose, and formats of their culminating experience, the DiP. Though not all institutions are able to completely redesign their DiP to be fully distinguished from a traditional dissertation, we have seen small shifts take place. For example, the purpose of DiPs has shifted from finding gaps in the literature to focusing on problems of practice. Inquiry questions have replaced traditional research questions as they focus on learning about problems of practice. Literature, however, is one area that might not have shifted as much. Some DiPs still require traditional, comprehensive reviews of extant literature while others might use literature to frame problems, and still others might include a review of the local context to situate the problem in both the literature and the local setting. Methodology is an area that has shifted towards applied methodologies, though traditional methodologies are still being used. Finally, the completed product might include recommendations like a traditional dissertation, or it might include multiple formats that can be used in practice. Table 2.1 offers a range of DiP formats starting with more traditional to non-traditional formats. Each row includes a description of how DiP components have shifted away from traditional roles towards a "scholarly endeavor that impacts a complex problem of practice" (CPED, 2010).

Table 2.1

DiP Formats and Purpose of Components–
2020 CPED Member Survey

	More Traditional 5-Chapter DiP	Less than 5-Chapter DiPs	DiP conducted by a Group of Students	Other, non-Traditional Formats
Purpose	Impact problem of practice within a practitioner setting	Impact problem of practice within a practitioner setting	Team-based collaborations to complete projects surrounding problem of practice	Document the scholarly development of leadership expertise in organizational improvement
Inquiry/ Research Questions	Focused on problem of practice	Focused on problem of practice	Collaboratively pursue the same questions but in varied settings/ contexts	Focused on problems of practice within a local context
Literature	Traditional literature review	Knowledge review or traditional literature review	Collaborative review of literature related to shared theme	Review of local context, literature related to theory of action/ improvement, conceptual frameworks
Methodology	Single or Mixed methodologies, applied methodologies	Applied methodologies, mixed methodologies, plans for action	Single or Mixed methodologies, applied methodologies depending on question being pursued	Improvement process, applied methodologies
Dissemination	Recommendations for practice	Contributions to practice and description of change process or application of findings	Contributions to practice: executive summaries, policy briefs, white papers, technical reports, etc.	Multiple formats and products depending on audience and nature of problem of practice

CPED will continue to survey its members to learn about the changes to the DiP, with a new survey launched beginning in 2023. Besides member surveys, CPED has learned much over the years from in-depth reviews of individual programs implementing the DiP. We have learned that programs might select a specific methodology to teach in the program that results in all students utilizing that methodology for the DiP. Arizona State University (ASU) was an early adopter of this format with their Action Research DiPs in their EdD in Innovation and Leadership. The DiP purpose connects applied research and inquiry cycles to the role of leadership and innovation for change. Students identify a problem of practice and utilize action research starting in their first semester. As they dig into the literature, they hone their action research cycles and work towards their DiP. The program employs a unique advising model called **Learner Scholar Communities** (Olson & Clark, 2009; Buss & Allen, 2020) to guide students through the process. The resulting document includes six chapters: Context and Purpose, Review of Supporting Scholarship, Research Design, Analysis and Results, Findings, and Conclusion. This model has resulted in three ASU graduates winning the CPED DiP Award.

At Virginia Commonwealth University (VCU), students engage in a team-based program evaluation. The faculty at VCU receive Requests for Assistance (RFAs) from local and regional clients. The faculty vet these RFAs and present those selected to current students to rank their interest in working on the specific evaluation project. Students are placed into teams, and a client/team relationship is built. Students participate in four courses across the program that prepare them to go to the client in the final year to conduct the evaluation. The final product is a report to the client and a presentation to the DiP committee. A student team from VCU won the first group CPED DiP award in 2014.

At the University of Pittsburgh, the faculty have chosen Improvement Science to be the single signature methodology that students learn. Students take four Practitioner Inquiry courses across three years. In the second, third, and fourth inquiry courses, students build the early sections of their DiP: *Naming and Framing the Problem of Practice, Developing a Theory of Improvement,* and

Designing a Plan-Do-Study-Act (PDSA) research design. The final product includes three additional sections: *PDSA Results, Learning and Actions, and Leadership Reflections.* The purpose of the DiP is to teach the skills, knowledge, and dispositions that a) improve leadership skills and b) can be applied to future problems of practice. Students present their work to a committee of two to three faculty members and one practitioner.

Western Carolina University (WCU) is the first and only institution to veer from the CPED language of "dissertation in practice". Instead, they use the term "disquisition" to symbolize a parting from the traditional dissertation and a unique conceptual change (Crow et al., 2016) aimed at moving student thinking away from numbers of chapters to focus on problems of practice and appropriate interventions that might improve them. The faculty have selected Improvement Science as the signature methodology that is combined with leadership strategies. Students use literature and local context to properly identify a problem and the roots of that problem in their organization. They implement improvement change ideas and report their work in a format of their choosing so long as it includes: statement of the problem of practice, theory of improvement, improvement process, evaluation of improvement methodology, implications, and recommendations. WCU won the CPED Program of the Year award in 2021.

These are just a few of the models that CPED members have developed. Many more ideas exist, such as portfolios, thematic DiPs, modified manuscript models, policy briefs, and more. At the very least, we have seen that these different models have similarities. First, they focus on a problem of practice (PoP)–language that was not used in education dissertations a decade ago. Second, they incorporate the idea of leadership development into the process of research so that research and inquiry become a tool of leadership. Third, literature no longer serves as a haystack where the researchers must dig for a hole they might fill with their own research. Rather, literature has become a tool (Perry et al., 2020; Perry, in press) that practitioners consult to help frame a deeper understanding of problems of practice and the interventions that might serve to improve them. Fourth, formats are changing. Though not as drastically as some might like to see, we notice that the chapters are different. As noted, the use of literature is different. Chapters are shorter in length. Chapter titles focus on non-traditional components like reflection. Final chapters go beyond suggestions for future action to demonstrations of action in practice, like reports given to school boards, presentations given at national professional conferences, or summaries to be shared with stakeholders. Fifth, committees are smaller and include a practitioner. Sixth, DiPs are often woven into the program design, not only so that students can finish within shorter timeframes (e.g., three years), but also to incorporate the teaching of research studies into the program to ensure practitioners learn the skills they need and are supported as they reach the data gathering and analysis process.

Each of these changes is significant if we look at them together and compare them to a traditional research dissertation. Yet, many program designers look only to cursory differences like chapter numbers and formats. With limitations in institutions, drastic changes in format can be difficult. Still, many faculty members have found creative ways to move the DiP process away from the traditional 5-chapter model to incorporate the skills, knowledge, and dispositions necessary to become a Scholarly Practitioner. Kennedy et al. (2018) recognize the forward-thinking changes that have taken place with their program and dissertation. Yet they also acknowledge that their faculty colleagues "are themselves steeped in technical rationality and have difficulty imagining alternatives [of dissertations]" (p. 6). Changing mindsets of faculty and administrators, who often have been trained in traditional ways, continue to be a challenge in distinguishing EdD and PhD programs and their dissertations. This challenge also extends to the preparation of new PhDs who will be teaching EdD students, but graduate with little understanding of the EdD.

Conclusion

In recent years, some EdD programs, as well as some online sites that help students seek out EdD programs, have been advertising education doctorate programs as the doctorate that "does not have a dissertation." This language is misleading and grounded in traditional and outdated values that privilege research for knowledge generation only. To claim that a program that offers the dissertation in practice is not offering a dissertation is harmful to the ongoing distinction of the EdD and the research efforts of EdD candidates. It undermines the work of CPED and its members with the notion that the EdD is a "watered-down PhD-lite." Rather, a dissertation in practice embraces two significant scholarly approaches–rigor and utilitarian applied research. It is the culminating experience that warrants "licensure" to become a Scholarly Practitioner.

References

Andrews, R., & Grogan, M. (2005, Spring). Form should follow function: Removing the EdD dissertation from the PhD straight jacket. *UCEA Review, 46*(2), 10-13.

Barton, Matthew D. (2005). Dissertations: Past, present, and future. *USF Tampa Graduate Theses and Dissertations.* https://digitalcommons.usf.edu/etd/2777

Buss, R. R., & Allen, J. G. (2020). Leader scholar communities: Supporting EdD students' dissertation in practice efforts. *Impacting Education: Journal on Transforming Professional Practice, 5*(3), 1–7. DOI:10.5195/ie.2020.98

Carnegie Project for the Educational Doctorate (CPED). (2010). *Design concept definitions.* Retrieved from http://cpedinitiative.org

Carter, M. C. (1956). A comparison of the doctoral requirements of forty-four institutions conferring both the degrees of doctor of philosophy in education and doctor of education. (Master's Thesis). https://digitalrepository.unm.edu/cgi/viewcontent.cgi?article=1075&context=educ_teelp_etds

Colwill, D. A. (2012). *Education of the scholar practitioner in organization development.* Information Age Publishing.

Cremin, L. (1978). *The education of the educating professions.* Paper presented at the American Association of Colleges for Teacher Education in Chicago, Illinois.

Crow, R., Lomotey, K., & Topolka-Jorissen, K. (2016). An adaptive model for a rigorous professional practice doctorate: The disquisition. In V. Storey & K. Hesbol (Eds.), *Contemporary Approaches to Dissertation Development and Research Methods* (pp. 205-220). IGA Global.

Ewell, S., Childers-McKee, C., Giblin, J., McNabb, J., Nolan, K., & Parenti,

M. (2022). Taking action: The dissertation in practice at Northeastern University. *Impacting Education: Journal on Transforming Professional Practice, 7*(1), 4–8. DOI: 10.5195/ie.2022.219

Foster, H. A., Chesnut, S., Thomas, J., & Robinson, C. (2023). Differentiating the EdD and the PhD in higher education: A survey of characteristics and trends. *Impacting Education: Journal on Transforming Professional Practice, 8*(1), 18–26. DOI: 10.5195/ie.2023.288

Freeman, F. N. (1931). *Practices of American universities in granting higher degrees in education.* University of Chicago Press.

Kennedy, B. L., Altman, M., & Pizano, A. (2018). Engaging in the battle of the snails by challenging the traditional dissertation model. *Impacting Education: Journal on Transforming Professional Practice, 3*(1), 4–12. DOI:10.5195/ie.2018.27

Ma, V. W., Dana, N. F., Adams, A., & Kennedy, B. L. (2018). Understanding the problem of practice: An analysis of professional practice EdD dissertations. *Impacting Education: Journal on Transforming Professional Practice, 3*(1), 13–22. DOI: 10.5195/ie.2018.50

McClelland, C.E. (1980). *State, society, and university in Germany,* 1700-1914. Cambridge University Press.

Olson, K., & Clark, C. M. (2009). A signature pedagogy in doctoral education: The leader–scholar. *Community Educational Researcher, 38*(3), 216–221. DOI: 10.3102/0013189X09334207

Perry, J.A. (2012). What history reveals about the education doctorate. In M. Macintyre Latta & S. Wunder (Eds.), *Placing practitioner knowledge at the center of teacher education: Rethinking the policy and practice of the Education Doctorate* (pp. 51-74). Information Age Publishing.

Perry, J.A. (2014). Changing schools of education through grassroots faculty-led change. *Innovation in Higher Education 39*(2), 155–168. DOI 10.1007/s10755-013-9267-y

Perry, J. A., Zambo, D., & Crow, R. (2020). *The improvement science dissertation in practice: A guide for faculty, committee members, and their students.* Myers Education Press.

Perry, J.A. (in press). *Reclaiming the education doctorate: A guidebook for preparing Scholarly Practitioners.* Myers Education Press.

Richardson, V. (2006). Doctoral education in education. In C. M. Golde, & Walker, G.E. (Eds.), *Envisioning the future of doctoral education: Preparing stewards of the discipline* (pp. 251-268). Jossey-Bass.

The Royal Literary Fund. (n.d.). *What is a dissertation? how is it different from an essay?* Retrieved April 22, 2023, from https://www.rlf.org.uk/resources/what-is-a-dissertation-how-is-it-different-from-an-essay/

#:~:text=The%20first%20usage%20of%20the,'%20%3D%20'to%20 debate'

Shulman, L. S., Golde, C. M., Bueschel, A. C., & Garabedian, K. J. (2006). Reclaiming education's doctorates: A critique and a proposal. *Educational Researcher, 35*(3), 25–32. DOI:10.3102/0013189X035003025

Storey, V.A., & Maughan, B.D. (2016). Dissertation in practice: Reconceptualizing the nature androle of the practitioner-scholar. In V.A. Storey (Ed.), *International Perspectives on Designing Professional Practice Doctorates* (pp. 213–232). Palgrave Macmillan. DOI:10.1057/ 9781137527066_13

Wergin, J. (2011). Rebooting the EdD. *Harvard Educational Review, 81*(1), 119–140. DOI: 10.17763/haer.81.1.fp775268x77n0122

CHAPTER 3

The Practitioner-Scholar and the DiP:

A Matched Pair to Redress Professional Marginalizations and Inequities

LESTER A. C. ARCHER, PHD; WES COTTONGIM, EDD

Over 100 years ago in 1921, Harvard University inaugurated and conferred the degree of doctorate in education (Perry, 2012). Designated as the EdD, the degree was conferred to legitimize a professional degree with a focus on developing educational concerns (Perry, 2012). Since its introduction, while discussion converges on its development as a practitioner-oriented degree, the EdD "suffers from questions of purpose, quality, and value" (Kerrigan & Mays, 2016, p. 147). Notwithstanding, the EdD provides an opportunity for practitioners to demonstrate their ability to pursue a practical project while not losing sight of the importance of scholarship.

The traditional features of doctoral education prepare students well for scholarly work. However, Hoffer et al. (2007) reported that roughly half of 45,000 students that earn a doctorate each year in the United States end up working in academia. In 2019, the Survey of Earned Doctors reported that 41% of all doctorate recipients said that their principal jobs in the United States would be in academia (National Center for Science and Engineering Statistics, 2019). In 2021, this number fell to 31% (NCSES, 2022). This statistic suggests a need for a terminal degree for professionals in private, nonprofit, and public organizations. Individuals in fields such as education, social services, business management, public policy, and other fields regularly seek EdD degrees (Archibald, 2010). This path has been shown to provide a more practitioner-based approach to the terminal degree. As a user-centered approach that is implemented in EdD coursework, the EdD degree provides practical measures, in a timely manner, to tactics used to address these problems of practice (Crow et al., 2019).

The EdD continues to afford working professionals and practitioners a gateway to reach the pinnacle of academia. In pursuit of the EdD degree, practitioners become informed by scholarship. Not only do they increase their knowledge of their field, but they also refine research skills and temper their dispositions. Perry (2012) noted that the EdD offers preparation that includes viewing problems of practice through theoretical as well as practical lens. EdD preparation continues to focus on improving practice and creating practitioner-scholars. Friel (2019) found that among EdD dissertations in higher education from 2007-2017, most authors focused on applied research in contrast to PhD dissertations that noted applied scholarship but reverted to more theory-based approaches.

The EdD has not been well defined; however, current efforts have begun to create distinctions from the PhD, which led to the emergence of a more *apropos* Dissertation in Practice (DiP). Early 20th century efforts to define the EdD created conflation with the PhD (Perry 2012; Tamin & Torres, 2022). Additionally, inconsistency of curriculum, program design, and intent of the myriad of EdD programs created different approaches. Differences in students selected for admission to various programs ranged widely since selection occurred at the departmental level (Neumann, 2005). Also, Neumann found that many EdD-granting institutions expected candidates to produce a dissertation. Some institutions treat the EdD dissertation similar to the PhD. As a counter to these issues, among others, the Carnegie Project on the Education Doctorate (CPED) has begun to distinguish and to encourage the development of the EdD as its own unique degree with underpinnings grounded in six principles (CPED, 2022; Perry, 2012).

Grounded in the work of Shulman (2005) and Shulman et al. (2006), steps have been made through the CPED and its consortium of universities to rethink, reimagine, and redesign the dissertation as one suitable for practitioners (Hochbein & Perry, 2013). Efforts to make the case for distinctions between the EdD and the PhD, as well as programmatic challenges, provided opportunities to refocus, redesign, and re-envision the EdD. These efforts made room to conceptualize the Dissertation in Practice (DiP) with a specific focus in the field of education. The rethinking, reimagining, and redesigning of EdD dissertations, known as "Dissertations in Practice," suits practitioners.

We organized this chapter as follows. In the first section we provide a brief list of definitions that apply to the EdD and the DiP. Next, there is discussion centered on the knowledge, skills, and dispositions the practitioner-scholar demonstrates while engaging with the DiP. Finally, we argue that practitioner-scholars should utilize the DiP to attend to marginalization and equity by eliminating *gap gazing* (Gutiérrez, 2008).

Before our discussion begins, we highlight some useful definitions to provide taken-as-shared meanings for important terms germane to the chapter: *Dissertation in Practice (DiP), the practitioner-scholar, the Doctorate in Education,* and *improvement science.* Similar to Shulman (2005), we define the **Dissertation in Practice (DiP)** as the scholarly endeavor and culminating experience which demonstrates the practitioner's scholarly ability to solve problems of practice. We follow CPED in their construction of the Scholarly Practitioner. The **practitioner-scholar** blends practical wisdom with professional skills and knowledge to name, frame, and solve problems of practice. We support CPED in their redefinition of the **Doctorate in Education (EdD)** which states, "The professional doctorate in education prepares educators for the application of appropriate and specific practices, the generation of new knowledge, and for the stewardship of the profession" (CPED, 2022). In addition, we understand the Doctorate in Education (EdD) as a terminal degree presented as an opportunity to prepare for academic, administrative, or specialized positions in education, that requires original research and often includes a clinical component (Council of Graduate Schools, 2007). We note **improvement science** as a methodological framework that guides practitioner-scholars to define problems, understand how a system produces the problem, identify changes to solve these problems, test the impact of the changes, and share the changes which lead to improvement (Cohen & Spillane, 1992).

Distinguishing the EdD from the PhD

The EdD and the PhD are both terminal degrees often sought by professional educators. These two degrees require a vast amount of coursework and a culminating project such as the DiP or the traditional five-chapter dissertation. The path to completion that doctoral students follow is strenuous, but they do differ to a degree in terms of application. Fulton et al. (2013) noted that the difference between a PhD and an EdD is the demonstration of knowledge production that makes a significant contribution to the profession.

The EdD serves as a terminal degree that has practical applications for real life scenarios. It is often well-suited for a practitioner due to the practicality of its course design. Grounded in principles of leadership, the EdD has been found to pay dividends in several professional fields. Many students enter EdD programs in a cohort design which allows them to progress through coursework with like-minded professionals. The EdD has been found to effectively prepare educators for the application of appropriate and specific practices, the generation of new knowledge, and for the stewardship of the profession (CPED).

Similar to the EdD, the PhD is also a terminal degree. However, a PhD degree is often sought by researchers and aspiring university faculty. The PhD degree is more traditional in its approach as it typically has a greater focus on program format, final project requirements, and required research hours (Buttram & Doolittle, 2015; Foster et al., 2023). In most cases, the culminating project–the dissertation–follows a more traditional five-chapter theory-based format (Friel, 2019). If set on a continuum, the traditional features of the PhD doctoral education prepare students well for scholarly work with an emphasis on research, while the EdD provides an opportunity for practitioners to demonstrate their ability to pursue a practical project while not losing sight of the importance of scholarship. In the role of the latter, the practitioner becomes a practitioner scholar (Wasserman & Kram, 2009).

Why the DiP is Important

Researchers and educators have sought solutions to the same problems that have plagued the field of education for decades. Thus far, their efforts have resulted in few solutions but have created new interventions, initiatives, and programs for our teachers to implement. Cohen and Spillane (1992) stated that education reformers are better at addition than subtraction. Their efforts simply lead to more work for an already overloaded workforce. The DiP is designed to address persistent problems with a practitioner approach (and viewpoint) that is more apt to find solutions.

Within academia, researchers view education through a different lens than an educator/practitioner views education. In a study performed at Vanderbilt University's Peabody College, the college faculty expressed that the primary objective of a DiP is for a student to have the opportunity to address complex educational problems. This objective is attained through the critical skills and knowledge that students obtained during the coursework and experiences within their program (Smrekar & McGraner, 2009).

The professional doctorate in education is designed to be practitioner focused. Because of that, the culminating project is designed to address issues as they relate to problems of practice in many forms. These issues may present themselves in the form of instructional issues, equity, ethics, social justice, personnel attrition, and much more. The professional doctorate in education prepares these leaders to make an impact on their communities, organizations, families, students, and other stakeholders. In order to have this impact, communicating the findings of their DiP is vital. The DiP is practical, but it has roots in research. The wisdom gained from that research allows practitioners to effectively minimize problems of practice (which are current and immediate) within their organizations.

The DiP allows candidates to explore real-world problems of practice within school settings, seek and apply solutions to these issues, and ultimately provide an applicable contribution to the field of education. Caboni and Proper (2009) indicated that the EdD candidate should be able to exemplify a skill set that revolves around deep knowledge and understanding of inquiry, organizational theory, resource deployment, leadership studies, and problems of educational policy and practice.

The DiP helps create practitioner-scholars who redress marginalization and inequities within professional settings. Militello et al. (2022), in their study of a reimagined EdD program, described how program students worked with multiple and diverse groups to address improved opportunities for students. One student focused on the assets of the community and supported principals to improve the experiences of ELL (English Language Learner) students. Another examined the teacher evaluation system in order to prioritize teaching practices and improvement so that all students could succeed. A third student worked with counselors to focus on the social and emotional concerns of students who struggle with the transition to high school.

Expectations of the Practitioner-Scholar

Discussions have led to the reinforcement of the construal of doctoral preparation from a project concerning theory advancement to one focusing on knowledge application. Emerging from the Consortium (CPED), the DiP for educational leaders affords practitioner-scholars a wide array of opportunities to become better leaders or, more specifically, change agents who will have an impact on PK-20 education (Hochbein & Perry, 2013). As change agents engaging in improvement, practitioner-scholars need to be able to carry out critical research that requires engagement in several activities that connect research skills and abilities to problems of practice (Hochbein & Perry, 2013). These activities include the ability to decipher, debate, and design. According to Hochbein and Perry (2013) deciphering involves "reading the work, understanding the contributions and limitations of the work, and then communicating these insights to other constituencies" (p. 186); debating includes the "abilities to debate both the ideological and methodological merits" of policies (p. 187); and designing incorporates the "application of knowledge from the research literature, both empirical and theoretical, towards developing a solution to an identified problem" and "to understand how to design evaluations of existing programs and new initiatives" (p. 187).

The DiP involves experiential learning. As Eyler (2009) explained, experiential education "takes students into the community, helps students both to bridge classroom study and life in the world and to transform inert knowledge into knowledge-in-use" (p. 24). Eyler further argued that experiential education has value that leads to more powerful academic learning. For Eyler, students apply experiential education to gain a greater understanding of their subject matter, to grow capacity in critical thinking knowledge application, and to ground themselves in learning in their workplaces. Experiential learning maps onto improvement science (IS) as a methodological framework for the DiP. The use of IS couples well with experiential learning. Buss (2018) noted that problems of practice "suggests a specific issue or concern that is rooted in a practitioners' workplace setting and warrants some type of resolution" (p. 24).

Doctoral candidates who engage the DiP should include, among others but not limited to, multiple methodological approaches such as improvement science and action research because of their affordances of cycles of research. The use of the IS framework supports the DiP because the "effectiveness as a practitioner-scholar involves ongoing inquiry, continuous learning, and application of research skills" (Patton, in Burkholder et al., 2019, p. xv). Using action research, students "learn to build knowledge networks, engage in experiential learning, and promote collaboration, inclusivity, and change" (Ewell et al., 2022, p. 5). Wasserman and Kram (2009) found among practitioner-scholars some who did not follow the traditional scholarly path had "a passion for approaching the field of practice but doing so from a scholarly perspective" (p. 23). Perry et al. (2020) argued that the DiP allows for practitioner learning. In fact, preparation lends itself to lifelong learning. Buss and Avery (2017) suggested that program components should be able to "develop scholarly and influential practitioners, individuals who would lead, innovate, conduct research, and collaborate in their workplace settings during the program and after completion" (p. 278). For Perry (2012), professional preparation in education provides practitioners "habits of hand, heart, and mind" (p. 43). In other words, to effect educational practice while engaging in the DiP process, doctoral students should be able to develop applicable knowledge, skills, and dispositions.

Knowledge

The DiP helps practitioner-scholars to continuously grow their knowledge. Wasserman and Kram (2009) uncovered scholars and practitioners who valued generating new knowledge, but how each group constituted new knowledge varied. By engaging in their research while in practice, practitioner-scholars are able to participate in an interactive process. These activities allow for knowledge growth that leads to greater understanding of their milieu. Using the DiP, practitioner-scholars are able to recognize and to grow their knowledge within their system. They can "direct their research to the improvement of practice, based on the needs of the organizations that they seek to help, and blend research methods and problems of practice" (Barnett & Muth, 2008, p. 11).

Knowledge growth dovetails with confidence and self-efficacy. Buss and Avery (2017) found that end-of-first year students developed confidence in leadership abilities, and they even indicated that others saw them as leaders. Kerrigan and Hayes (2016) found that in a sample of EdD students, their research showed self-efficacy increased as they completed research courses. However, these researchers did not find a positive relationship between interest in research and research self-efficacy.

Skills

The DiP helps practitioner-scholars not only to increase knowledge but also to hone their skills. Earlier in this chapter, we posited that the DiP includes experiential learning, which provides opportunities for students to engage in community, to bridge classroom study to milieu, and to transform "inert knowledge into knowledge-in-use" (Eyler, 2009, p. 24). Leaders should engage in the community in order to hone skill development, among others. Leadership skills include the ability to collaborate, to communicate, and to connect with experts and the larger community while building communities of practice (Buss & Avery, 2017). The DiP approach naturally supports collaboration. As Kernaghan (2009) pointed out, the academic and the practitioner in a common space can combine the "conceptual, theoretical, empirical and practical considerations" (p.

504). Bridging classroom study to milieu includes the development of methodological skills.

The DiP should demonstrate that practitioners recognize the importance of using literature to inform the project, framing research questions to pursue knowledge, collecting data appropriate to answer research questions, and interpreting the data to provide meaning to the project. In addition, issues relating to validity should be incorporated. Taken together, practitioner-scholars should demonstrate methodological skills that support the examination of a focal problem with broad knowledge of the problem of practice (Barnett & Muth, 2008). According to the CPED framework, careful selection of methods and methodological understanding helps to ground the DiP, which, in turn, acts as a demonstration of transforming "inert knowledge into knowledge-in-use" (Eyler, 2009, p. 24). Knowledge-in-use translates to research skills that "must be connected to practice in meaningful ways" (Buss, 2018, p. 24).

Dispositions

The DiP allows for practitioner learning (Perry et al., 2020), which suggests a mind-set of iterative inquiry. Patton posited that practitioner-scholars should develop a mind-set of inquiry (Burkholder et al., 2019). In fact, Patton, as cited in Burkholder et al. (2019), put forward eight essential habits that accompany the development of a mind-set of inquiry. For Patton, these eight habits of highly effective practitioner-scholars encompass: 1) savvy and discriminating research consumption, 2) asking meaningful and important questions, 3) critical thinking skills, 4) advanced observational skills, 5) astute observational skills, 6) rigorous meaning-making skills, 7) integrating theory and practice, and 8) systematic evaluative thinking.

Among the dispositions is the ability to collaborate and confer within a community. The CPED framework provides for collaborative scholarly relationships which include "scholarly writing projects, vertical labs, and electronic networks" (Barnett & Muth, 2008, p. 28). EdD students have expressed positive comments as it relates to navigating collaborative networks (Godwin & Meek, 2016). Eyler (2009) noted that students in experiential education learn as workers or community participants with a need to know in order to get a job done (p. 29). Practitioner-scholars reflect on practice, expose themselves to alternative perspectives, and learn to challenge the opinions of others (Pilkington, 2009).

In their report on restructuring curriculum, Ewell et al. (2022) found that action research as a methodology encouraged doctoral students to engage in cycles of inquiry, promote new learning, and promote shared and co-created knowledge (p. 5). Their sample of DiPs highlight how practitioner-scholars redress marginalization and inequities within professional settings. One example includes the establishment of a mentoring program for Black female students in a private research university. Another example is the implementation of an in-house coaching model to onboard new employees in a Northwestern for-profit company. Yet another example was the implementation of a "Professional Development series to improve the delivery of teaching and learning for students with Autism Spectrum Disorder in a Northeastern, urban, public, K-8 school" (p. 8). These projects exemplify a wide focus on marginalized groups.

Who Benefits from a DiP

As previously mentioned, the DiP is a culminating academic exercise used to solve real-world issues that practitioners face in their day-to-day work settings. These problems of practice reinforce the progress practitioners make toward work goals. For instance, Johnson (2022) found that among library and information DiPs, the problems explored were more practical in nature that related to the delivery of health information and the impact of existing services. Lewis et al. (2021) demonstrated that a pitch presentation to administrators can be used to introduce a DiP as beneficial to their respective institutions.

Practitioners pursuing their EdD have substantial experience in the field of education. They are more likely to be less interested in research as an end in itself (Costley & Lester, 2012). Traditionally, the practitioner-scholar most likely will stay within their current role once they have completed their coursework. Some doctoral students (particularly those with an education background) have complained that the scholarly view they encounter in their coursework, while de-emphasizing the normative, the personal, the particular, and the experiential, implies the loss of something essential for education (Butlerman-Bos, 2008).

Practitioners tend to be more interested in compelling and effective real-world solutions rather than purely theoretical representations (Costley & Lester, 2012). These practitioners benefit from the scholarly knowledge they attain during their program, but losing the non-tangibles that are important for their positions in a traditional dissertation is undesirable. In the field of education, research is distinctly more analytical that focuses on the process required to produce valid explanations of the educational phenomena (Butlerman-Bos, 2008). Practitioners are more concerned with the question of what is best for students.

The DiP to Redress Marginalization and Inequities Within Professional Settings

Taken together, the designing, framing, and presenting of a DiP represent the merging of high caliber scholarship and practical significance. Notions of high caliber scholarship include framing appropriate research questions, reading pertinent literature, and deploying applicable methodology. Framing appropriate questions will be reflected in the caliber of questions posed and pursued. Reading pertinent literature is about becoming informed in the area of concern, giving care to theory, and recognizing what is applicable and what is important for the given localized context.

In the localized context, the practitioner-scholar should utilize the DiP as a fundamental tool to redress marginalization and inequities. Tamim and Torres (2022) noted that DiPs "address existing workplace problems in comparison to traditionally structured dissertations" (p. 2). The existing workplace becomes the localized context of the practitioner-scholar. The problem of practice becomes clear. Practitioner-scholars should equip themselves with the knowledge, skills, and dispositions to examine marginalization and inequities in their contexts. Practitioner-scholars are equipped with the tools to examine marginalization and inequities while avoiding *gap gazing* (Gutiérrez, 2008).

Rocehelle Gutiérrez (2008) described *gap gazing* in the mathematics education literature. For Gutiérrez, researchers unconsciously normalize the "low achievement" of non-White students, and such normalization perpetuates myths that the problem and solution is "technical" (p. 359). The foundational theoretical lens supports deficit thinking while ignoring students' identities and agency. In addition, viewing through a *gap gazing* lens suggests that marginalized students are not worth studying in their own right—between-group variance trumps within-group variance.

The localized context should be the proving ground to move away from *gap gazing* to address issues of identity and power. In a localized context, the problem of focus could examine what identities all students bring to the milieu that strengthens their sense of being as well as their individual agency. Practitioner-scholars have opportunities to examine and to recognize the linguistic and cultural resources that marginalized students bring not only to the mathematics classroom but also to other disciplines of mathematics (Gutiérrez, 2008). However, these opportunities need not be discipline bound. As Gutiérrez argued, instead of an achievement-gap lens, "a research agenda that focuses on advancement, on excellence, and on gains within marginalized communities" should be able to focus on excellence and gains. Here, excellence means high performance and gains is interpreted as "significant growth in student achievement over time" (p. 362). Gillham et al. (2019) found that among 19 dissertations, most authors identified their problems of practice based on a need to take action and guided by their professional roles. However, many of the authors failed to specify how their study would impact their localized context. These findings suggest that once marginalization and inequities are investigated, the impact of the DiP should be identified, and follow-up studies should be conducted.

Persistent marginalization and inequities continue in the form of *gap gazing* and deficit thinking. Gutiérrez (2008) sent out a clarion call for more research on effective teaching and learning environments. There should be more robust understanding of the complex roots and perpetuation of educational environments that encompass a wider spectrum of students that include ELL and working-class students. The DiP is designed to address persistent problems. Solutions can be found and should be scaled up. Here, we use scaling up to mean the practitioner-scholar collaborating with dissertation advisors, involving participants, and focusing intensely on the localized context.

As a practitioner-scholar, Sawkins (2020) investigated how a localized context afforded migrant women an opportunity for learning. Sawkins drew on observational and interview data of migrant women whose investment in language and literacy learning helped to develop their confidence, identity, and social relationships. The investment enabled these women to overcome barriers to social capital.

We noted earlier in this chapter that the primary objective of a DiP benefits and offers advantages for doctoral students to pursue opportunities to address complex educational problems. The DiP allows doctoral candidates to explore real-world problems of practice within school settings, to seek and apply solutions to these issues, and to provide applicable contributions to the field of education. The DiP for educational leaders affords Scholarly Practitioners many opportunities to become better leaders or, more specifically, change agents who will have an impact on PK-20 education (Hochbein & Perry, 2013).

Conclusion

The DiP should be highly distinguished. The DiP is a natural tool that practitioner-scholars can use because it becomes is applicable (Fulton et al., 2013; Johnson, 2022). One application is the use of the DiP to redress marginalization and inequities within professional settings. The DiP has a practical component and contributes to the practitioner's toolbox. The knowledge, skills, and abilities are significant because of their localized focus. The traditional PhD focuses more on theoretical knowledge and is research-based. The EdD, with the DiP in mind, has a practical application that often focuses on a problem of practice and provides a contribution to the field. The distinction is in the practicability of the project. Not only does the DiP become a finished academic product but also, it becomes the start of an iterative process of inquiry.

References

Archbald, D. (2010). "Breaking the mold" in the dissertation: Implementing a problem based, decision-oriented thesis project. *Journal of Continuing Higher Education, 58*(2), 99–107. https://doi.org/10.1080/07377361003617368

Barnett, B.G., & Muse, I. D. (1993). Cohort groups in educational administration: Promises and challenges. *School Leadership, 3*(4), 400-415. https://doi.org/10.1177/105268469300300405

Barnett, B. G., & Muth, R. (2008). Using action-research strategies and cohort structures to ensure research competence for practitioner-scholar leaders. *Journal of Research on Leadership Education, 3*(1), 1-42. https://doi.org/10.1177/194277510800300101

Burkholder, G. J., Cox, K. A., Crawford, L. M., & Hitchcock, J. H. (Eds.). (2019). *Research design and methods: An applied guide for the scholar-practitioner.* Sage.

Buss, R. R. (2018). Using action research as a signature pedagogy to develop EdD students' inquiry as practice abilities. *Impacting Education: Journal on Transforming Professional Practice, 3*(1), 23-31. https://doi.org/10.5195/ie.2018.46

Buss, R. R., & Avery, A. (2017). Research becomes you: Cultivating EdD students' identities as educational leaders and researchers and a "learning by doing" meta-study. *Journal of Research on Leadership Education, 12*(3), 273-301. https://doi.org/10.1177/1942775116674463

Butlerman-Bos, J. A. (2008). Will a clinical approach make education research more relevant for practice? *Educational Researcher, 37*(7), 412–420. https://doi.org/10.3102/0013189X08325555

Buttram, J. L., & Doolittle, V. (2015). Redesign of EdD and PhD educational leadership programs. *International Journal of Educational Reform, 24*(3), 282-308. https://doi.org/10.1177/105678791502400306

Caboni, T., & Proper, E. (2009). Re-envisioning the professional doctorate for educational leadership and higher educational leadership: Vanderbilt University's Peabody College EdD program. *Peabody Journal of Education, 84*(1), 61-68. https://doi.org/10.1080/01619560802679666

Carnegie Project on the Education Doctorate (CPED). (2022). *The CPED Framework©.* https://www.cpedinitiative.org/the-framework

Cohen, D.K., & Spillane, J. P., (1992). Chapter 1: Policy and practice: The relations between governance and instruction. *Review of Research in Education, 18*(1), 3-49. https://doi.org/10.3102/0091732X018001003

Costley, C., & Lester, S. (2012). Work-based doctorates: Professional extension at the highest levels. *Studies in Higher Education, 37*(3), 257–269. https://doi.org/10.1080/03075079.2010.503344

Council of Graduate Schools (2007). *CGS task force report on the professional doctorate.* Council of Graduate Schools.

Crow, R., Hinnant-Crawford, B.N., & Spalding, D. (2019). *The educational leader's guide to improvement science: Data, design and cases for reflection.* Myers Education Press.

Dewey, J. (1916). *Democracy and education: An introduction to the philosophy of education.* Free Press.

Ewell, S., Childers-McKee, C., Giblin, J., McNabb, J., Nolan, K., & Parenti, M. (2022). Taking action: The dissertation in practice at Northeastern University. *Impacting Education: Journal on Transforming Professional Practice, 7*(1), 4-8. http://doi.org/10.5195/ie.2022.219

Eyler, J. (2009). The power of experiential education. *Liberal Education, 95*(4), 24–31.

Foster, H. A., Chesnut, S., Thomas, J., & Robinson, C. (2023). Differentiating the EdD and the PhD in higher education: A survey of characteristics and trends. *Impacting Education: Journal on Transforming Professional Practice, 8*(1), 18-26. https://doi.org/10.5195/ie.2023.288

Friel, W. (2019). *Theory and practice in doctoral dissertation research, 2007-2017: A content analysis by degree type* [Unpublished doctoral dissertation]. Seton Hall University.

Fulton, J., Kuit, J., Sanders, G., & Smith, P. (2013). *The professional doctorate: A practical guide.* Palgrave Macmillan.

Gillham, J. C., Williams, N. V., Rife, G., & Parker, K. K. (2019). Problems of practice: A document analysis of education doctorate dissertations. *Impacting Education: Journal on Transforming Professional Practice, 4*(1), 1-9. https://doi.org/10.5195/ie.2019.85

Godwin, M. L., & Meek, J. W. (2016). The Scholarly Practitioner: Connections of research and practice in the classroom. *Teaching Public Administration, 34*(1), 54–69. https://doi.org/10.1177/0144739415593337

Gutiérrez, R. (2008). A gap-gazing fetish in mathematics education? Problematizing research on the achievement gap. *Journal for Research in Mathematics Education, 39*(4), 357-364. https://doi.org/10.5951/jresematheduc.39.4.0357

Hochbein, C., & Perry, J. A. (2013). The role of research in the professional doctorate. *Planning & Changing, 44*(3/4), 181-194.

Hoffer, T., Hess, M., Welch, V., Jr., & Williams, K. (2007). *Doctorate recipients from United States universities: Summary report, 2006.* National Opinion Research Center.

Johnson, F. (2022). Dissertations into Practice: 10 years on, 40 articles later. *Health Information & Libraries Journal, 39*(1), 79–81. https://doi.org/10.1111/hir.12422

Kernaghan, K. (2009). Speaking truth to academics: The wisdom of the practitioners. *Canadian Public Administration/Administration publique du Canada, 52*(4), 503–23. https://doi.org/10.1111/j.1754-7121.2009.00099.x

Kerrigan, M. R., & Hayes, K. M. (2016). EdD students' self-efficacy and interest in conducting research. *International Journal of Doctoral Studies, 11*, 147-162. htttp://ijds.org/Volume11/IJDSv11p147-162Kerrigan1975.pdf

Lewis, T., Puckett, H., & Siegel, D. J. (2021). Making our pitch: Engaging practitioner supervisors in the development of the dissertation in practice. *Journal of Research on Leadership Education, 18*(2). https://doi.org/10.1177/19427751211055087

Militello, M., Argent, J., & Tredway, L. (2022). A better EdD by design: An inquiry-focused, equity-based dissertation to change leadership practice. *Journal of Research on Leadership Education, 18*(3). https://doi.org/10.1177/19427751221087728

National Center for Science and Engineering Statistics, National Science Foundation. (2019). *Doctorate recipients from U.S. universities: 2019.* https://ncses.nsf.gov/pubs/nsf21308/

National Center for Science and Engineering Statistics, National Science Foundation. (2022). *Doctorate recipients from U.S. universities: 2021.* https://ncses.nsf.gov/pubs/nsf23300/

Neumann, R. (2005). Doctoral differences: Professional doctorates and PhDs compared. *Journal of Higher Education Policy and Management, 27*(2), 173-188. https://doi.org/10.1080/13600800500120027

Passaretta, G., Trivellato, P., & Triventi, M. (2019). Between academia and labour market—the occupational outcomes of PhD graduates in a period of academic reforms and economic crisis. *Higher Education, 77*, 541-559. https://doi.org/10.1007/s10734-018-0288-4

Perry, J. A. (2012). To Ed.D. or not to Ed.D.? *Phi Delta Kappan, 94*(1), 41–44. http://doi.org/10.1177/003172171209400108

Perry, J. A., Zambo, D., & Crow, R. (2020). *The improvement science dissertation in practice: A guide for faculty, committee members, and their students.* Myers Education Press.

Pilkington, R. M. (2009). Practitioner research in education: The critical perspectives of doctoral students. *Studies in the Education of Adults, 41*(2), 154-174. https://doi.org/10.1080/02660830.2009.11661579

Sawkins, T. (2020). *Reimagining an employment program for migrant women: From holistic classroom practice to arts-informed program evaluation* [Unpublished doctoral dissertation]. Simon Fraser University.

Shulman, L.S. (2005). Signature pedagogies in the professions. *Daedalus, 134*(3), 52-59. https://www.jstor.org/stable/20027998

Shulman, L. S., Golde, C. M., Bueschel, A. C., & Garabedian, K. J. (2006). Reclaiming education's doctorates: A critique and a proposal. *Educational Researcher, 35*(3), 25–32. https://doi.org/10.3102/0013189X035003025

Smrekar, C., & McGraner, K. (2009). From curricular alignment to the culminating project: The Peabody College EdD capstone. *Peabody Journal of Education, 84*(1), 48-60. https://doi.org/10.1080/01619560802679641

Tamim, S., & Torres, K. M. (2022). Evolution of the dissertation in practice. *Impacting Education: Journal on Transforming Professional Practice, 7*(1), 1-3. https://doi.org/10.5195/ie.2022.267

Wasserman, I. C., & Kram, K. E. (2009). Enacting the scholar—practitioner role: An exploration of narratives. *The Journal of Applied Behavioral Science, 45*(1), 12-38. https://doi.org/10.1177/0021886308327238

SECTION 2:

Evaluation and Important Traits of the DiP

CHAPTER 4

Evaluating the DiP:
The Development of a Rubric

LYNN HEMMER, PHD; SUHA R. TAMIM, EDD;
KELLY M. TORRES, PHD

Since its inception in 2007, the Carnegie Project on the Education Doctorate (CPED) has aimed to strengthen the Professional Doctorate by establishing a common definition and design concepts, and developing working principles to ensure rigor and quality (Perry, 2015). Along with these efforts, CPED created the Dissertation in Practice (DiP) Award in 2012 to spotlight exemplary dissertations that align with the envisioned principles of the professional doctorate. For that purpose, a committee was formed to set assessment criteria that were later disseminated to CPED members for feedback. The initial performance criteria revolved around an understanding of the problem of practice, ethics and integrity of action, effective communication, integration of theory and practice for the advancement of knowledge, evidence of potential impact, and appropriate use of methods of inquiry (Storey et al., 2015). However, as Storey et al. (2015) acknowledged, specifying what the DiP should look like and how to measure its impact is challenging, with various possible designs, the necessity of reflection, and the creation of new knowledge that is significant to practice and profession-specific.

Rubrics play a vital role in evaluating dissertation awards since they provide a structured and objective framework for assessing the quality and merit of Scholarly Practitioner-focused research.

However, it is important to note that when the committee applies a rubric to a dissertation submitted for the CPED DiP award, we are determining how each aspect of the dissertation fits into the descriptors outlined in the rubric and not "judging it" (Brookhart, 2013, p. 4). The rubric is designed to be descriptive, with each level category characterized and informed by CPED's framework and guiding principles, yet general enough to allow for a variety of methodological approaches and dissertation products. According to Tan (2020), "rubrics convey expectations and ambitions" (p. 79). By aligning the descriptors to CPED's framework and guiding principles, the rubric offers an explicit portrayal of what CPED anticipates from Dissertations in Practice. Dissertations often involve complex research processes and focuses. As a result, the inclusion of objective rubrics helps establish clear criteria and expectations for evaluating various research components.

While creating a rubric is often seen as a "relatively simple task" (Goldberg, 2014, p. 1), as evidenced by the work of the original DiP award committee and the committees thereafter, there is complexity in the development process and in improving the rubric. As mentioned prior, the original committee sought feedback from the CPED membership at large before finalizing the initial rubric. Because this work centered on awarding an exemplar Dissertation in Practice, a rubric had to be designed that, in essence, would help committee members to make a dichotomous decision such as accepted/rejected. Scale points were assigned that were intended to help differentiate the alignment of evidence to CPED guiding principles. Since the initial rubric was created, it has undergone revision and refinement each year. Through this continuous improvement process, it is our hope that we can extend and clarify expectations. However, as Storey et al. (2015) explained, as much as committee members agree on the criteria and process of evaluation, ambiguity and perception of overgeneralization will exist (Storey et al., 2015).

The DiP Award Process

As new committees formed yearly, and before selecting DiP award winners, members would frequently meet to revisit the DiP evaluation rubric and discuss the evaluation process. Once the committee agrees on the rubric criteria, and per CPED deadlines, a call for submission is sent out asking nominees to submit a synopsis of their dissertation and, prior to the 2023 award year, with a nomination letter from their dissertation chair. The synopses are blindly reviewed and scored by the DiP award committee members. Accordingly, finalists with the highest scores are selected and asked to submit their full dissertations. Then, the committee determines the number of finalists after deliberations over the initial synopses scores. A second round of review and scoring follows to select the winner based on the highest score and further deliberations. It is important to note that, over the years and with the increase of CPED members, the number of submissions increased, as did the number of the DiP awards committee members to ensure multiple scores for each submission.

Rubric Refinement and Revision

While the submission process is streamlined, the evaluation process is more complex. As previously mentioned, each year after completing the rounds of evaluation, committee members discuss improvements to the rubric and incorporate them in the following year's evaluation cycle. Shortly after the October Convening (when the award is presented), the committee meets to discuss what worked well and what challenges were encountered when applying the rubric. These open discussions often include ways in which to improve consistency amongst the readers/reviewers, challenges in how terms and principles are interpreted, and alignment between CPED principles, rubric, and submissions.

In the spring, prior to the call going out, the committee meets again to discuss desired changes to the rubric. Below, we share some of the changes that have occurred over the last few years in the committee's attempt to bring clarity to the CPED expectation of what an exemplar Dissertation in Practice looks like (Figure 4.1). For example, over the last several years, the DiP award committee has undertaken the initiative to update the award evaluation rubric to better encompass alternative forms of dissertations. Particularly, in prior years, the evaluation criteria were more aligned with traditional research studies, potentially placing award submissions that reflected alternative forms of research at an unfair disadvantage. For the purpose of this chapter, we share more insight focused on the times and rubric changes during which we served as co-chairs of the committee.

Figure 4.1 *Timeline of Rubric Changes*

The Dissertation in Practice Award Rubric Changes

2012	2016	2019	2020	2022
Initial Performance Criteria	**Incorporated CPED's guiding principle of social justice**	**Terms Defined** **Expectation of Alignment with CPED Definitions**	**Alternative Dissertation Formats**	**Increase and Diversified Committee Membership**
An understanding of the problem of practice, ethics and integrity of action, effective communication, integration of theory and practice for the advancement of knowledge, evidence of potential impact, and appropriate use of methods of inquiry		Reciprocity and Critical Inquiry defined / Expectation of evidence of alignment	Improvement science / Focus on purpose of dissertation and less on structure / Focus on evidence of intervention and practice improvement	Interpretation, conceptual and theoretical nuances, desirable consistency in scoring

Timeline Rubric Changes

In 2019, some terms used in the rubric were defined for clarity and consistency in scoring, such as Reciprocity and Critical Inquiry, which were incorporated in 2016 to reflect CPED's guiding principle of social justice (Tamim et al., 2021). Additionally, the call for nominations was revised to ask for a clear discussion of the Problems of Practice (PoP) as persistent, contextualized, and embedded in practice, in alignment with CPED's definition (CPED, n.d., Design Concepts section), and based on Leach et al.'s (2019) study on the evidence of explicit framing of problems of practice in DiPs per the CPED definition that found the majority of DiPs relied on evidence from the literature with little systematically collected contextual evidence. Furthermore, some criteria on the rubric were separated, such as key findings and implications; the rationale being that key findings represent a generation of knowledge, whereas implications point to actions taken or to be taken to improve the PoP as products of the dissertation. Moreover, as member institutions vary in the dissertation formats, the criterion of experimenting with distinctive or alternative designs was incorporated. However, in 2020, the committee decided to remove this criterion and place emphasis on the purpose of the dissertation instead of its format and updated the call for submission (see Figure 4.2).

Figure 4.2

Comparison Between Original and Updated Call Text

Original text	Updated text
Methods description that includes the research design, participants, data sources, data collection procedures, and data analysis. Varied conceptualizations and methodologies are welcome and encouraged.	Methods description that includes the research design, data sources, data collection procedures, and data analysis. Varied conceptualizations and methodologies are welcome and encouraged. *(The word participants was removed. Not all alternative formats may include participants).*
Summary of key findings.	Summary of impact on the problem of practice.
Implications for practice such as: • What generative impact will this work have on practice, policy, and/or future research? • What impact does this work have on the future work and agendas of the scholar practitioner? • How does this work demonstrate the scholarly practitioner's ability to solve or contribute to the solution of problems of practice? • What, if any, action pieces have been generated?	Resulting Professional Practice Product in the form of an action plan, policy development, technical report, improvement plan, etc. that impact practice. *(changed to include a variety of products)*

Part of the 2019-2020 End of Year report.

Figure 4.3 shows the scoring guide used in the 2020 award cycle. As part of the elements, the terms that were defined in 2019 remained a focus was added on purpose of the dissertation and intervention or practice improvement added.

Figure 4.3

2020 DiP Award Finalist Scoring Guide

The Dissertation in Practice:	Exemplary (9-10)	Proficient (8-6)	Developing (5-3)	Poor (2-0)
Frames the problem of practice as a persistent, contextualized problem embedded in the work of the professional practitioner.				
The problem of practice demonstrates reciprocity[1] with the field.				
Identifies a theoretical or conceptual framework that frames the problem of practice with support from the literature.				
Demonstrates use of rigorous, appropriate, and ethical methods of critical inquiry[2] to address the identified complex problem of practice.				
Demonstrates the integration of both theory and practice in the interpretation of the summary of the impact on the problem of practice to advance professional knowledge and to impact the field.				
Demonstrates the goals of the problem-based thesis as involving decisions, changed practices, better organizational performances, and application of a theory of change.				
Engages in creative, innovative, or interdisciplinary inquiry.				
Researches with distinctive designs or alternatives to traditional doctoral dissertation format or product (e.g., alternatives to five chapters; additional reflective elements relating to personal reflections on the learning journey how the student's or field partner's ideas have changed).				
Discusses a Professional Practice Product in the form of an action plan, policy development, technical report, improvement plan, etc. that impacts practice and makes a contribution to the field beyond the DiP.				
Demonstrates the scholarly practitioner's ability to communicate effectively to an appropriate audience to advance professional knowledge and impact the field.				
TOTAL (/100)				

2020 Score Guide

[1] Reciprocity: Research should involve an essentially collaborative relationship between researcher and the research participants in which each contributes something the other needs or desires. (Trainor & Ahlgren-Bouchard, 2013)

[2] 3 Critical inquiry: Takes into account how our lives are mediated by systems of inequity such as classism, racism, sexism, and heterosexism (Marrais & Lapan, 2004).

The 2021 DiP award committee developed criteria to advance thinking and possibilities about what a culminating product looks like and accomplishes in EdD programs. As part of this effort, rubrics for both the synopsis and full dissertation submissions were revised to better align with CPED working principles for program design. A rubric review process was crafted that focuses on the essential questions of: "Do the rubrics focus on the elements of a DiP?" and "Should the rubrics include more in terms of what is exemplary, proficient, developing, and poor?." Based on these focuses, the award rubric was modified to contain specific elements for each evaluation criterion. The central evaluation criterion of the updated rubric included: (1) explanation of the study's PoP, (2) explanation of significance of guiding questions and/or rationale, (3) explanation of the knowledge that frames the complex PoP, (4) description of the resulting professional practice product, and (5) explanation for next steps for professional practice. Further, the rubric scores were updated for more salient criterion to contain higher point values in their overall rubric weighting score.

In 2022, the committee itself underwent changes to its membership. As CPED membership continued to grow and diversify, so should the committee's membership. As such, four new members were welcomed to the committee. With our newest committee members, we included representation across the United States, as well as representation from international members. Part of welcoming new members to the committee involved explaining the rubric(s) previously used. These conversations opened ways in which to interpret CPED principles, conceptual nuances, and desirable consistency in scoring. The rubric revision process focused on the interpretation of CPED principles, conceptual and theoretical nuances, and desirable consistency in scoring (Figure 4.4). The changes to the rubric were made to continue to reflect ways in which to keep moving towards clarifying the CPED principles and evidence of such within the dissertation.

Figure 4.4 *Example of Revised Elements*

Revised Elements	Elements
Explanation of the study's Problem of Practice (PoP). (2 pages)	Explanation of the study's Problem of Practice (PoP). (2 pages)
The Problem of Practice aligns with the CPED's Design-Concepts in which the scholarly practitioner blended "practical wisdom with professional skills and knowledge to name, frame, and solve problems of practice" using "a critical and professional stance with a moral and ethical imperative for equity and social justice"	*Alignment with CPED PoP design concept*
The Problem of Practice is framed as persistent and substantially contextualized and emanates from the scholarly practitioner's direct and lived observations with their context of professional practice	*Framed as persistent, contextualized; embedded in the work of the professional practitioner*
Demonstrates reciprocity with the field and the community it seeks to serve	*Demonstrates reciprocity with the field*
Provides a logical explanation of the PoP and its defining and enabling conditions (e.g. empathy interviews, analysis of relevant data, cycles of research, systems map, fishbone diagram, or other evidence) that support the DiP inquiry	*Provides a causal analysis (e.g. fishbone diagram)*
Demonstrates alignment between the general larger PoP (e.g. historical, economic, anthropological, sociological lenes, and various learning theories)to the local context and conditions of the PoP	*Demonstrates alignment between the general larger PoP to the local context of the PoP*

Clarifying CPED Principles and Evidence

Another change to the rubric included a description/explanation of what constitutes the different scaling marks (i.e. 10-9; 8-6). However, the committee opted to reduce score scale spread to 3, 2, 1, 0 to address previous concerns related to inter-rater reliability (Figure 4.5).

Figure 4.5

Scoring Guide

3	2	1	0
Clear evidence of alignment of the PoP to the CPED's design-concepts	Some evidence of alignment of the PoP to the CPED's design-concepts	Little evidence of alignment of the PoP to the CPED's design-concepts	Minimal to no evidence of alignment of the PoP to the CPED's design-concepts

Scoring Guide for Award Year 2022

Conclusion

Each year, revisions are essential given that rubrics contribute to the continuous improvement of the evaluation process itself. It is important to note here, that each year new members join the committee and others leave, which brings new perspectives on the evaluation process; this also presents challenges to the consistency of the evaluation. By regularly reviewing and updating rubrics, evaluators can refine the assessment criteria, align them with evolving research standards, and incorporate emerging scholarly practices. This iterative process ensures that the evaluation of dissertation awards remains relevant and up-to-date and reflective of impactful research being conducted within the field.

References

Brookhart, S.M. (2013). *How to create and use rubrics for formative assessment and grading.* ASCD.

Carnegie Project for the Education Doctorate (CPED) (2022). *The CPED framework.* https://www.cpedinitiative.org/the-framework

Leach, L. F., Baker, C., & Leamons, C. G. (April, 2019). *Beyond anecdotal evidence of problems of practice: A document analysis.* Annual Meeting of the American Educational Research Association, Toronto, Canada. Online Paper Repository. https://doi.org/10.3102/1441945

Perry, J. A. (2015). The Carnegie Project on the Education Doctorate. *Change: The Magazine of Higher Learning, 47*(3), 56–61. https://doi.org/10.1080/00091383.2015.1040712

Storey, V. A., Caskey, M. M., Hesbol, K. A., Marshall, J. E., Maughan, B., & Dolan, A. W. (2015). Examining EdD dissertations in practice: The Carnegie Project on the Education Doctorate. *International HETL Review, 5*(2). https://www.hetl.org/examining-edd-dissertations-in-practice-the-carnegie-project-on-the-education-doctorate/

Tamim, S. R., Torres, K., Finch, M., Bartlett, J., Everson, K., Hemmer, L., Leach, L., Lomotey, K., Nix, J., & Tolman S. (2021, Winter). The Carnegie Project on the Education Doctorate and the dissertation in practice principles. In N. Hafenstein (Ed.), *Perspectives in gifted education: Influences and impacts of the education doctorate on gifted education II* (Vol.8). Office of the Daniel L. Ritchie Endowed Chair in Gifted Education, University of Denver.

Tan, K. (2020). *Assessment rubrics decoded: An educator's guide.* Routledge. https://doi.org/10.4324/9780429022081

CHAPTER 5

The Problem of Practice:
The Core of the Practitioner-Oriented EdD Dissertation in Practice

KOFI LOMOTEY, PHD

Within practitioner-oriented EdD programs, the focus is on preparing educational leaders to identify, describe, analyze, and address Problems of Practice (PoPs) that they observe in their workplace. The intent is to prepare practitioners to improve practice, or as the Council of Graduate Schools (2007) indicated, the purpose of these programs is "preparation for the potential transformation of [the] field of professional practice" (p. 6).

The PoP is at the core of the practitioner-oriented EdD dissertation exercise and of the EdD degree program in education. Quite a bit of research has been done in the past 10 years looking at aspects of the PoP in practitioner-oriented EdD degree programs, including studies that have: (1) defined PoPs (Belzer & Ryan, 2013); (2) explored the impact of the reconceptualization of the PoP on course development and student support systems (Blevins et al., 2022); (3) shown how scholar practitioners select PoPs (Gillham et al., 2019; Ma et al., 2018); and (4) enumerated what scholar practitioners study (Gillham et al., 2019).

In this chapter, after briefly defining a PoP, I discuss: (1) selecting a PoP, (2) Improvement Science (IS) and the PoP, and (3) framing a PoP, using an equity, ethics, and social justice lens.

Defining a PoP

By definition, a PoP is a significant challenge identified by a *scholar practitioner*[1] that substantially impacts the teaching-learning process, directly or indirectly. The magnitude of the PoP is measured by the impact that successfully addressing it will have on that educational process. My discussion is focused on the development of PoPs within practitioner-oriented EdD programs that are geared toward preparing practitioners to lead primary, secondary, and tertiary educational institutions.

Many traditional EdD programs have been challenged in preparing (prospective) school leaders to address PoPs–the issues these leaders deal with daily in their workplace. Too often, school leaders have not been adequately prepared to be practical problem solvers. In many instances, they have been much better prepared to become academics or researchers.[2]

Since 2007, The Carnegie Project on the Education Doctorate (CPED) has been working diligently with faculty in practitioner-oriented EdD programs to ensure that these programs address the unique needs of educational leaders at all levels. My colleague, Jess Weiler and I have spoken to this important role played by CPED (2021).[3] I now consider factors associated with pursuing a PoP, beginning with a brief discussion of the PoP selection process.

Selecting a PoP

Much of what a scholar practitioner is engaged in from the time they consider enrollment in a practitioner-oriented EdD degree program until commencement, ideally, should be geared toward selecting, studying, and addressing a consequential PoP. While such programs have fundamental objectives related to increasing the knowledge of scholar practitioners in the broad areas of leadership, inquiry, and more, an additional significant and aligned focus should be on better preparing scholar practitioners to identify and address consequential PoPs. The successful experience in this endeavor should substantially increase the scholar practitioner's ability to identify, describe, analyze, and address PoPs as they emerge within their workplace or laboratory of practice.

In many cases, a scholar practitioner who is enrolled in a practitioner-oriented EdD program, is employed at least to some degree, in administration—either officially by title, or less formally, with leadership as a part of what they do—as part of their responsibilities. In our EdD program at Western Carolina University (WCU), we discourage applicants from pursuing our degree if they are not presently in some type of leadership role. (We also discourage applicants who indicate that their ultimate goal is to be an academic.)[4].

In practitioner-oriented EdD programs, wherein scholar practitioners are not currently in a leadership role (or fulfilling some significant leadership responsibility), they typically are close enough to the pulse of the institution to be able to ascertain the issues that negatively impact its operation. Accordingly, they have a head start when enrolling in a practitioner-oriented EdD program. Still, such programs have a responsibility to encourage each scholar practitioner to think more concretely about far-reaching PoPs–even during the recruitment, application, and enrollment processes.

The earlier a scholar practitioner identifies a significant PoP on which they desire to focus, the more opportunities they have to utilize program resources [e.g., peers, faculty, (required and supplemental) readings, assignments, (small and large) class discussions, and guest lectures] to better understand the PoP. This early introduction also provides an opportunity to formulate a fitting intervention to address the PoP.

Rick Mintrop (2016) raised three considerations when searching for a PoP. He suggests first taking into consideration: (1) the amount of available time to pursue the PoP and (2) the human and material means at your disposal to address the PoP. Second, he urged the scholar practitioner to consider to what extent is the local issue being pondered a reflection of a larger problem in the parent organization (e.g., the school district or the university system). Finally, Mintrop's advice speaks to the need to understand the protocol or routines being undertaken in the institution that are reflective of the PoP being explored.

In summarizing his treatise, Mintrop (2016) stated that several factors indicate the appropriateness of a potential PoP:

- Is the PoP a result of a clear need within the institution?

- Can you address the PoP from where you sit?

- Is there adequate time and resources available to address the PoP?

- Is the PoP linked to the direction in which the institution seeks to go?

- Are there practices connected to the PoP that can readily be addressed?

- Is the PoP one that will likely persist if not addressed?

Improvement Science and the PoP

In many practitioner-oriented EdD programs, including the program at WCU, the preferred methodology is improvement science (IS) (Bryk et al., 2015; Crow et al., 2016; Hinnant-Crawford, 2020; Langley et al., 2009; Sparks, 2013). Brandi Hinnant-Crawford (2020) described IS as:

> ... a methodological framework that is undergirded by foundational principals that guide scholar-practitioners to define problems, understand how the system produces the problem, identify changes to rectify the problems, test the efficacy of those changes, and spread the changes (if the change is indeed an improvement). (p.1)

Hinnant-Crawford (2020) goes on to contend that with IS, one can effectively pursue social justice ends and reform schools more effectively and efficiently. Unlike traditional research methodologies, IS can serve as a bellwether, enabling one to progress through course correction systematically. In IS, to effectively address issues of equity, ethics, and social justice, she says, the scholar practitioner constantly asks these questions: Who is involved and who is impacted?

Framing a PoP

Evidence-based identification of the PoP occurs at the beginning of the process of developing a Dissertation in Practice (DiP). This selection is followed by the internalization of an in-depth understanding of the nature of the problem and an exploration of effective strategies to address the problem. The process of preparing a DiP culminates in the implementation, systematic evaluation, and adjustment of one or more selected improvement strategies or interventions. The selection of an applicable PoP evolves out of: (1) practical wisdom, (2) professional practice, and (3) institutional and individual commitments to social justice, equity, and ethics. The intent in addressing a far-reaching PoP is to (1) gain the skills necessary to be able to disrupt and improve the situation through investigations within the institution and (2) to acquire and apply relevant knowledge to subsequent challenges. Critical thinking, knowledge of the field(s), and some give-and-take are necessary.

The scholar practitioner develops a perspective on the problem and leads a team (ideally of program faculty and practitioners) in framing the problem in a way that enables the team to identify, design, implement, and assess appropriate interventions. While previous literature is utilized, it is not employed to develop an argument but, instead, to support and inform the process. According to Hochbein and Perry (2013), "Scholarly Practitioners need to apply the findings of research literature in the design of practical solutions to address pressing universal problems of practice" (p.187).

In practitioner-oriented EdD programs, we seek to prepare education leaders who can apply theory to authentic situations in order to address meaningful PoPs. This process, in part with the utilization of relevant coursework, helps to prepare individuals to better serve as leaders in education. We understand, in concert with CPED, that "[the EdD is] the highest-quality degree for the advanced preparation of school practitioners and clinical faculty, academic leaders, and professional staff for the nation's schools and colleges and the organizations that support them" (Perry, 2012, p. 42). I turn now to a discussion of the significance of equity, ethics, and social justice within the process of formulating and addressing a PoP.

When I refer to an equity, ethics, and social justice lens, I am denoting a structure or schema in which we imbed a focus on equity, ethics, and social justice within the discussion of the formulation of a PoP. It is a fundamental component of the framework of the PoP. Relatedly, program faculty must link the PoP with the degree program. *The PoP (and the DiP) cannot be successfully focused on equity, ethics, and social justice if the degree program is not similarly focused.*

Weiler and I have contended (2021) that if we are genuinely concerned with the development of scholar practitioners, we must also be concerned with the development of equitable, ethical, and socially just leaders. As we stated it:

> An orientation toward scholarly practice must accompany an orientation toward equity and justice . . . programs that develop scholar-practitioners, but do not develop students' orientation toward equity, are complicit in maintaining the oppressive status quo, albeit through scholarly means. (p.127)

As CPED has indicated, in preparing what they refer to as scholarly practitioners, we are, by definition, preparing individuals who, in fact, understand the importance of equity, ethics, and social justice, and who strive toward enhancing these ideas in the workplace.

Many practitioner-oriented EdD programs *articulate* a focus on equity, ethics, and social justice with limited evidence of such. If a practitioner-oriented EdD program seeks to be focused on equity, ethics, and social justice, the focus must permeate the *entire* program, from recruitment to commencement. This is of paramount importance as long as we live in a society, indeed in a world, where people continue to be oppressed based upon illegitimate forms of exclusion (DeMatthews and Mawhinney, 2014). On this matter, Hinnant-Crawford (2020) has forcefully posited:

> Our educational system is broken. Despite all we know about teaching and learning, our educational system continues to advantage some while relegating others. Deficit ideology pervades the minds of educators at all levels, and practices and policies stemming from such understandings continue to reproduce inequalities within our society. Students of color, particularly Indigenous,

Black, and Latinx students, continue to be overrepresented in special education and underrepresented in gifted programs. These underserved populations, as well as LGBTQ and poor students are also more likely to be recipients of punitive discipline policies. The achievement disparity between White, middle-class students and their peers (students of color and non-affluent Whites) reflects the inequity in opportunity. (p. 203)

A focus on equity, ethics, and social justice should permeate all aspects of these programs. Illustrations of such inclusions follow.

Recruitment materials should clearly articulate an equitable, ethical, and socially just focus, so that prospective scholar practitioners know from the onset that such a focus is a fundamental part of the program. Marketing materials should indicate that the program is committed to preparing leaders to disrupt and dismantle educational programs that are oppressive to any group(s). Recruitment materials should include statements indicating that participants are encouraged to increase their understanding, appreciation, respect, and embracing of people who are different from them. Such materials should also focus on the program's emphasis on scholar practitioners being critically self-reflective.

In the **admission process**, the focus on equity, ethics, and social justice should be clear. If there is literature to be evaluated by the applicants, as part of the screening process, these materials should include writings that address issues of social justice and candidates should be asked to critically reflect on them. Where face-to-face interviews are held, a discussion of equity, ethics, and social justice issues should be included. These exercises provide opportunities for the program faculty to gauge the degree to which applicants are aware of, concerned about, and involved in addressing issues of equity, ethics, and social justice; they provide a baseline for beginning the discussion.

The **program orientation** should include a focus on equity, ethics, and social justice, emphasizing the centrality of these ideas throughout the program. There should be an opportunity to discuss equity, ethics, and social justice issues. New Student Orientation is not too early a time to consider equity, ethics, and social justice issues in one's workplace that may generate an appropriate PoP.

Coursework centered on issues of equity, ethics, and social justice should not be limited to a course on social justice–no more than there should only be one leadership course or only one inquiry course. *Issues of equity, ethics, and social justice should permeate the curriculum.* Indeed, a course focused on equity, ethics, and social justice (e. g., Leadership for Social Justice in Education, a course offered within the WCU program) is important, but—given the state of U.S. society, with continuing social injustices—a consideration of equity, ethics, and social justice should be addressed throughout the curriculum. An examination of injustices in U.S. schools may suggest an idea for a PoP for a given scholar practitioner to pursue.

A **DiP** framed with equity, ethics, and social justice addresses a PoP that has implications for the honest, decent, and fair treatment of all peoples within the institution–and ideally beyond. The DiP so framed, spotlights the issues and demands of leaders in education and *the institutions in which they work.* It sheds additional, directed, and effective light on efforts to address a particular organizational quandary–a PoP–taking into consideration equity, ethics, and social justice ramifications.

A Note of Caution: Constraints in Selecting a PoP

Mintrop (2016) posed a few cautions in the selection process. First, specifically as it relates to equity-focused PoPs, too often the source is not at the local level but is at a higher level (e.g., the district or the university system). In fact, Mintrop contended that such an issue is not a PoP at all. He says that a PoP, by definition, is local *and can be addressed at the local level.*

Mintrop also argued that change is not only difficult, but it is often incremental and thereby frustrating. Finally, he contended that the proposed intervention intended to address the PoP must be practical or realistic if it is to be effective on any level. The scholar practitioner must ask the question: Can it realistically be carried out?

Summary

In 2009, the CPED envisioned the characteristics of graduates of CPED influenced practitioner-oriented EdD programs. They said that those graduates would be able to:

1. blend practical wisdom with professional skills and knowledge to name, frame, and solve PoPs;

2. use practical research and applied theories as tools for change because they understand the importance of equity and social-justice; and

3. disseminate their work in multiple ways, and recognize their obligation to resolve problems of practice by collaborating with key stakeholders, including the university, the educational institution, the community, and individuals (p.1)

A PoP is identified, described, analyzed, and addressed within a DiP—a formal, problem—based discourse or treatise. Within the DiP, there is a discussion of methods and strategies used to bring about change and to assess whether the change is, in fact, an improvement. Through the identification, description, analysis, and addressing of a meaningful PoP, the scholar practitioner can document the scholarly development of leadership expertise in organizational improvement. A social justice framework informs this exercise with a focus on equitable and ethical practice and the dismantling and transformation of existing oppressive educational systems. The intervention aimed at addressing the PoP—as well as the entire DiP and associated activities—contributes a concrete good to the larger community and the dissemination of new relevant knowledge. With the cultivation of this type of knowledge and skill base, we are preparing high-quality leaders in education, including principals, curriculum leaders, superintendents, and other pre-K-12 central office administrators, community college presidents, and other community college administrators, four-year college and university administrators, teacher educators, evaluators, and more.

Graduates of practitioner-oriented EdD programs must be prepared to display equitable, ethical, and socially-just leadership. As CPED indicated, our goal in practitioner-oriented EdD programs is to "increase the likelihood that EdD candidates graduate with the capacity to transform educational practice" (Perry, 2013, p.

114). Linking abstract and down-to-earth skills equips scholar practitioners to more effectively identify, analyze, deliberate on, and frame investigations focused on highly significant PoPs.

I close with the sobering words of Hinnant-Crawford (2020):

> . . . we have to be audacious enough to believe we can save education. No matter how bleak or how big, how wicked, or how complex the problem, we have to have faith that we have the knowledge, the power, the tools, and the capacity to tackle it. But first, we must have the will. We must name the problem, and we must see the system. (p. 204).

Endnotes

[1] At WCU, we refer to our EdD students as scholar practitioners, emphasizing the importance of the integration of practitioner-oriented research methods, such as improvement science, within their day-to-day leadership practices. This notion is quite like the concept of scholarly practitioners who "blend practical wisdom with professional skills and knowledge to name, frame and solve problems of practice. They use practical research and applied theories as tools for change because they understand the importance of equity and social justice. They disseminate their work in multiple ways, and they have an obligation to resolve problems of practice by collaborating with key stakeholders, including the university, the educational institution, the community, and individuals." (CPED, 2010)

[2] There are several disciplines wherein research and professional practice doctorates exist side by side–sometimes within the same institution. In most cases, the curricula are very different, focusing on the expectations for graduates of the respective programs. For example, the graduate of a PhD program in biomedicine is expected to advance knowledge in medicine, while an MD recipient is expected to apply existing knowledge in medicine. Similarly, in business, a PhD is a research degree for candidates who seek to pursue careers in academia and/or conduct research that contributes to business knowledge or theory. A DBA is a professional doctorate in business with a focus on advancing theoretical knowledge and its use in business practice. Although some content may overlap, in each of these illustrations the preparation for the researchers and the practitioners needs to be different–and it is.

[3] In 2007, CPED–committed to practitioner-oriented EdD programs–began to fill a void in these programs, providing guidance to existing and developing programs seeking to address the needs of education practitioners. The consortium–now with more than 100 institutions–is continuing to help to redesign these programs to be more practitioner-oriented. CPED has six guiding principles that direct its work with its member institutions, with a focus on: (1) equity, ethics, and social justice, (2) constructing and applying knowledge, (3) collaboration and communication skills, (4) analyzing and addressing PoPs, (5) a professional knowledge base, and (6) professional knowledge and practice. (Carnegie Project on the Education Doctorate, n.d.)

[4] We discourage aspiring academics from enrolling in our EdD program because, while they will likely gain many of the skills to serve successfully as university faculty, our goal is not to prepare our students for tenure track faculty positions. The focus on a PoP is significantly different from that which is the emphasis with a traditional PhD dissertation and program (i.e., applied versus theoretical).

References

Belzer, A., & Ryan, S. (2013). Defining the problem of practice dissertation: Where's the practice, where's the problem. *Planning and Changing,*

44(3), 1095-207.

Blevins, B. E., Cooper, S., Papadakis, L. K. C., Earl, J., Howell, L., Lively, C. & Werse, N. R. (2022). Reframing the problem of practice: Transitions in Baylor University's EdD in learning and organizational change program. *Impacting Education, 7*(1), 32-41. https://doi.org/10.5195/ie.20 22.230

Bryk, A. S., Gomez, L. M., Grunow, A. and LeMahieu, P. G. (2015). *Learning to improve: How America's schools can get better at getting better.* Harvard Education Press. https://doi.org/10.17763/1943-5045-85.4.675a

Carnegie Project on the Education Doctorate. (n.d.). *About CPED.* https://cped. memberclicks.net/assets/resource-center/docs/cped_framework.pdf

Carnegie Project on the Education Doctorate. (2009). *Working principles of the professional practice doctorate in education.*

Carnegie Project on the Education Doctorate. (2010). *Design concept definitions.* http://cpedinitiative.org/design-concept-definitions/

Council of Graduate Schools. (2007). *Task force report on the professional doctorate.* Council of Graduate Schools.

Crow, R., Lomotey, K., & Topolka-Jorissen, K. (2016). An adaptive model or a rigorous professional practice doctorate: The disquisition. In V. Storey & K. Hesbol (Eds.), *Contemporary approaches to dissertation development and research methods* (pp. 205-220). IGI Global. https://doi.org/10.4018/978-1-5225-1624-8.ch024

DeMatthews, D., & Mawhinney, H. (2014). Social justice leadership and inclusion: Exploring challenges in an urban district struggling to address inequities. *Educational Administration Quarterly, 50*(5), 844–881. https://doi.org/10.1177/0013161X13514440

Furman, G. (2012). Social justice leadership as praxis: Developing capacities through preparation programs. *Educational Administration Quarterly, 48*(2), 191–229. https://doi.org/10.1177/0013161X11427394

Gillham, J. C., Williams, N. V., Rife, G., & Parker, K. K. (2019). Problems of practice: A document analysis of education doctorate dissertations. *Impacting Education, 4*(1), 1-9. https://doi.org/10.5195/ie.2019.85

Hinnant-Crawford, B. N. (2020). *Improvement science in education: A primer.* Myers Education Press.

Hochbein, C. & Perry, J. A. (2013). The role of research in the professional doctorate. *Planning and Changing, 44*(3/4), 181-195.

Langley, G. J., Moen, R. D., Nolan, K. M., Nolan, T. W., Norman, C. L., & Provost, L. P. (2009). *The improvement guide: A practical approach to enhancing organizational performance (2nd ed).* Jossey-Bass. https://doi. org/10.1080/10686967.1998.11919154

Ma, V. W. Dana, N. F., Adams, A., & Kennedy, B. L. (2018). Understanding the problem of practice: An analysis of professional practice EdD dissertations. *Impacting Education: Journal on Transforming Professional Practice, 3*(1), 13-22. https://doi.org/10.5195/ie.2018.50

Mayer, G. (2023, 9 January). After condemning 'trendy ideology' in higher ed, Florida's governor targets a small college. *The Chronicle of Higher Education.*

Mintrop, R. (2016). *Design-based school improvement: A practical guide for education leaders.* Harvard Education Press.

Perry, J. A. (2012). To Ed.D. or not to Ed.D.? *Phi Delta Kappan, 94*(1), 41-44.

Perry, J. A. (2013). Carnegie Project on the Education Doctorate: The education doctorate–a degree for a time. *Planning and Change, 44*(3/4), 113-126.

Schueler, M. (2023, 19 January). Florida Gov. Ron DeSantis' war on 'woke ideology' in higher education threatens academic freedom. *Orlando Weekly.*

Solochek, J. S. (2023, 9 January). Florida higher education under fire as 'woke' by DeSantis, appointees. *Tampa Bay Times.*

Sparks, S. D. (2013). "Improvement Science" seen as an emerging tool in K-12 spheres. *Education Week, 33*(6), 5-6.

Weiler, J. & Lomotey, K. (2021). Defining rigor in justice-oriented EdD programs: Preparing leaders to disrupt and transform schools. *Educational Administration Quarterly, 58*(1), 110-140. https://doi.org/10.1177/0013 161x211050926

CHAPTER 6

Context and Conditions of the DiP

SUHA R. TAMIM, EDD, MPH; CHRIS SUMMERS, EDD;
LESLEE SCHAUER, EDD; VERONICA RAMON, EDD;
LYNN HEMMER, PHD

In their book, *The Improvement Science Dissertation in Practice,* Perry et al. (2020) recounted the initiative that led to the birth of the Carnegie Project for the Education Doctorate (CPED) and the re-establishment of the EdD as "the professional doctorate in education" (p. 6). They noted that one model of EdD does not fit all because educational practitioners vary in their needs. They said that "the profession of education spans PK-12 schooling, post-secondary education, out-of-school learning, non-profit leadership, and beyond" (Perry et al., p. 5). These settings represent learning organizations that are complex systems by nature. Reigeluth and Duffy (2019) explained:

> A classroom is part of a school, a school is part of a school district, a school district is part of a community, which is part of a state, which is part of a region, which is part of a country, which is part of our planet, which is part of the universe. (Reigeluth & Duffy, 2019, p. 4)

Similarly, Senge (2012) described three nested systems in learning organizations. The learning classroom consists of teachers, students, and parents; the learning school consists of superintendents, principals, administrators, board members, trustees, etc.; and the learning community consists of the local, regional, or international environment the learning organization exists in. Bryk et al. (2016) added goals, ideas, tools, and technologies as layers of complexities to these systems; they stressed the importance of analyzing the educational systems to understand how they operate and to determine the root causes of problems.

Selecting a problem of practice (PoP) for the Dissertation in Practice (DiP) in these complex educational systems can sound overwhelming for education practitioners. Therefore, it is essential to consider one that is "persistent, contextualized, and ... embedded in the work of a professional practitioner" (CPED, 2022, Design Concepts Upon Which to Build Programs). Even then, several plausible PoPs could exist in a particular educational work setting. In this regard, Mintrop (2016) specified that a good problem of practice is one that is urgent, within the sphere of influence of the investigator; has clear indicators, a problem that can be explored within the time frame and resources available during the study; and one that aligns with the organizational goals. Additionally, he highlighted the need to frame the PoP and define it to determine its structure and its environment that will, in turn, direct the appropriate solutions.

On the other hand, the inquiry process in a DiP aims to improve learning by changing current practices. Far too often, change initiatives fail because they are implemented without a true understanding of the nature of the desired transformation and its inherent complexities (Bryk et al., 2016). Successful change occurs at the interconnection of teaching and learning, organizational and social infrastructure, and the system's relationship with its environment (Reigeluth & Duffy, 2019). In other words, a change in one part of the system will cause a change in the other parts. DiPs are designed for a specific local context, one that is replete with history and with culture. Within that context exists conditions, some supporting change and others challenging change. Consequently, the DiP context and conditions become important elements.

Context of the Dissertation in Practice (DiP)

At its most general, context has been defined as "the interrelated conditions in which something exists or occurs" (Merriam-Webster dictionary, n.d.). A slightly more nuanced definition is that context is the physical environment, the physical attributes of boundaries and structures, in which practice and proposed change takes place (McCormack et al., 2002). Øvretveit (2011) explained context as "all factors that are **not** [emphasis added] part of the quality improvement intervention itself" (p. 118). These factors can include social elements (Squires et al., 2015), policy pressures and expectations (Braun et al., 2011), along with environmental physical attributes of the setting. McCormack et al. (2002) goes on to explain that in order to understand context, one must also understand the social, cultural, and structural boundaries; all of which are integral parts when setting one's sight on effecting change.

Context also considers the specifics of the larger organizational framework, capturing factors such as leadership structure, practice characteristics, and factors that may directly relate to the experiences of stakeholders (e.g., teachers and students), as well as external influences such as sources of financing and community involvement (Tomoaia-Cotisel et al., 2013). As such, the success of an action (e.g., intervention, scale, evaluation) to address a PoP depends not just on what the action is, but the fidelity of how a DiP is designed and conducted (Elonga Mboyo, 2021). While the scholarly practitioner should identify the contextual factors that will influence their design of the DiP, they also need to take into consideration the conditions which may influence how DiP activities occur in their specific context.

Conditions of the Dissertation in Practice (DiP) to Effect Change

The conditions in which a DiP are to occur are important considerations because they relate to the demands encountered by the scholarly practitioner in the workplace that is also serving as the site of research. As McCormack et al. (2002) explained, there are leadership and evaluative conditions which exist within the context, meaning that the conditions regarding the authority to define and solve different local problems need to be understood by the scholar-practitioner. As expectations of what the scholar-practitioner should achieve through a DiP come into view, so must one seek to develop new conditions to accept changes. However, scholar-practitioners seeking to effect change within their local context must know what conditions exist for change. Øvretveit (2011) further explained that for scholar-practitioners who aim to conduct some type of quality improvement research, one must first "understand which conditions influence improvement and how they do so" (p. 118).

Below, three scholar-practitioners (co-authors), Chris, Leslee, and Veronica, share their direct experiences as they designed and conducted a DiP to address a specific PoP within the context of their respective professional practices. They then described dynamics and interrelationship conditions that influenced their DiP activities as they sought to effect change locally. While the stories presented do not describe in full the context and conditions of their respective DiPs, they do offer examples of why and how context and conditions are important to consider.

Context of Chris' DiP

In 2014, I was hired by a south Texas urban school district as director of curriculum and instruction. Of 2,000 students enrolled, 92% were identified as low socioeconomic, and 61% at-risk. The district was performing below state averages on state assessments, with data revealing significant performance gaps in all content areas. The district had a high teacher turnover rate averaging 20% the three years prior to my arrival, with 31%, on average, of district teachers having five or fewer years of experience. We were starting every school year not only with newly hired teachers, but many were beginning teachers. Furthermore, there was no teacher induction program in place to support these new teachers. So, in August 2014, we pieced together an initial induction program and I turned to the literature to help me better understand teacher attrition and teacher induction, before embarking on my DiP study.

Teacher attrition negatively impacts student success, contributes to a school climate of instability, and redirects funds toward recruitment that might be better spent on student learning (Barnes et al., 2007; Carver-Thomas & Darling-Hammond, 2019). Research reveals half of all teacher attrition occurs in just 25% of all public schools: those with high-poverty, high-minority students and in urban and rural areas (Ingersoll et al., 2018), which grounded the contextual basis for my DiP. Concerning me was how to best support teachers new to the district and new to the profession. I know effective teacher induction programs have been shown to improve new teacher retention rates by 20%, accelerate professional growth, provide a positive return on investment, and increase teacher effectiveness (Ingersoll & Strong, 2011).

Conditions of Chris' DiP

My DiP was a professional practice dissertation designed to enhance and impact the immediate practice of a school district and our support of beginning teachers. I used a three-fold design challenge focused on developing, scaling, and improving a teacher induction program. The first two design challenges were critical context and condition components of the DiP, allowing me to understand the existing and shifting conditions that would influence any improvement to the teacher attrition rate in my district. Important to these design challenges was understanding the conditions for the systemic and cultural transformation that occurred through the implementation and improvement of the teacher induction program along with understanding the systemic importance of a comprehensive system of teacher support and development.

Grounding the work of developing and refining a teacher induction program within the context of a DiP allowed me to bring a research basis to the work of changing habits and practices in the district. Instead of it being a "pet project" or one person's vision, the work became the collective emphasis for improving the teaching and learning in the district and bringing stability to the teaching staff of the district. The DiP format required district leaders to be intentional about bringing current, peer-reviewed research to our decisions about organizational change, adult learning, and the systemization of best practices in support of beginning teachers.

Chris' DiP Context and Conditions Combined

Along with the geographical (urban, south Texas), school district demography (high poverty, high at-risk, low performance) contexts, my DiP was further contextualized by structural factors of frequent leadership turnover, absence of a guaranteed and viable curriculum, and the lack of a comprehensive teacher induction program, which contributed to a high rate of new teacher attrition. As an appreciation for a system and theory of knowledge relative to the needs of new teachers came into focus, conditions of the DiP took shape. These conditions included steps taken during the research timeline to create essential experiences of mentoring, release time, communities of practices, and situated learning; that in turn allowed for an increased capability and likelihood for improvement for the district's new teacher attrition rate.

Context of Leslee's DiP

Texas Senate Bill 1746 was passed in 2019, which added Indicator #14, children of incarcerated parents to state-defined criteria for students considered to be at risk for school failure. This policy label centered children of incarcerated parents and the premise that additional supports were needed to ensure their success academically, socially, and emotionally. At that time and during this study, I was an education specialist at a state-sponsored educational service center (ESC) and was responsible for providing training and support to school districts.

The context of my DiP was two-fold, personally and professionally. When I was three, my father was sent to prison, and from my reflective perspective, the school district was unsure of what services would meet my specific needs because they most likely were unaware of my circumstances. While I learned self-sufficiency and resiliency, I realize now that I might have carried a slew of other red flags, and still there were no additional supports provided. At the ESC, a Counselor Cooperative was operated, where any of 46 districts and charters in the ESC's region can opt in to the paid network to receive training/participate in monthly meetings. When Indicator #14 was released, the educational specialist team met with the Cooperative and found there was a dearth of information relative to children of incarcerated parents. One question asked repeatedly was, "How do we properly identify these students?" We had no clear response or guidance to offer. Training and professional development focused on how school counselors can help these students was nonexistent. I envisioned this DiP as a way to respond to and address the needs of school counselors who were tasked with identifying and serving these students.

Conditions of Leslee's DiP

The purpose of my DiP was to develop a professional development (PD) experience focused on the advancement of school counselors' knowledge concerned with a deeper awareness and understanding of holistic supports for children of incarcerated parents. Three phases were designed to align with four goals of the study. Two iterations of the PD were delivered to the ESC Cooperative.

I engaged with six school counselors (focus group; attended two iterations of the PD) and eight community stakeholders (interviews) who served as advocates for children of incarcerated parents. Analysis of focus group and interview data, along with policy and setting artifacts resulted in three overarching conditional outcomes. I was able to: (a) identify knowledge (and absence) of the prevalence of the population, (b) describe characteristics and needs of children of incarcerated parents, and (c) identify community supports that currently exist. With the professional development experience serving as an intervention, there were three additional conditions the school counselors desired: 1) move beyond the theory to application; 2) create engaging activities; and 3) provide practical tools to use.

Knowing the existing and desired conditions for school counselor professional practice allowed for a deeper understanding of what knowledge and resources school counselors were aware of, while creating new information for a research-based school counselor professional development. The DiP was designed to be able to develop, test, implement, and spread change but more importantly, to allow the change to be informed by the experiences of stakeholders who needed to be familiar with the needs of these children.

Leslee's DiP Context and Conditions Combined

My DiP revolved around an overlap between my personal and professional contexts. The personal context of a childhood experience of having a father who was incarcerated served as a partial motivation for me to center children of incarcerated parents in my DiP. Professionally, the passage of Senate Bill 1746, alongside my role and responsibilities as an education service specialist, influenced how I considered approaching the DiP to effect change for school counselors. Several conditions unfolded as the DiP was conducted. These conditions included me having to be responsive to participant needs by using participant feedback to adapt the professional development iterations, while remaining in compliance with the organizational structure.

Context of Veronica's DiP

My dissertation in practice (DiP) conducted during the 2022-2023 school year (SY) reflects my experience as the current Chief Support Services Officer in a rural, small district in South Texas (1450 students; 97% Hispanic; 82% economically disadvantaged; 50% at risk of school failure) to improve an existing peer-to-peer student mentoring program, herein known as the P^3 program. In 2017, the P^3 program was conceptualized as part of a broader district dropout initiative to support early literacy development for elementary students who were at risk of school failure. At that time, we sought to anchor early literacy development with positive school experiences and as such, positioned the program around supportive peer-to-peer student relationships. From 2018-2019 SY to fall 2019, the P^3 program was in full operation. In early 2020 school districts closed due to the COVID-19 global pandemic, effectively pausing the P^3 program for a year. The P^3 program resurfaced in fall 2021, now conceptualized as a viable option to support students who not only were struggling with academics, but who needed social-emotional support. Of concern was that the program was still being delivered from a stance of what was possible and not from a clear plan or purpose.

Conditions of Veronica's DiP

No logic model or formal program plan existed for the P³ program; this absence complicated an understanding of the relationship between essential P³ components and their outcomes, which according to Peyton and Scicchitano (2017) makes planning for an improvement, problematic. The DiP was used to gain a better understanding of the vision, process, and outcomes of the P³ mentoring program in order to create a logic model that can then be used to guide future evaluations and improvements. Without a formal understanding of what the P³ program entails, and how and what it is designed to accomplish, certain influences (e.g., stakeholder's understanding, COVID-19 learning loss) may trigger changes in its design, complicating its utility to serve as a mechanism to prevent students from dropping out of school.

The conditions of my DiP included using a four-phase process to crystalize the program vision and process that in turn translated to the development of a logic model: (1) establishing assumptions about the program; (2) comparing program artifacts to these assumptions; (3) using varied stakeholder vantage points (coordinator, superintendent, site teachers and administrators, parents and students); and (4) analyzing select activities relative to program purpose. Although initial conditions for the DiP were set as part of the research design, they did not consider what happens with key stakeholders (those with institutional and programmatic memory) who leave the district before data is collected. Some might chalk this up as a limitation to the study and leave it at that. However, for my DiP, designed with a limited number of possible participants (stakeholders) to begin with, I had to shift my thinking and approaches to consider ways in which to continue to move the work forward. This included acknowledging the gap in historical knowledge of the program and then focus more on the here, now, and future of the P³ program.

Veronica's DiP Context and Conditions Combined

I first describe the context of DiP using descriptors of small, rural, school district in south Texas, and I use state demographic labels to describe the students we serve; however, neither capture the depth of context for why this DiP was important to conduct. To illustrate context in more depth, I then describe how my district sought to find value, scope, and continued refinement of an existing program that was envisioned to serve a vulnerable population within the district—the student at risk of dropping out of school. The conditions of my DiP were reflective of seeing this as an opportunity to effect change and as such, I designed the DiP to take into account a relatively small number of participants due to district size. However, during the study, personnel changes occurred and changed the conditions of my DiP.

Conclusion

Context is increasingly being discussed when pursuing a DiP. Scholar-practitioners often describe context in descriptive detail relative to the setting in which the study takes place. However, context extends beyond the environmental factors of geography and demographics of a site; it includes social, cultural, economic, political, and historical factors that shape a DiP's purpose, significance, and methodological approach used to address a PoP. Context is more than an objective and tangible phenomenon; rather, it indicates what is important to scholar-practitioners and how they attach significance to their study. As evidenced in the experiences shared by Chris, Leslee, and Veronica, context was described not only according to their respective environmental settings, but also in terms of complex, multilayered personal and professional situational boundaries, replete with organizational culture and traditions, cannon of local and broad knowledge, and professional authorities representing normative agencies, all of which contributed to why their respective PoP was studied.

Creating change through a DiP requires the scholar-practitioner not only to understand the importance of context, but also recognize the opportunity or constraint for change and position it as something accessible and understood by others. To influence change through a DiP, there exists conditions of leadership, capacity for change, and culture that need to be considered, especially when designing opportunities for change to happen. The research design of a DiP often considers involving others to help identify the PoP, develop a solution, and implement a change. In doing so, the specific conditions necessary to create change depend not solely on the change itself but also on the people who are included in the study. However, conditions of a DiP may shift, sometimes rapidly, as the study is being completed.

Some conditions are recognized and accounted for during the design of the DiP. Chris, Leslee, and Veronica designed their studies understanding structural, procedural, cultural, and leadership conditions that influenced how they designed their DiPs and planned for change. They designed their DiPs to include using participant feedback to design and develop: a mentoring experience (Chris), professional development (Leslee) and a logic model (Veronica). However, other conditions manifested themselves *during* the study. A DiP research design cannot always foresee conditions that arise out of common occurrences within the practitioners setting, of difficulties in planning for long-term impact amidst ongoing policy changes (student achievement scores for Chris; system change for Leslee), or personnel changes (Veronica). When conditions shift, the scholar-practitioner will need to shift as well.

References

Barnes, G., Crowe, E., & Schaefer, B. (2007). *The cost of teacher turnover in five school districts: A pilot study*. National Commission on Teaching and America's Future.

Braun, A., Ball, S. J., Maguire, M., & Hoskins, K. (2011). Taking context seriously: Towards explaining policy enactments in the secondary school. *Discourse (Abingdon, England)*, *32*(4), 585-596. https://doi.org/10.108 0/01596306.2011.601555

Bryk, A. S., Gomez, L. M., Grunow, A., LeMahieu, P. G. (2015). *Learning to improve: How America's schools can get better at getting better*. Harvard Education Press.

Carnegie Project for the Education Doctorate (2022). *The CPED Framework*. https://cped.memberclicks.net/the-framework

Carver-Thomas, D., & Darling-Hammond, L. (2019). The trouble with teacher turnover: How teacher attrition affects students and schools.

Education Policy Analysis Archives, 27(36), 36. https://doi.org/10.14507 /epaa.27.3699

Elonga Mboyo, J. P. (2021). Theorizing context in educational leadership from a relational critical realist perspective. *Research in Educational Administration & Leadership, 6*(3), 724-740. https://doi.org/10.30828/ real/2021.3.7

Ingersoll, R. M., Merrill, E., Stuckey, D., & Collins, G. (2018). *Seven trends: The transformation of the teaching force.* https://repository.upenn.edu/ cpre_researchreports/108

Ingersoll, R. & Strong, M. (2011). The impact of induction and mentoring programs for beginning teachers: A critical review of the research. *Review of Education Research, 81*(2), 201-233. https://doi.org/ 10.3102/0034654311403323

McCormack, B., Kitson, A., Harvey, G., Rycroft-Malone, J., Titchen, A., & Seers, K. (2002). Getting evidence into practice: The meaning of context. *Journal of Advanced Nursing, 38*(1), 94-104. https://doi.org/ 10.1046/j.1365-2648.2002.02150.x

Merriam-Webster online dictionary. (n.d.). Context. In *Merriam-Webster. com dictionary.* https://www.merriam-webster.com/dictionary/context

Mintrop, R. (2016). *Design-based school improvement: A practical guide for educational leaders.* Harvard Education Press.

Øvretveit, J. (2011). Understanding the conditions for improvement: Research to discover which context influences affect improvement success. *BMJ Quality & Safety, 20*(Suppl 1), i18-23. https://doi.org/10.1136/bm jqs.2010.045955

Perry, J. A., Zambo, D., & Crow, R. (2020). *The improvement science dissertation in practice: A guide for faculty, committee members, and their students.* Myers Education Press.

Peyton, D. J., & Scicchitano, M. (2017). Devil is in the details: Using logic models to investigate program process. *Evaluation and Program Planning, 65,* 156-162. https://doi.org/10.1016/j.evalprogplan.2017.08.012

Reigeluth, C. M., & Duffy, F. M. (2019). The school system transformation process: Guidance for paradigm change in school districts. In M. J. Spector, B. B. Lockee, & M. D. Childress (Eds.), *Learning, design, and technology: An international compendium of theory, research, practice, and policy* (pp. 1–32). Springer. https://doi.org/10.1007/978-3-319-17727-4_96-1

Senge, P. M. (2012). *Schools that learn: A fifth discipline fieldbook for educators, parents, and everyone who cares about education.* Crown Business.

Squires, J. E., Graham, I. D., Hutchinson, A. M., Michie, S., Francis, J. J., Sales, A., Brehaut, J., Curran, J., Ivers, N., Lavis, J., Linklater, S., Fenton, S., Noseworthy, T., Vine, J., & Grimshaw, J. M. (2015). Identifying the domains of context important to implementation science: A study protocol. *Implementation Science: IS, 10*(1), 135-135. https://doi.org/10.1186/s13012-015-0325-y

Tomoaia-Cotisel, A., Scammon, D. L., Waitzman, N. J., Cronholm, P. F., Halladay, J. R., Driscoll, D. L., Solberg, L. I., Hsu, C., Tai-Seale, M., Hiratsuka, V. & Shih, S. C. (2013) Context matters: the experience of 14 research teams in systematically reporting contextual factors important for practice change. *The Annals of Family Medicine, 11*, S115–S123.

CHAPTER 7

Knowledge that Frames the DiP:

Traditional Indigenous Knowledges— A Foundation of the Dissertation in Practice

WALTER KAHUMOKU III, PHD; LORI IDETA, EDD

In training school administrators for leadership, Shulman and colleagues (2006) contended that an educational doctorate had lost its meaning. At the time, for colleges and schools of education, demarcation between a PhD—which produced new knowledge and prepared scholars for life as an academic-researcher—and an EdD—which focused on developing practitioner stewards—was indistinguishable (Burgess & Wellington, 2010; Maxwell, 2003; Perry, 2013; Taylor & Storey, 2011). As a response, the Carnegie Project on the Educational Doctorate (CPED) convened a national dialogue where stakeholders engaged in addressing two fundamental questions: "What are the knowledge, skills, and dispositions that professionals working in education should demonstrably have?" and "How do we prepare them to have these?" (Perry, 2013, p. 114). An underlying premise for these discussions was: to "meet the complex needs of our communities, it requires an innovative mindset that can be responsive to a generative culture of leadership that fosters change" (Twomey et al., 2017, pp. 19-20).

For people of color and specifically those who identify as Indigenous, Tribal, Aboriginal, and/or Native to the lands on which they have resided for generational millennia, this chapter examines how Indigenous traditional knowledges are activated in a Dissertation in Practice (DiP). The question guiding this chapter is: what aspects of an EdD program founded on social justice include and integrate the milieu of traditional Native knowledges and wisdoms that abound in the Indigenous peoples of the Pacific? This chapter presents the University of Hawai'i, Mānoa (UHM), College of Education's Educational Doctorate in Professional Practice (UHM-COE's EdD) program as an exemplar regarding how it has instituted learning environments that allow for and uphold the use of traditional, Indigenous knowledges as means of developing leader-practitioner-scholars. This is a story of an EdD program that has, since 2011 purposefully sustained growth environments where amalgams of professional, cultural and linguistic, and theories and research methods, seek to resolve key problems-of-practice impacting education in the islands (Twomey & Lambrev, 2018).

The Complexity of Determining Indigeneity

Before describing the program's determinatives, 'Indigenous/ Native' and 'Indigenous/Native Knowledges' need to be framed. When formulating its Declaration of Indigenous Rights, delegates to the United Nations encountered difficulty defining the term "Indigenous." Many terms used to describe Indigenous peoples were created and imposed by colonizers (Indigenous Foundations, 2023). Agreement on an accepted meaning and how to measure its existence was tenuous (Weaver, 2001). Conventionally, 'Indigenous' refers to a people who have lived in and have a relationship with a place for generational millennia (United Nations, 2006) and for the purposes of this chapter, we interchange the use of terms such as Indigenous, Native, Aboriginal, and Tribal out of respect for the complexity and multiplicity of identities among peoples across the world.

In addition, UHM-COE's EdD Program embraces the constant, competing tensions—rightful access to lands and waters; validity of Native ways of knowing, believing, and being; linguistic and educational sovereignty; self-government and determination; among others—that are a part of Indigenous students' lives. In turn, this program embraces research on problems-of-practice that are driven by critical needs in their Native communities.

Degai et al. (2022) guide our work when they share the following wisdom:

> While working with Indigenous communities, one has to be mindful of the systemic trauma they have experienced in their history, and allow time, and channel resources so that these communities can heal and reconcile with their land, histories and languages that were disrupted due to colonization (p. 2).

Likewise, in this learning ecosystem, Native researchers integrate both contemporary research methods and theory as well as their cultural knowledges, frameworks, cosmologies, epistemologies, and the like throughout their study (Degai et al., 2022; Hunt, 2014; Jessen et al., 2022; Tom et al., 2019) so that "Indigenous traditional knowledge not only sustains Indigenous and local communities in their daily lives, but is also a key element of their identity and self-determination" (United Nations, Department of Economic and Social Affairs: Indigenous Peoples, 2006, p. 7). The faculty and mentors in this EdD believe that:

> the production of Indigenous knowledge does not involve "saving" Indigenous people but helping construct conditions that allow for Indigenous self-sufficiency while learning from the vast storehouse of Indigenous knowledges that provide compelling insights into all domains of human endeavor. (Kincheloe & Steinberg, 2008, p. 135)

The Program: University of Hawai'i, College of Education, EdD Doctorate in Professional Educational Practice

Since accepting the first cohort in 2011, a total of 112 students have entered this EdD—30 students in Cohort I, 27 in Cohort II, 29 in Cohort III, and 26 in Cohort IV. Its student-program completion rate (total number of students who started coursework divided by degree completers) is 82.56% through the first three cohorts (Cohort IV is in the process of completing their dissertations). Using self-identified data, 43.75% of participants identified as Native Hawaiian and/or Pacific Islander (e.g., Chamorro, Samoan, Chuukese, Palauan), .08% as Filipino, and 70+% as female.

The UHM-COE's EdD Program, founded on the tenets of CPED, has continually supported its students to address issues of educational social injustice in Hawai'i. The program continues to normalize dissertations written partially/entirely in an Indigenous language, as well as the use of traditional cultural knowledges and theoretical constructs that honor traditional Native ways of understanding, believing, and being. These foundational principles have been recognized in a recent accreditation report as one of the premier programs offered by UH's College of Education (AAQEP Accreditation Report, 2021).

Renormalizing Indigenous/Native Knowledge

"For Indigenous research to be beneficial, one must research with a paradigm that accounts for Indigenous ways of knowing" (Thomas, 2022, p. 84). This program intentionally selects faculty and community mentors who willingly incorporate theoretical frameworks and constructs readings and critical discussions that espouse traditional Native knowledges—cultural, linguistic, historic, spiritual, and others—held by peoples of the Pacific. Dissertation chairs and committee members come from a well-formed network of minority and Native scholar-practitioners to constitute dissertation committees.

This targeted selection allows Indigenous students to accept and embrace traditional Native knowledge as ways that shape their studies. A Chamorro student originally from Guam explains:

> Chamoru ontology prioritizes a communal, place-based identity; Chamoru axiology honors relationship and reciprocal care. The ethos underlying Chamoru epistemology, ontology, and axiology is known as inafa'maolek (to make good), a holistic philosophy which promotes harmonic interdependence among all beings living and non-living, human and non-human, and events in the past, present, and future. It is an ethos of direct, lived experiences in our spaces (ordinary and non-ordinary, natural, and supernatural), practicing harmonious relationships and reciprocal actions for the well-being of the whole rather than the individual (Perez-Iyechad, 2009, as cited by Hattori, 2014, pp. 6-7).

This EdD program has also created and sustained protocols that integrate Native well-being concepts to embolden its students. At program events and at the start of several courses, the cohort will intone a Hawaiian 'oli or chant to respect ancestors that reside in a place of learning. Native wise sayings are shared during class discussions and 34 of 112 dissertations have integrated them in framing dissertation chapters. Guest speakers present both in their Native language as well as in English with an understanding that translation can be offered when appropriate and needed. Purposefully, the UHM-COE's EdD continues to renormalize the Indigeneity of its students.

Contesting the Canons of Accepted/Acceptable Research

To sustain teaching and learning that honors the ancient wisdoms of the people of Moana Nui (Pacific Ocean), this EdD Program (and its five directors) has continuously challenged the canons of valid, trustworthy academic investigations. While such contested debates have not led to quick adoption nor inclusion by this university and others, this program has remained steadfast in its commitment of Indigeneity and Native knowledges. For example, instead of requiring program participants to adopt well-established, accepted ways of conducting qualitative research—ethnography, phenomenology, case study, and the like—students and their dissertation chairs incorporate Indigenous ways that refine their research. Two DiPs utilized the ancient Kanaka (Native Hawaiian) art form of lei-making to guide their studies. Alencastre (2015), the program's first DiP of the Year award, shared:

> The analogy of lei-making became instrumental in personally connecting to the intentionality and complexities that emerged within each phase of this study. Articulating and extending the familiar processes and procedures of lei making as a traditional and valued custom contributed to the mauli ola of this study—its wellbeing and success as I assumed the role of participant researcher. (p. 32)

Another noted: "In this research, I embraced the work of Vaughan (2016) and the concept of "he haku aloha: research as lei-making" (p. 28) and Alencastre's (2015) metaphor of lei-making in research to provide a framing for the moʻolelo examined within" (Reid-Hayes, 2020, p. 2).

As shown in Keliʻikipikāneokolokaka's (2020) dissertation, native knowledge also framed why a study should benefit communities that want education to uphold their Indigeneity:

The process of kūkulu kuapā was the inspiration for my development of the Kūkulu Kuapā Framework that serves as the conceptual framework for this dissertation. The first four chapters represent a different stage of the kūkulu kuapā process (see Figure 1.5). The method of inquiry from the introduction to the data collection creates the kuapā, establishing the necessary conditions for analysis and synthesis. The resulting iʻa (findings and conclusions) harvested from this metaphorical loko iʻa have the potential to feed those who are ... applying Papakū Makawalu to their contexts. (p. 6)

Culturally embedded knowledge also brings purpose to the research. An author writes: "moʻo, used as a root word, encompasses an Indigenous view of this work. The title, Moʻohelu is an account. ... The introduction is the Moʻolelo Hoʻolauna, a story of introduction. ... Chapter 1 is the Moʻolelo Moʻokūʻauhau, the genealogy of this project" (Ikeda, 2014, p. 5). The genealogical importance of this Moʻo concept to Native Hawaiians offers one of a few justifications for conducting their research. Many students face similar questions about the validity of research not intended to sustain the well-being of those who are being investigated.

Another spoke to academic investigations as grounded in a commitment to ancestors, sharing "I bring and honor my kūpuna, their ʻike, and their hopes and dreams. ... I am but a part of a ʻmoʻokūʻauhau of intellectual traditions' from which I directly benefit and to which I bear the responsibility to mālama and hoʻoulu in pono ways" (Gapero, 2019, p. 1). Just as Native Hawaiians have been assimilated into life as Americans, and education became (and in many ways still is) one of the colonizing apparatuses that denounced Hawaiian ways of being, thinking, and knowing, devoting to ʻike Hawaiʻi (traditional knowledges) cares for the well-being of the Indigenous population in these islands.

Yet another student contended that the purpose of their research was to counter prevailing myths about the lands to which they were born and currently resides.

> Wai'anae 'Āina Momona is an offering akin to Indigenous Research because it focuses on righting the wrongs and implementing change. It is the way for a kama'āina (Native born) ma kēia āina nei (from *this* beloved place) to express the richness of Wai'anae as seen through an insider's view. (Wakinekona, 2017, p. 48)

These investigations have added meaning and import when these traditional understandings guide why, what, and how research is conducted.

> The closest translation and cultural pratice resembling talanoa in my Chuukeseouter island language is the concept of arekirek. ... Arekirek is more appropriate for a research process which requires informality and a sense of equality between the researcher and respondents. In fact, when invited into a process of arekirek ... participants share equal responsibility to seek answers to whatever problem is being addressed. (Raatior, 2017, p. 23)

When research is intended to counteract a legacy—often traumatic and at times, horrific—of imposed Western education that imposed non-Native beliefs through norms of acceptable beliefs and behaviors embedded in educational practices, it is extremely powerful. A scan of 112 dissertations produced by the first three cohorts identified 104 that addressed injustices in the island's educational systems and processes. Of these, 67 utilized a form of critical theory, culture-based theory, or other theoretical constructs, to shape their research.

Instead of simply completing the dissertation to attain a degree, this EdD recognizes: "Honoring these and other cultural norms led to engaging encounters, sharing of meaningful stories, new or stronger relationships, and other rich and sometimes unexpected outcomes" (Hattori, 2014, p. 39). Gapero (2019) states:

> The prioritization of the interdependence of intention and aligned outcomes seeks to maintain alignment with discovery that is driven by necessity, sustaining the very 'ōiwi mindset that knowledge worth gaining should have an authentic and appreciable application, as opposed to learning for the mere sake of learning. (p. 29)

Contesting standard research methods by allowing Native wisdoms to permeate the investigatory process has empowered this EdD program's participants to boldly explore and bring evocative solutions to some of the most challenging problems of practice facing Hawai'i's educational arenas. The following is an excerpt from a student's introduction to their dissertation.

> Dedication
> I am from Hawai'i
> I am from Papahanaumoku and Wākea
> I am from lāhui, 'Ōlelo, and Mo'okū'auhau
> Generations and Generations of Kānaka
> From The Great Dying of 1780 to the Overthrow of 1892
>
> … my mother, who had been conditioned to believe that Hawaiians, and all things Hawaiian, were inferior, had no interest in Hawaiian issues or Hawaiian language. Instead, she believed that my brothers and I should receive a traditional, western education. (Sarsona, 2017, p. 1)

Traditional Indigenous Intelligence as Data

In addition to culturally significant wisdom applied to research methods, dissertation chairs and committees have explored traditional knowledge as data. As Wakinekona (2017) illustrated, collecting mana'o (thoughts/beliefs) from Native Hawaiian kūpuna (elders) in the community concerning the state of education was vital to understanding what was problematic with the current ways in which children (the majority were Kānaka/Native Hawaiian) are schooled. These data points also pointed to solutions that would replace pronounced Americanized education processes with curriculum, instruction, and assessments that provide contexts around the strengths of this community—its history, language, traditions, and others.

In examining young Hawaiian males in higher education, Akiona (2018) collected information from 'ohana (families) about the importance of a higher education experience and degree. "Some of the familial influence was direct encouragement through dialogue, and at other times, it was indirect through observations of actions and circumstance" (Akiona, 2018, p. 67). In this case, their dissertation chair guided them to examine 'ohana mo'olelo (family stories) that uncovered key understandings about Native masculinity as related to schooling, jobs and careers, and family wellbeing.

Another student looked at how cultural protocols shape rigorous ways to collect research information:

> He mea nui ka 'o'ole'a ma luna o ia mau a'oākumu i 'ike i ka hana 'oia'i'o maoli o ke kūlana kumu, 'a'ole he hana ma'alahi a pono e mākaukau pono ma ka no'ono'o, ma ka 'ike, ma ka na'au, a me ka 'uhane pū kekahi. *Rigor is important in preparing for the reality and challenges of teaching, so preparation needs to be cognitive, emotional, and spiritual.* (Alencastre, 2015, p. 54)

Even traditional Kānaka belief in the power of Moi 'Uhane (dream state) challenges what is commonly held as appropriate research data. Reid-Hayes (2020) argued that dreams were integral to her autoethnography:

> However, it became clear that there was a philosophical disconnect. Autoethnography would not provide the foundation in 'ike kūpuna that my transformation would require. ... It became clear that I would need to listen to my kūpuna and step into the "life changing ceremony" (Wilson, 2008, p. 61) of Indigenous research. (p. 47)

In its attempts to contest the established epistemological proposition that scientific knowledge is superior to that produced by Indigenous people (Turnbull, 2009), this program has advocated for power ontologies that embrace Native wisdom as valid data. "Indigenous and non-Indigenous scholars demand the inclusion of Indigenous knowledges into our academic and scientific discourses, mainly in response to the large-scale dismissal of Indigenous knowledges in these very discourses" (Knoff, 2015, p. 179).

> ... my deepest desires to de-educate myself and re-claim my Indigenous identity and roots. By de-education I mean the process by which I am beginning to disclaim every Western-focused,

American-influenced, post-colonialist epistemology which I have learned in the American school system since my childhood. Throughout my 50 years of formal education, I have not claimed any expertise in any of the knowledge, skills, values that are authentically ours in the Northwest islands of Chuuk. (Raatior, 2017, p. 54)

Traditional Indigenous Approaches to Analysis and Reporting

A strong tenet of UHM-COE's EdD is for students to utilize the authentic voices of their study's participants. Dissertation committees and chairs are encouraged to assist student researchers who conduct qualitative studies to integrate Indigenous processes in their data analyses and reporting. Because "Hoolono, to listen in Hawaiian Epistemology is a critical principle" (Patria, 2014, p. 55), Patria deployed hoʻolono, or highly sensitive listening, to delineate the multiple and layered meanings of what was being shared by their study's participants.

My analysis of the data would include the cultural construct of kaona, or the hidden or veiled meanings, a unique feature of Hawaiian Epistemology. This effort would require a deeper examination beyond the surface of the storyteller's words to arrive at their message, their truth, their breath. (Patria, 2014, p. 56)

Sarsona (2017) listened to and honored the histories of four Native Hawaiian female educational leaders, in the Kanaka tradition of Aloha aku, Aloha mai (reciprocation). After writing her findings, she asked each of her participants to verify her telling of their life stories (a step beyond verifying data through member checking).

This program continues to support students to use cultural accountability measures to analyze and report on the data collected through their studies. Such research analysis techniques may one day alter dependence on scientific objectivity as a means of conducting valid, valuable research. Reid-Hayes (2020), who examined her own life stories and moi ʻuhane or dreams as a way to map the changes to her pedagogy with kindergarteners, recommends:

As a researcher, I wanted to explore the use of Indigenous methodologies that were unfamiliar and provocative. I intended to step away from traditional forms of qualitative research and reporting to explore methods rooted in moʻolelo, moʻokūʻahuhau, and personal reflection. As an individual, I hoped to discover a place where I could embrace my own Indigeneity. (p. 151)

Conclusion

After centuries of dissemination, colonization, and denial, research and approaches that attend to social injustices occurring in the education of Native peoples here in Hawaiʻi are surfacing. UHM-COE's EdD continues to shape learning spaces that support focus "on local Indigenous ideas, practices and visions of education that hold direct benefit for Indigenous peoples and broader impacts for all peoples" (Turnbull, 2009, p. 1). Moreover, the program honors and celebrates Indigeneity. Keliʻikipikāneokolohaka (2020) presents: "Indigenous research paradigms ... (that) aim to honor and elevate Indigenous knowledge and work to bring forth new knowledge that empowers the Indigenous collective" (p. 35); thereby " ... shifting the lens, or interpretation of research, from an Anglo view to an Indigenous view is a way to free ourselves and connect to the ʻike that we learn at home ... rising up and waking up of liberating knowledge" (Ikeda, 2014, p. 18).

This EdD elevates traditional knowledges of the Pacific's Native Peoples by contesting the canons of standard research protocols and processes, embracing Indigenous wisdoms as data, and employing Native approaches to data analysis and reporting. It does so by selecting faculty and committee members (mentors) who offer readings, teach courses about, and conduct discussions on how to utilize Native axiologies, epistemologies, and ontologies to conduct investigations of merit and worth to their students' communities. The program also lives its commitment to Indigeneity in the ways it begins events and courses through ʻoli and orients students to value their Native worth. Most importantly, the program continues to believe in an inherent sense of kuleana, of responsibility, to honor and uphold the traditional wisdom of those who generationally have existed on their home islands for millennia.

The authors of this chapter recognize the importance of walking this type of journey with the program's students, especially those of Native ancestry. A chair wrote about their student's dissertation process:

> Nearing the end of the journey—some 160 pages into the text and about a month before her dissertation presentation—she hurried to write, rewrite and rewrite again her methods chapter. The discouraging demands of time, getting it right by trying "to make you [her dissertation chair—me] proud," and hoping to just be done with this darn thing, crashed in on her. What advice I offered seemed to be challenging; what corrections she made seemed wrong and worse, woefully inadequate. She wept ... her sobs echoing through the empty zoom space with deafening alacrity. And yet ... we are here ... the "defense" magnificently traversed and the final perfunctory edits and additions to the text managed with pro-like efficiency. (Reid-Hayes, 2020, p. ix)

The intent of the UH EdD is to create space for Indigenous knowledge to flow, reshape, and reveal ancient ʻike which affirms Native approaches, methodologies, and conclusions within an EdD dissertation. One will note that this chapter does not pretend to present a prescribed checklist or cookbook recipe approach on how to successfully create safe spaces for Indigenous knowledge to flourish. Rather, this viewpoint sought to share this EdD's journey and as such, hopes to highlight, lift up, inspire, and enlighten. We as authors believe strongly that others who seek to do the same must be in relationship and conversation with the Indigenous peoples of that land in order to humbly respect their history, knowledge, and eternal wisdoms. We acknowledge, honor, and celebrate Indigenous epistemologies as a way to address problems of practice on equal footing with Western-based solutions.

References

Akiona, L. (2018). *Where are the brothers? Native Hawaiian males and higher education* (ISBN No. 978-0-438-47714-8) [Doctoral dissertation, the University of Hawaiʻi at Mānoa]. ProQuest Dissertations.

Alencastre, M. (2015). *E hoʻoulu ʻIa nā kumu mauli Ola Hawaiʻi: Preparing Hawaiian cultural identity teachers* (ISBN No. 978-1-321-96555-1) [Doctoral dissertation, the University of Hawaiʻi at Mānoa]. ProQuest Dissertations.

Association for Advancing Quality in Educator Preparation (AAQEP). (2021). *University of Hawaiʻi Visiting Committee AAQEP Accreditation Report.*

Burgess, H., & Wellington, J. (2010). Exploring the impact of the professional doctorate on students' professional practice and personal development: Early indications. *Work based learning e-journal, 1*(1), 160-176.

Degai, T., Petrov, A. N., Badhe, R., Egede Dahl, P. P., Döring, N., Dudeck, S., ... & Strawhacker, C. (2022). Shaping Arctic's tomorrow through Indigenous knowledge engagement and knowledge co-production. *Sustainability, 14*(3), 1331.

Gapero, Kaʻulu (2019). *Developing educator identity, perspective, and praxis to advance learning for ʻŌiwi Hawaiʻi leaders* (ISBN No. 9798698531760) [Doctoral dissertation, the University of Hawaiʻi at Mānoa]. ProQuest Dissertations.

Hattori, M. (2014). *Culturally responsive educational technology* (ISBN No. 978-1-321-46316-3.) [Doctoral dissertation, the University of Hawaiʻi at Mānoa]. ProQuest Dissertations.

Hunt, S. (2014). Ontologies of Indigeneity: The politics of embodying a concept. *Cultural geographies, 21*(1), 27-32.

Ikeda, C.K. (2014). *Ka moʻohelu o ke alana: The accounting of a culture-based education professional development course* (ISBN No. 978-1-321-46323-1) [Doctoral dissertation, the University of Hawaiʻi at Mānoa]. ProQuest Dissertations.

First Nations & Indigenous Studies: the University of British Columbia. (2023). *Terminology.* Which terms should I use? https://indigenous-foundations.arts.ubc.ca/terminology/

Jessen, T. D., Ban, N. C., Claxton, N. X., & Darimont, C. T. (2022). Contributions of Indigenous knowledge to ecological and evolutionary understanding. *Frontiers in Ecology and the Environment, 20*(2), 93-101.

Keliʻikipikāneokolohaka, R. (2020). *Papakū makawalu: A portal for hānau ma ka lolo* (ISBN No. 9798698531838) [Doctoral dissertation, the University of Hawaiʻi at Mānoa]. ProQuest Dissertations.

Kincheloe, J. L., & Steinberg, S. R. (2008). Indigenous knowledges in education: Complexities, dangers, and profound benefits. In N. K. Denzin,

Y. S. Lincoln, & L. T. Smith (Eds.), *Handbook of critical and indigenous methodologies* (pp. 135-156). Sage.

Knopf, K. (2015). The turn toward the Indigenous: Knowledge systems and practices in the academy. *Amerikastudien/American Studies, 60*(2/3), 179-200.

Kovach, M. (2010). Conversation method in Indigenous research. *First Peoples Child & Family Review, 5*(1), 40-48.

Maxwell, T. (2003). From first to second generation professional doctorate. *Studies in Higher Education, 28*(3), 279-291.

Maxwell, T. W. (2011). Australian professional doctorates: Mapping, distinctiveness, stress and prospects. *Work based learning e-journal, 2*(1), 24-43.

Patria, S. M. (2014). *Moʻolelo, storytelling: Storytellers of Hawaiʻi give voice to the utilization and preservation of a Hawaiian tradition in urban high schools* (ISBN No. 978-1-321-46355-2) [Doctoral dissertation, the University of Hawaiʻi at Mānoa]. ProQuest Dissertations.

Perez-Iyechad, L. (2009). *Inafaʻmaolek: Striving for Harmony*. Guampedia. http://guampedia.com/inafamaolek/

Perry, J. A. (2013). Carnegie Project on the Education Doctorate: The education doctorate, a degree for our time. *Planning and Changing, 44*(3/4), 113.

Raatior, V. (2017). *Successful practices of Micronesian college students in Hawaiʻi: Utilizing positive deviants to develop strength-based student support services in higher education* (ISBN No. 978-0-355-60083-4) [Doctoral dissertation, the University of Hawaiʻi at Mānoa]. ProQuest Dissertations.

Reid-Hayes, D. E. K. (2020). *There is beauty in the space between child and teacher: A moʻokūahuhau of a kanaka ʻōiwi early childhood educator (an ʻōiwi moʻolelo research study)* (ISBN No. 9798698532309) [Doctoral dissertation, the University of Hawaiʻi at Mānoa]. ProQuest Dissertations.

Sarsona, M.R.W. (2017). *Alakaʻina: Female leadership in Native Hawaiian education: Examining the lives of three female leaders in Native Hawaiian education* (ISBN No. 978-0-355-60095-7) [Doctoral dissertation, the University of Hawaiʻi at Mānoa]. ProQuest Dissertations.

Shulman, L. S., Golde, C. M., Bueschel, A. C., & Garabedian, K. J. (2006). Reclaiming education's doctorates: A critique and a proposal. *Educational Researcher, 35*(3), 25-32.

Taylor, R., & Storey, V. A. (2011). (Re) designing and implementing the professional doctorate in education: Comparing experiences of a small independent university and a large public university. *International Journal of Educational Leadership Preparation, 6*(3), n3.

Thomas, D.S. (2022). Applying one dish, one spoon as an Indigenous research methodology. *AlterNative: An International Journal of Indigenous Peoples, 18*(1), 84-93.

Tom, M., N., Huaman, E. S., & McCarty, T. L. (2019). Indigenous knowledges as vital contributions to sustainability. *International Review of Education, 65*(1), 1-18.

Turnbull, D. (2009). Introduction: futures for Indigenous knowledges. *Futures, 41*(1), 1-5.

Twomey, S. J., Lambrev, V., Leong, K., Watanabe, J., Baxa, G. V., Noh, E., & Hampton, C. (2017). The EdD consultancy project: Social justice leadership practice. *Educational Perspectives, 49*(1), 19-26.

Twomey, S. J. & Lambrev, V. (2018). *University of Hawai'i at Mānoa, EdD Program of the Year Application.*

United Nations, Department of Economic and Social Affairs: Indigenous Peoples (2006). *Permanent Forum on Indigenous Issues: Report on the fifth session* (15-26 May 2006). https://www.un.org/development/desa/indigenouspeoples/unpfii-sessions-2.html

Vaughan, M. B. (2016). He lei aloha 'āina. In Oliveira, K-A. R. K. N., & Wright, E. K. (Eds.), *Kanaka 'ōiwi methodologies: Mo'olelo and metaphor* (pp. 42-52). University of Hawai'i Press.

Wakinekona, L.L. (2017). *Wai'anae 'āina momona: A vision of strengths and place-based learning* (ISBN No. 978-0-355-60111-4) [Doctoral dissertation, the University of Hawai'i at Mānoa]. ProQuest Dissertations.

Weaver, H. N. (2001). Indigenous identity: What is it, and who really has it. *American Indian Quarterly, 25*(2), 240-255.

Wilson, S. (2008). *Research is ceremony: Indigenous research methods.* Fernwood Publishing.

CHAPTER 8

Focal Patterns of Action

STACY LEGGETT, EDD

L earning leaders frequently encounter scenarios where actions within a given context lead to predictable reactions. I ask a class of graduate students who are also educators, "What happens when you give fourth-graders dowel rods?" They reply in one voice, "Sword fights." I follow with a story about a new teacher who directs seventh-grade students, "Go get your workbooks." I pause the story and ask students to predict what happens next. Quickly, they anticipate the chaos and instructional time lost. These repetitive cause-and-effect interrelationships are *patterns of action*. Doctorate in Education programs, focused on improving educational outcomes for students, are often most concerned with patterns of action involving problems of practice.

In problem-based patterns of action, a leader may frame problems and design solutions emotionally, intuitively, or rationally; often, there is some combination. The leader may respond *emotionally* by reacting from gratitude, fear, or other emotions (Lerner et al., 2015). They may respond *intuitively* based on heuristics (internal decision-making rules) from previous observations and experiences (Mintrop & Zumpe, 2016). Veteran educators might intuitively recognize a problem related to school culture and implement a professional-learning strategy without understanding the underlying causes and defining the relationship between the problem and the potential solution.

Leaders may also respond to problems of practice **rationally**. Rational responses are the result of filtering available information to understand the problem and then identifying a change most likely to improve outcomes. Successful individuals tend to have good intuition about the cause-and-effect relationships in their work. However, Mintrop and Zumpe (2016) guided leaders to disrupt intuitive decision-making with inquiry-oriented thinking patterns aligned with rational patterns of action: recognizing problems, identifying possible solutions, considering the advantages and disadvantages of potential solutions, and implementing the change most likely to result in improved outcomes.

Focal patterns of action critical to Dissertations in Practice (DiPs) are the cause-and-effect interrelationships the project seeks to understand and improve. Practitioner-scholars seek to understand the focal patterns of action, including the relationships among the problem, the context, the theoretical and empirical knowledge base, the outcomes, and the impacts on current or future practice. Four possible DiP approaches are inquiry-oriented, evaluative, policy, and theoretical studies, but programs may also provide other routes (Storey & Hesbol, 2014; Storey & Maughan, 2014; Storey et al., 2015). The product itself might closely resemble a traditional, five-chapter dissertation, but it might also be a series of articles, a portfolio, an executive summary, a policy brief, a combination of these products, or another non-traditional format (Storey & Maughan, 2014; Storey et al., 2015).

The political landscape often pushes for quick and substantial change in education, which Bryk et al. (2015) called "going fast and learning slow" (p. 6). The pace and load of educational leadership also create constraints, driving leaders to make decisions quickly. Making decisions too quickly can result in:

- Not understanding the problem

- Not knowing relevant information

- Ignoring the perspectives of some groups

- Assuming a one-size-fits-all stance that ignores the importance of context, and

- Failing to align practices with the knowledge base

DiPs provide structures for explicating and framing problems to help us move "toward learning fast and implementing well" (Bryk et al., 2015, p. 7). These frameworks usually include some patterns of action. This chapter examines how practitioner-scholars engage in inquiry-oriented patterns of action to articulate their disciplinary, focal patterns of action.

DiP Patterns of Action

Students take on the dual roles inherent in the name practitioner-scholar when completing a DiP. They frequently serve in practitioner roles such as teacher, administrator, or support staff in pre K-12, higher education, or associated settings. As scholars, they review the literature to frame the problem, develop their hypotheses, and situate findings within the literature (Perry et al., 2020). In this duality of roles, they engage in dual patterns of action: one set of practices associated with their method of inquiry and another disciplinary set of behaviors. The first set of inquiry-oriented patterns of action leads to identifying a solution matching the problem (Figure 8.1). The second set of inquiry-oriented patterns of action leads to explicating the focal pattern of action.

Figure 8.1

Inquiry-Oriented Patterns of Action Associated with Matching Problems and Solutions

| Identify the problem of practice | Frame the problem of practice | Select change mostly likely to improve outcomes |

Note. This figure illustrates three inquiry-oriented patterns of action supporting the framing of the problem.

Matching Problems and Solutions

In completing a DiP, practitioner-scholars seek to understand and impact a problem of practice in their local context. How these processes occur depend to a certain degree on the program framework. The three inquiry-oriented patterns of action in Figure 8.1 are associated with matching problems and solutions: identifying the problem of practice, framing the problem, and selecting the change most likely to impact outcomes positively.

Identifying Problems of Practice. Practitioner-scholars filter through complex information to identify and understand problems of practice. How we filter the data cannot be separated from who we are and the experiences we bring. Our previous experiences with cause-and-effect relationships allow us to identify relevant data, recognize patterns and trends in the data, and connect those patterns to the knowledge base and to practice. We often identify problems of practice intuitively. At the school level, our gut may tell us there is a problem with student engagement in the classroom or cause us to question our effectiveness in using 1:1 devices. At the district level, we may recognize patterns of learning needs among new school administrators or disproportional student suspension rates. In higher education, program faculty may detect a lack of horizontal and vertical curricular alignment.

Similarly, practitioner-scholars often start their journeys intuitively recognizing a problem of practice, but the intuitive problem may not align with the inquiry method or parameters. The practitioner-scholar may focus on a symptom of the problem. Engaging in root cause analyses, systems mapping, and process mapping may be helpful. Second, the practitioner-scholar may need to break down a complex problem into more manageable pieces. Third, there may be many complex problems with various possible solutions. When selecting problems, prioritize the "pebble in your shoe," an issue affecting success that, if addressed, can catalyze significant growth (Donaldson, 2008).

Framing the Problem. Framing the problem includes identifying possible changes, the likely outcomes of each, and the likelihood the change will improve practice. The characteristics and experiences of the scholar-practitioner influence how they frame and identify problems. Engaging in a DiP process also influences the response to the problem of practice. DiPs require practitioner-scholars to match problems with solutions. For inquiry-oriented projects, the process occurs sequentially: identifying a problem and then implementing a possible improvement. The following practices can help students select an appropriate problem and solution.

- Identify problems of practice suggested by the patterns and trends within data.

- Select a problem and change appropriate for the practitioner's role, which impacts their sphere of influence and access to organizational resources.

- Select a problem and change appropriate for the program timeframe. Programs have varying timelines and benchmarks for completing the work.

Selecting a Change. When the DiP requires students to implement a change, the practitioner-scholar should identify the change most likely to impact practice within the frame of the study. Addressing a problem of practice can be challenging when working with complex and adaptive problems. When we enter a dark room, there is often a simple solution to our problem: flip a light switch. When we flip the light switch, we usually see an immediate change in our setting, which we know is a direct response to our action. In educational organizations, the problems keeping us awake at night are much more complex. The changes we implement may not immediately impact outcomes, and the emerging changes may result from other factors. There are further reasons our problem-solving may not be optimal: competing logics, unclear objectives, and insufficient time (Mintrop & Zumpe, 2019). Leaders should also be aware of some common, faulty heuristics when selecting changes.

- Solutionitis (Bryk et al., 2015): the tendency to implement solutions before fully understanding the problem.

- The professional development heuristic (Mintrop & Zumpe, 2016): the tendency to describe problems as the absence of something and provide professional development to fill the void.

- Correlation/causation fallacies: the tendency to interpret the correlation of variables as a causal relationship, which can lead to implementing changes that do not address the cause of the problem.

- Biases: the tendency to make decisions based on preconceived ideas. Making decisions based on biases yield problem-solving processes that ignore the perspectives of stakeholder groups. Biases take multiple forms, including social bias and confirmation bias.

- Groupthink: prioritizing consensus as a group over optimal decision-making (Janis, 1972).

- Overgeneralizations: the tendency to make conclusions that are too broad. For example, we may apply solutions from other contexts to our own, ignoring the importance of contextual factors. They may also include making assumptions within our own context.

Explicating the Focal Pattern of Action

Scholar-practitioners can use the five inquiry-oriented processes in Figure 8.2 to define, refine, communicate, and evaluate focal patterns of action while clarifying the relationships among the problems, changes, and desired outcomes. Students may use these representations independently to reflect on their projects, but as practitioners, they must realize the importance of collaborative problem-solving. To this end, practitioner-scholars should clarify who will be involved in defining the focal pattern of action and establish processes for maintaining engagement early.

Figure 8.2

Explicating the Focal Pattern of Action

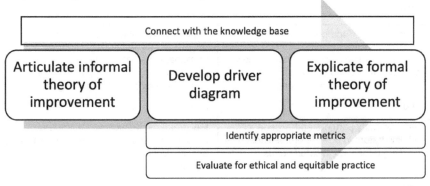

Note. This figure illustrates five inquiry-oriented patterns of action supporting the explication of the disciplinary focal pattern of action.

Numerous organizational improvement models (improvement science, quality improvement, design-based improvement) prescribe articulating a theory of improvement. A theory of improvement is the hypothesis conveying the interrelationships among the problems of practice, the proposed changes, and the desired outcomes. Articulating this theory is not about developing the perfect theory of improvement but creating an explicit, evidence-based understanding of the interrelationships critical to successful change. Therefore, the practitioner-scholar should collaborate with stakeholders to revisit and update the theory of improvement as understanding deepens.

Articulating an Informal Focal Pattern of Action. The first step in explicating a focal pattern of action is articulating an informal theory of improvement as an if-then statement. The statement is worded as a hypothesis and assumes positive outcomes. For example, a doctoral graduate addressed the learning needs of new administrators through an improvement science project (Table 8.1).

Table 8.1

Informal Theory of Improvement for Administrator Support Network (ASN)

If district administrators	Then new school administrators will
create a collegial support cohort for new school administrators aligned with the principles of adult learning theory	participate in a network providing professional and emotional support from other new school administrator colleagues
and	and
use university partners and experienced administrators to provide professional learning targeting indicated needs	feel greater self-efficacy in their readiness to lead and manage responsibilities effectively as guided by their professional standards
and	and
establish relationships with new school administrators,	connect with the district administrator and be more willing to reach out for support when needed.

Note. Adapted from *Closing the Preparedness-Readiness Gap in New School Administrators* [Doctoral dissertation, Western Kentucky University] by M. W. Stephanski, 2022, ProQuest Dissertations & Theses Global. Adapted with permission.

Developing Driver Diagrams. Developing a driver diagram is the second step toward defining a theory of improvement. Driver diagrams help us understand problems of practice, identify possible changes, determine our theories of improvement, and identify possible metrics (Perry et al., 2020). They help us to know what changes we must implement. The following process is essential in developing driver diagrams.

1. Articulate a measurable goal or aim.

2. Identify the change that must occur to accomplish the goal.

3. Identify **primary drivers**, the key conditions that must change to achieve the aim.

4. Identify **secondary drivers**, the conditions in the causal pathway between the change and primary drivers; they are immediately affected by the proposed change and, in turn, have the potential to impact the primary drivers.

An initial driver diagram may include many possible changes, but leaders must collectively revise and narrow it to focus on the desired change. The driver diagram should address at least one cause from the root cause analysis.

Figure 8.3 illustrates the driver diagram for an Administrator Support Network (ASN). The hypothesis undergirding the ASN study was that administrators with stronger relationships within the district and greater self-efficacy would be more likely to experience feelings of success and stay—these elements being the primary drivers (Figure 8.3). For these conditions to improve, the scholar-practitioner proposed the implementation of the ASN—the change. The scholar-practitioner defined three critical components that she would facilitate to complete the causal pathway from the change to the aim—the secondary drivers.

Figure 8.3

Driver Diagram for ASN

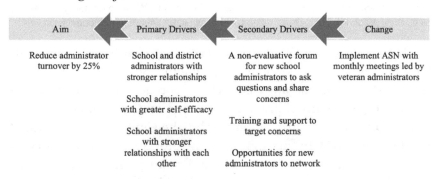

Note. Adapted from *Closing the Preparedness-Readiness Gap in New School Administrators* [Doctoral dissertation, Western Kentucky University] by M. W. Stephanski, 2022, ProQuest Dissertations & Theses Global. Adapted with permission.

Figure 8.4 illustrates the implementation of schoolwide Positive Behavior Intervention Supports (PBIS). For this example, the desired outcome was to reduce office discipline referrals. Reducing office discipline referrals can result from either the students not engaging in behaviors leading to office referrals or teachers responding differently to student behavior and not sending them to the office—the primary drivers. In this case, the changes were actions initiated by the PBIS team. The secondary drivers were the teacher behaviors resulting from the PBIS team initiatives and influencing the primary drivers.

Figure 8.4

Driver Diagram for Schoolwide PBIS at Title I High School

Aim	Primary Drivers	Secondary Drivers	Changes
Reduce office discipline referrals by 25% across all accountability subgroups	Students meet expectations for positive behavior Teachers only write referrals for major behavior infractions	**Teachers will** • support, teach, and recognize positive expectations • understand and follow discipline flowchart	**The PBIS team will** • develop resources for teaching expectations and provide professional learning to teachers on using resources • create a reward system • develop a discipline flow chart with teacher input and provide training

Note. Adapted from *Implications of the Improvement Science Process on SWPBIS Implementation at a Title I High School* [Doctoral dissertation, Western Kentucky University] by C. Rich, 2022, ProQuest Dissertations & Theses Global. Adapted with permission.

Distinguishing primary and secondary drivers can be challenging due to the complexity of problems. Sometimes the causal relationships are not apparent. One approach to consider when addressing problems of practice related to teaching and learning is to take a leadership-driven approach (The Center for Educational Leadership, 2013). In this approach, the practitioner-scholar makes leadership behaviors core. Instead of thinking, "If ..., then ...," students frame their hypothesis as, "If school leaders ..., then teachers will ..., then students will ...." With this approach, leadership behaviors become the secondary drivers, teacher behaviors are the primary drivers, and student behaviors are the outcomes. A similar approach can be taken where the scholar-practitioners facilitate the secondary drivers, and the primary drivers are the actions of the participants.

There is not a single approach to distinguishing primary and secondary drivers. Each DiP is unique. Considering the causal pathway from the change to the aim and selecting the key change drivers to the desired aim may yield varying results.

Conveying a Formal Theory of Improvement. Individuals engaged in continuous improvement may use a logic model format to express a formal theory of improvement and provide a visual overview of focal patterns of action for evaluation and design purposes by illustrating the interrelationships among inputs, activities, outputs, and outcomes. They may also explicitly state the metrics, rationale, and assumptions. Documenting these interrelationships can surface the assumptions and underlying rationale to deepen the understanding of all stakeholders and identify faulty inferences. As the practitioner-scholar and stakeholders review new evidence and their learning deepens through the DiP process, the formal theory of improvement should be a dynamic representation (Perry et al., 2020) reflecting the new understanding. Logic models should include the following items.

- **Inputs:** Resources needed for effective implementation.

- **Activities:** Steps needed to accomplish desired outcomes.

- **Outputs:** Metrics directly related to the activities that occur.

- **Outcomes:** Desired indicators of success.

- **Rationale:** Explanation of why the proposed project should lead to the desired outcomes in the project's context.

- **Assumptions:** The underlying ideas and beliefs regarding the likely outcomes of the program or change.

Figure 8.5 provides a logic model template with examples or types of each component.

Figure 8.5 *Logic Model Template*

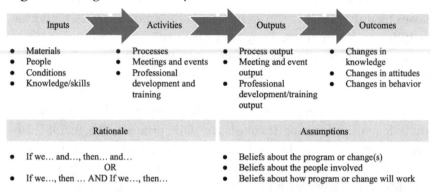

Figure 8.6 provides a completed logic model template for the ASN described in the section on driver diagrams. In logic models, outcomes may include short-, mid-, and long-term outcomes, so the ASN Theory of Improvement (Figure 8.6) has additional outcomes when compared to the ASN Driver Diagram (Figure 8.4).

Figure 8.6 *ASN Theory of Improvement*

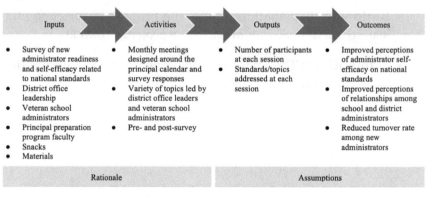

Figure 8.6 Note. Adapted from *Closing the Preparedness-Readiness Gap in New School Administrators* [Doctoral dissertation, Western Kentucky University] by M. W. Stephanski, 2022, ProQuest Dissertations & Theses Global. Adapted with permission.

A second example of a theory of improvement is in Figure 8.7. This theory of improvement guided the PBIS project in Figure 8.4. Practitioner-scholars and their practitioner collaborators should engage in an ongoing process of comparison among the driver diagram, theory of improvement, and project actions. The driver diagram and theory of improvement are dynamic documents that may likely require revision as the practitioner-scholar's understanding of interrelationships develops.

Figure 8.7

Schoolwide PBIS at Title I High School Theory of Improvement

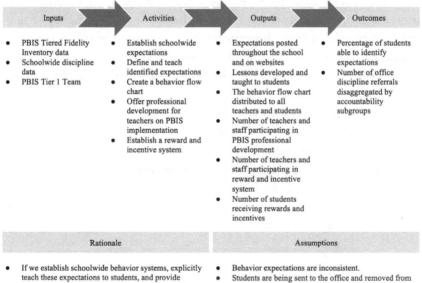

Note. Adapted from *Implications of the Improvement Science Process on SWPBIS Implementation at a Title I High School* [Doctoral dissertation, Western Kentucky University] by C. Rich, 2022, ProQuest Dissertations & Theses Global. Adapted with permission

Identifying Appropriate Metrics as Indicators of Success. Bryk et al. (2015) tell us we cannot improve at scale what we cannot measure. We cannot engage in continuous improvement without appropriate measures. The driver diagram and logic model can help define essential **improvement** metrics to evaluate the outcomes, drivers, and processes. The outcome measures will tell us if the change was successful. Outcome measures are those measures most readily available in education settings. The **outcome** measure may have been the evidence that alerted us to the problem of practice, but the availability of the evidence creates challenges for use in improvement. For example, when implementing a new administrator induction program to reduce administrator turnover, waiting to review turnover data at the end of the year does not provide sufficient evidence for continuous improvement.

The **driver** measures tell us if it is working. One driver to increase administrator retention is improved self-efficacy, measured through surveys, interviews, focus groups, or other metrics. A monthly survey that only addresses self-efficacy might tell us if what we are doing is successful or not, but alone, it might not tell us why.

The **process** measures tell us how it is working (Hinnant-Crawford, 2020). This third type of measure provides feedback on our "how" or processes. Feedback on administrator support network sessions might let us know the groups are too large, the topics are not the most pressing, the learning is not worth the cost of being out of their building, or perhaps just the opposite. Examples are provided in Table 8.2.

Table 8.2

Examples of Improvement Metrics

	Outcomes Measures	Driver Measures	Process Measures
New Administrator Support Network	• Turnover rate among new administrators	• Number of participants at each session • Participant self-ratings on efficacy regarding standards/topics addressed at each session • Participant responses regarding the development of a network	• Participant responses to survey on monthly meeting topics, format, logistics • Focus groups or interviews of participants
Implement Schoolwide PBIS at Title I High School	• Percentage of students able to identify expectations • Number of office discipline referrals disaggregated by accountability subgroups	• External feedback on implementation fidelity • Number of teachers and staff participating in PBIS professional development • Number of teachers and staff participating in reward and incentive system • Number of students receiving rewards and incentives	• Stakeholder surveys on implementation • Teacher focus group on implementation • External feedback on implementation fidelity

Note. This table provides examples of three types of improvement data for two projects. Some data sources may contain data relevant to drivers and processes.

Connecting with the Knowledge Base. Reviewing the literature should occur throughout the process. Specifically, the literature can deepen understanding of root causes and previously successful changes. Perry et al. (2020) provided the following purposes for using the literature in an improvement science DiP.

- Identifying the problem and explicating the rationale,

- Situating the problem in the broader context,

- Identifying root causes of the problem,

- Developing and supporting the theory of improvement,

- Recognizing what the field does not know,

- Framing study of intervention or investigation, and

- Serving as an analytic starting point. (p. 96)

As students complete their DiPs, they should use each of these purposes as a lens for reviewing the body of knowledge.

Evaluating Patterns of Action for Ethical and Equitable Practices. In developing, implementing, and evaluating focal patterns of action, scholar-practitioners must adhere to ethical and equitable practices. By nature, DiPs often occur within the practitioner-scholar's workplace, requiring them to reflect on the ethical nature of the work from multiple perspectives. The literature surrounding inquiry-oriented research and DiPs offers some critical areas of ethics and equity to consider. The considerations and questions from Biag (2019), Perry and Zambo (2019), and Perry et al. (2020) were selected and modified to align with the two stages of developing inquiry-oriented patterns of actions in Figure 8.8.

Figure 8.8

Examples of Questions to Consider Related to Ethics and Equity

Matching Problems to Solutions	Explicating Theory of Improvement
Are the purpose, rationale, and framing of the problem ethical and equitable (Perry & Zambo, 2019; Perry et al., 2020)? How does our understanding of the problem keep the needs of our most vulnerable students at the center? How do my identity and experiences influence my perceptions of the problem (Biag, 2019)?	How does our role create ethical or equitable concerns? How are we ensuring that data collection and use are ethical and equitable? (Perry & Zambo, 2019; Perry et al., 2020) How are we engaging diverse groups and incorporating their experiences? How does our theory of action promote the inclusion of diverse communities and groups? (Biag, 2019)

Designing research as a practitioner-scholar requires attention to the ethics and equity of the project. For example, suppose a principal is leading a project with teachers whom they directly supervise. How can the principal ensure that the project's implementation and evaluation are conducted ethically and equitably? If an assistant principal needs de-identified data, how can the assistant principal ensure an undue burden is not placed on an employee? If a counselor conducts a survey of new teachers regarding their perceptions of support from administrators, how does the counselor ethically report findings without jeopardizing their employment? These questions will differ depending on the nature of the study. Still, they illustrate the importance of questioning issues of ethics and equity related to the framing and methods of the study concurrent with our positionality. The goal of the DiP is to impact practice to promote equitable outcomes, but issues of ethics and equity occur at each step along the pathway from the proposed change to the desired aim.

Conclusion

Defining, implementing, and evaluating the focal theories of action associated with DiPs are usually predicated on the implementation of inquiry-oriented theories of action related to the approach and format of the project. Engaging in action research, improvement science, evaluation, or other types of practitioner scholarship requires a focus on the discipline of the content, such as new administrator support and schoolwide PBIS. Concurrently, students are also immersed in the inquiry methods of their work. As students engage in these processes, they develop disciplinary expertise while, hopefully, habituating problem-solving practices for future inquiry.

Application Questions

1. How would you describe your decision-making on your DiP at this point: emotional, intuitive, rational?

2. Consider the knowledge base and the seven instances where practitioner-scholars should engage with the literature. How strongly have you connected with the literature for each?

3. After considering the questions related to ethics and equity, what changes should you make in your theory of action?

4. How does your theory of action connect with the root cause analysis?

5. How will you measure outcomes, drivers, and processes? What will your metrics be? What will they tell you?

6. Engage in each of the eight inquiry-oriented patterns of action as a reflection tool: (a) identify the problem, (b) frame the problem, (c) select the solution most likely to bring improvement, (d) create a table aligning your theory of action to the knowledge base, (e) articulate an informal theory of action, (f) develop your driver diagram, (g) explicate your formal theory of action as a logic model, (h) identify appropriate metrics, and (i) evaluate your project for issues related to ethics and equity.

7. Follow-up to Question 6 with your practitioner collaborators on the project within your context.

References

Biag, M. (2019). Navigating the improvement journey with an equity compass. In R. Crow, B. N. Hinnant-Crawford, & D. T. Spaulding (Eds.), *The educational leader's guide to improvement science: Data, design and cases for reflection* (pp. 91-124). Myers Education Press.

Bryk, A. S., Gomez, L. M., Grunow, A., & LeMahieu, P. G. (2015). *Learning to improve: How America's schools can get better at getting better.* Harvard Education Press.

The Center for Educational Leadership. (2013). *Creating a theory of action: Learning tools.* https://k-12leadership.org/tools/creating-a-theory-of-action/

Donaldson, G. A. (2008). *How leaders learn: Cultivating capacities for school improvement.* Teachers College Press.

Hinnant-Crawford, B. N. (2020). *Improvement science in education: A Primer.* Myers Education Press.

Janis, I. L. (1972). *Victims of groupthink: A psychological study of foreign-policy decisions and fiascoes.* Houghton Mifflin.

Lerner, J. S., Li, Y., Valdesolo, P., & Kassam, K. S. (2015). Emotion and decision making. *Annual Review of Psychology, 66,* 799-823. https://doi.

org/10.1146/annurev-psych-010213-115043

Mintrop, R., & Zumpe, E. (2016). Making intuitive theories of action explicit. In R. Mintrop (Ed.), *Design-based school improvement: A practical guide for education leaders* (pp. 43-56). Harvard Education Press.

Mintrop, R., & Zumpe, E. (2019). Solving real-life problems of practice and education leaders' school improvement mind-set. *American Journal of Education, 125*(3), 295-344. https://doi.org/125.000-000.10.1086/702733

Perry, J., & Zambo, D. (2019). Understanding the role of improvement science in EdD programs. In R. Crow, B. N. Hinnant-Crawford, & D. T. Spaulding (Eds.), *The educational leader's guide to improvement science: Data, design, and cases for reflection* (pp. 166-188). Myers Education Press.

Perry, J. A., Zambo, D., & Crow, R. (2020). *The improvement science dissertation in practice: A guide for faculty, committee members, and their students.* Myers Education Press.

Rich, C. (2022). *Implications of the improvement science process on SWPBIS implementation at a Title I high school* (Publication No. 215) [Doctoral dissertation, Western Kentucky University]. https://digital-commons.wku.edu/diss/215/

Stephanski, M. W. (2022). *Closing the preparedness-readiness gap in new school administrators* (Publication No. 223) [Doctoral dissertation, Western Kentucky University]. https://digitalcommons.wku.edu/diss/223/

Storey, V. & Hesbol, K. (2014). Can the dissertation in practice bridge the researcher practitioner gap? The Education Professional Practice Doctorate and the Impact of the Carnegie Project on the Education Doctorate Consortium. *Journal of Public Relations Research, 35*(3), 324-347. https://doi.org/10.3138/jspr.35.3.324

Storey, V. A., & Maughan, B. D. (2014). *Beyond a definition: Designing and specifying Dissertation in Practice (DiP) models* [Conference paper]. A Knowledge Forum on the EdD. https://www.researcgate.net/publication/282612699_Beyond_a_definition_Designing_and_specifying_Dissertation_in_Practice_DiP_models_Process_and_Product

Storey, V. A., Caskey, M. M., Hesbol, K. A., Marshall, J. E., Maughan, B., & Dolan, A. W. (2015). Examining EdD dissertations in practice: The Carnegie Project on the Education Doctorate. *International HETL Review, 5*(2). https://www.researchgate.net/publication/273381580_Examining=_EdD_Dissertations_in_Practice_The_Carnegie_Project_on_the_Education_Doctorate

CHAPTER 9

Dissertation in Practice Methodologies

SARAH A. CAPELLO, PHD; EDWIN NII BONNEY, PHD;
MAXWELL M. YURKOFSKY, EDD

As other chapters in this book have noted, there has been a surge of interest over the last 20 years in the education doctorate (EdD) related to revisiting its purpose, program design, and curriculum. Notably, the Carnegie Project on the Education Doctorate (CPED) (2022) and other EdD scholars (Allen et al., 2016; Perry, 2012; Perry & Imig, 2008; Shulman et al., 2006) have argued that the EdD should be a doctorate in professional practice that is closely aligned with the problems of practice (PoPs) practitioners face and that prepares them to be transformative leaders. Reforming the EdD has led scholars and practitioners to rethink many components of the EdD including the dissertation in practice (DiP) (Belzer & Ryan, 2013; Perry et al., 2020; Tamim & Torres, 2022). EdD dissertations have historically mirrored PhD dissertations that are: focused on specialized original research, heavily theoretical, based in scholarly research, book-length, and disconnected from practitioners' work and career goals as well as the communities they serve (Perry et al., 2020). However, revised EdD DiPs:

- Center on a localized PoP that is based in students' professional practice;

- Allow students to draw on their existing professional knowledge, skills, and experiences and combine those with new learning through applied inquiry;

- Bridge the researcher-practitioner divide;

- Generate knowledge that can be used to initiate organizational change; and

- Encourage collaboration between the scholar-practitioner and community members involved in and impacted by the PoP (Perry et al., 2020; Tamim & Torres, 2022).

Conceptual shifts in understanding the EdD and the DiP have impacted how EdD scholars, faculty, and administrators think about research methodologies for practitioners and have led to important questions for the field to consider such as: *Do practitioners need to choose a specific methodology for their DiP? How much training do EdD students need in traditional research methodologies? What content should be taught and how?* (Bengtson et al., 2016; Capello et al., 2023; Firestone et al., 2021; Hochbein & Perry, 2013). While practitioners can and do take various perspectives in their work, they may not align themselves with a particular methodology or epistemology for the duration of their career. They also may not view a PoP along distinct methodological lines and may need to collect and review various forms of available data in order to make well-informed decisions related to policy and practice. For example, a scholar-practitioner might use a variety of designs and methods for different purposes while conducting their DiP. They may begin the inquiry with a mixed methods approach to learn about the root causes of the PoP, or they may be able to accomplish this task through qualitative interviews. As the inquiry progresses, the scholar-practitioner might collect quantitative data to measure the effect of a particular intervention implemented to address the problem.

Despite these realities and complexities, there are multiple benefits to understanding methodological differences and drawing on one for the DiP. Identifying a methodological approach can help scholar-practitioners frame their inquiry and narrow the scope of the DiP. Furthermore, methodology guides the scholar-practitioner in knowing whether change is occurring and how to evaluate that change. Finally, methodology informs data collection and analysis as well as the conclusions scholar-practitioners can draw. As we discuss in more detail below, quantitative and qualitative methodologies are associated with various research purposes, forms of data, data collection instruments, and data analysis procedures. It is important to align the purpose of the DiP, inquiry question(s), and data collection and analysis procedures with the appropriate methodology in order to conduct a valid and robust study. It is not appropriate to thoughtlessly mix and match elements of the research design. Cobbling together a DiP with unaligned research design elements (e.g., purpose, data collection instruments, data analysis procedures) will result in an invalid study that is not useful to anyone and could cause harm to the population(s) associated with the PoP.

Methodological Considerations

Therefore, what is important to consider when choosing a methodological approach for the DiP? Oftentimes, the DiP topic, inquiry questions, or research goals can serve as a guide to choosing a methodology. Table 9.1 below offers some guiding questions to consider when choosing a DiP methodology.

Table 9.1

Questions to Consider When Choosing a DiP Methodology

What does the scholar-practitioner want to know? (I.e., what is the inquiry question(s)?)	Certain questions are often aligned with particular methodologies. For example, "how" and "why" questions often frame qualitative DiPs. "How much", "to what extent", or "what is the relationship between x and y" questions often guide quantitative DiPs.
What is the goal or purpose of the DiP?	DiPs have varying purposes from being descriptive, evaluative, exploratory, or explanatory. Descriptive and evaluative DiPs are often mixed methods while exploratory DiPs are often qualitative, and explanatory DiPs are quantitative.

What is the PoP topic?	Certain PoPs may orient themselves toward particular methodologies. DiPs focused on topics that are associated with numerical data (e.g., test scores, attendance and discipline rates) or common educational variables (e.g., gender, SES, race) are good candidates for quantitative methods. DiPs focused on topics that are not easily quantified might be better suited for qualitative methods.
How has the PoP topic been studied previously?	The research and professional literature can provide a good starting point for choosing a methodology. For example, if the topic has typically been studied using mixed methods, the researcher could follow in that tradition.
What is the scholar-practitioner's positionality toward or relationship with potential research participants?	Qualitative methodologists have a close relationship with research participants and may seek to conduct research with them, share preliminary findings, and consider their own role, power, and/or privilege in relation to the participants. Quantitative methodologists often work with aggregated data that may be anonymized. They may not know whose data are included in their sample or have a close researcher-participant relationship with them. Quantitative methodologist may however want to consider how their positionality shapes how they interpret findings from analyzed aggregated data.
What is the scope of the inquiry?	DiPs that seek to study a sample and make inferences to a larger population are generally quantitative. DiPs that do not seek to generalize findings are typically qualitative.
Will a particular research design be used?	Research designs are often associated with specific methodologies. Survey research, experimental and quasi-experimental, secondary data analysis, and content analysis are often associated with quantitative methodology. Case study, ethnography, phenomenology, narrative inquiry, and grounded theory are associated with qualitative methodology. Improvement science, action research, program evaluation, and designed-based research are associated with mixed methodology.
What data will be used?	Quantitative methodology utilizes numerical data, qualitative methodology primarily utilizes non-numerical data but may include some numerical data. Mixed methods incorporate both.

It is important to note that there is flexibility when choosing a methodological approach, and the suggestions listed above are simply guidelines. A given PoP can be studied using different methodologies, but the key is to ensure that all elements of the research design are aligned.

Finally, we recommend that students and DiP chairs converse at the early stages of the DiP process about both the appropriateness of the chosen methodology and the student's and chair's comfort level with the desired methodological approach. It may not be feasible for a student to learn the requisite data collection and analysis techniques to be able to carry out the desired research in the allotted DiP timeframe. Furthermore, not all EdD faculty feel confident supervising a DiP that is outside their methodological expertise.

Brief Overview of a Quantitative DiP

Quantitative research methodology is based in positivist and post-positivist paradigms that view: the world as knowable through objective, scientific inquiry; human behavior as predictable; and actors in the world as generalizable across cases. The undergirding logic of quantitative methodology is that the characteristics of a population can be closely estimated by taking a random, representative sample, studying the sample characteristics, drawing conclusions, and inferring that the characteristics of the sample are representative of the population. A quantitative approach to a DiP can be useful for inquiring into many different problems in virtually any context. PK-12 and higher education institutions often collect and store large amounts of quantitative data on student demographics, grades, attendance, discipline, retention, and graduation as well as a host of other student, faculty, staff, and institutional characteristics and outcomes. Furthermore, practitioners often have access to and work closely with these data as part of their everyday responsibilities for descriptive, explanatory, or evaluative purposes. A descriptive, quantitative DiP could map the extent of learning loss across a district by examining patterns in the district's data related to grade, school, content area, and groups of students. This DiP could help school leaders understand the scope of the learning loss, identify particular sub-groups or grade levels that have been severely affected, and provide insight for remediation efforts.

When practitioners are interested in learning what factors may be contributing to or causing a particular outcome, they may use a quantitative approach and attempt to isolate one or more variables they believe is causing a given phenomenon, gather quantifiable data on those variables, and then analyze the data using statistical tools to look for a hypothesized relationship among the variables. This is commonly done in DiPs through intervention-based research. In this case, the scholar-practitioner implements a new initiative or intervention on a small scale that she believes will affect an outcome and takes occasional measurements—often before, during, and after the intervention—to learn if and how the intervention affects the intended outcome. Finally, if a school leader has implemented a new program and wants to know how well it is working, he could use quantitative methods to evaluate the program. An evaluative DiP might examine the effects of an after-school tutoring program for elementary children. Evaluative DiPs often utilize a predetermined standard for the operation of the program or policy being evaluated, and then collect data from a variety of sources to determine whether or not the program is meeting the desired standards.

Quantitative DiPs can be prime opportunities for practitioners to draw on existing institutional data they already work with or could easily obtain, blend their practitioner wisdom with scholarly knowledge to develop change ideas, utilize existing data analysis skills while supplementing those with newly-learned statistical tools, analyze large datasets quickly, make inferences about the population under study, and solve PoPs. If the goal of a DiP is: (1) to learn about particular characteristics of a local sample or population; (2) to test out a hypothesis by isolating one or more potential variables impacting an outcome and identifying relationships among those variables; or (3) to draw conclusions about the local population, then a quantitative DiP may be appropriate.

Quantitative DiP Example

Meghan, an elementary school principal, was concerned about a consistent decline in reading scores in her school on a state-mandated test. Seeing her DiP as an opportunity to learn more about this problem and a potential solution, Meghan began her DiP work by disaggregating her school's reading achievement data by grade level, student gender, and socioeconomic status (SES) for the past 10 years. This analysis revealed that third grade students who were male and low-income historically scored the lowest on the state assessment. She also noticed that third grade typically had the highest proportion of new teachers, many with less than two years of teaching experience. Armed with this knowledge and evidence from a review of the research on literacy instruction, Meghan decided to implement five professional development (PD) sessions, each based on a tenet of the science of reading, for the third-grade teachers. Prior to offering the PD, Meghan administered a pre-survey that asked teachers to rate their knowledge of the five tenets on a Likert scale. After reviewing the pre-survey results, Meghan finalized the PD sessions, focusing on knowledge gaps she found on the pre-survey. Meghan and her literacy coach offered one session each month from October to February. After the final session, Meghan asked her teachers to take a post-survey, which included the same questions as the pre-survey. Meghan conducted a t-test to look for statistically significant differences in the pre- and post-survey scores that would indicate teacher growth in knowledge of the science of reading. Although the scores between the two tests were not statistically significant, she did find increases in mean scores from the pre- to the post-test, which indicated that teachers' knowledge did increase through the PD. Although it is not part of her DiP, Meghan will continue to follow the third-grade teachers to learn if their students' scores improve on the state reading assessment, which could justify continued offering of the PD or expanding it to other grade levels.

Brief Overview of a Qualitative DiP

Qualitative research methodology is situated within interpretivist/constructivist, critical, or post-modernist/post-structuralist research paradigms. Unlike quantitative research where the inquiry purpose may be to predict, control, or generalize, the purpose of qualitative research is to describe, understand, interpret, deconstruct, problematize, or empower. In this tradition, practitioners view reality as local and subjective such that there can be multiple realities and co-created or co-constructed meaning and knowledge. For example, within critical paradigms, the scholar-practitioner understands that there are multiple realities that are situated within existing systems and power dynamics that privilege and oppress certain types of knowledge and truth, such that knowledge is never objective. Qualitative methods also emphasize the positionality of the practitioner and encourage the student to be reflexive about their organizational position, power, responsibility, and relationship to others within their context as well as to DiP participants. Scholar-practitioners who are particularly interested in learning about the PoP from the perspective of study participants, inquiring into and implementing solutions with participants, or who have PoPs that center on critical topics, are well-positioned to use a qualitative approach for their DiP.

Several qualitative research designs are particularly useful for a DiP: basic qualitative research, case study, action research and its variants, and phenomenology. Alternative DiP formats, such as documentaries and other creative and artistic works, often fall within this methodology. Scholar-practitioners using qualitative methodology choose a design depending on their inquiry question, worldview, and positionality. For example, a student who believes that meaning and knowledge are co-created and constructed, might ask questions about how individuals or groups make sense of a program or a policy and how they experience it. This scholar-practitioner might select a phenomenological research design where they conduct multiple interviews with a person or group that has had direct experience with the PoP while also exploring their own experience with the PoP.

Irrespective of research design, there is considerable overlap in the qualitative data collection and analysis tools scholar-practitioners employ in their DiP inquiry. Most qualitative research designs could include: interviews or focus groups, observations and field notes, documents or artifact analysis, coding, theming, or any variation of inductive and deductive data analysis. Students might draw on several of these tools at different stages of the DiP process for various purposes. For example, they may first conduct observations in their place of practice to learn more about the PoP. Then, they may supplement findings from the observations with interviews with organizational members who are positioned at different levels or who have varying experiences with the PoP. Once the scholar-practitioner has a holistic understanding of the PoP, they could use a focus group to learn about potential solutions from those within the organization and use any of the tools to collect and analyze data on the effectiveness of the implemented solution.

Qualitative DiP Example

Teisha is a program coordinator for a community center that offers arts programs for middle and high schoolers in Crow City. Over the past four years, she has noticed a steady drop-off in participation in the arts programs offered at the center. She thought perhaps the youth were no longer interested in programs the center sponsored, so she began her DiP inquiry by inviting current program participants and their families to complete an open-ended questionnaire that asked about the arts offerings and programs they participated in at the center: what they enjoyed, whether there were other art programs they were interested in, and what barriers prevented them from participating. Teisha asked participants to share their names in a separate form if they would be willing to engage in a follow up focus group. Ten parents and 16 middle and high school-aged youth participated in two separate focus group discussions with Teisha and her staff.

After transcribing and analyzing the focus group data, Teisha learned several key pieces of information. First, both parents and youth were satisfied with the center's programming, but parents were often unaware of current offerings. One parent also remarked that a local bus route used to stop at the community center but had been rerouted. This parent relied on public transportation, and it was not until she purchased a vehicle that she was able to bring her kids back to the center. Teisha was unaware of this change in the bus route, but, when she checked with the city, she noticed the route had changed about four years ago—the time when the drop-off in youth participation began. In addition to parent feedback, youth study participants shared that they were interested in creating art in public spaces outside the center with their friends. Teisha and her staff invited the middle and high schoolers back to brainstorm ideas for a community public art project and then implemented two of the ideas the following summer. After unveiling the new art project, Teisha asked the youth who participated in the project to write about or create a visual describing their experiences. She used thematic analysis to explore common themes among the student artifacts and concluded that the project helped to connect youth to their community, privilege the participants' voices, raise youth awareness of the center's programs, and increase participation in the center's programs.

As part of her DiP dissemination work, Teisha shared her findings with the community center director who alerted the city about the bus route while Teisha and her staff talked with the local school district about offering a bus line that brought kids to the community center after school. She and her team also visited schools to talk with students about the arts program and the public art projects. They also increased advertisements about the community center's programs on social media. Although the bus route still does not pass by the community center, participation in the art program increased.

Brief Overview of a Mixed Methodology DiP

A mixed methods DiP can be viewed as a middle ground between quantitative and qualitative methods, epistemologies, and paradigms. In fact, it may be one of the most practical methodologies for practitioners since they often have access to secondary data useful for quantitative analyses but may need to collect qualitative data to understand the nuances of the PoP or the effects of the solution. Mixed methodology allows practitioners to take practical, real-world approaches to identifying and solving problems. Rather than operating within a purely positivist (or post-positivist) or constructivist (or interpretivist, post-modernist, post-structural, or critical) paradigm, mixed methods DiPs take a "needs-based or contingency" approach to selecting research methods (Johnson & Onwuegbuzie, 2004, p. 17). This means combining qualitative and quantitative methods in a way that results in "complementary strengths and non-overlapping weaknesses" based on the questions scholar-practitioners are interested in investigating (Johnson & Onwuegbuzie, 2004, p. 17). Firmly grounded in pragmatist philosophy, mixed methods research adopts the stance that the value of any approach to inquiry can be evaluated based on the practical consequences that flow from using that method in real-world settings. Pragmatists thus evaluate a round of inquiry by considering both whether they have solved the problem and whether they like the new problems they have created through their inquiry (Schön, 1995, p. 31).

While the mixed methods DiP affords the scholar-practitioner the opportunity to draw on elements of quantitative and qualitative methodologies to better understand the PoP or assess a change idea, it is imperative that researchers purposefully and thoughtfully integrate qualitative and quantitative inquiry questions, data collection methods, and analytic strategies. Scholar-practitioners may take a sequential approach to integrating qualitative and quantitative forms of inquiry. This involves using qualitative methods in the first phase of the DiP inquiry and quantitative methods in the second phase (or vice versa). Alternatively, mixed methods researchers might adopt a concurrent approach, where they use quantitative and qualitative methods simultaneously. In either case, mixed methods researchers might also choose to give quantitative and qualitative methods equal status, or have quantitative (or qualitative) methods play a dominant role in the research design, with qualitative (or quantitative) methods playing a secondary role.

Consistent with its roots in pragmatism, a mixed methods approach is often necessary for DiPs that are focused primarily on generating change in real-life settings. For that reason, mixed methods approaches may be particularly well suited for improvement science, action research (and other forms of participatory research), or design-based research DiPs, since each of these methodologies are about enacting positive change in organizations.

Mixed Methods DiP Example

Laura, a district-level administrator in a small rural district, was concerned about stagnating writing scores across her system. She engaged in a mixed methods study to inquire into and address this problem aligned with the improvement science process. Improvement science typically involves three primary stages: 1) identifying a problem and seeing the system that contributes to that problem, 2) developing a theory of improvement to address the problem, and 3) implementing iterative tests of change and spreading successful changes across an organization (Bryk et al., 2015; Hinnant-Crawford, 2020; Perry et al., 2020).

Laura relied on a concurrent mixed methods research design during the later stages of the improvement science process, which involves conducting iterative tests of change, typically using a plan-do-study-act (PDSA) cycle. Based on her analysis of the problem, Laura worked with her team to come up with the following change idea: an end-of-class instructional routine that embeds writing skills in other content areas (i.e., math, science, and social studies). She decided to pilot that routine with two science teachers and two social studies teachers. Laura relied on quantitative methods to help her answer the question: Is this change idea working, and for whom? Specifically, she developed a weekly survey where pilot teachers shared how often they were using the writing routine and how effective they found it to be, as well as a bi-weekly writing assessment scored using a 5-point writing rubric. From this data, Laura learned that social studies teachers found the routine more helpful and used it more than the science teachers, suggesting some kind of adaptation for science teachers was needed. At the same time, Laura also engaged in qualitative inquiry to understand how the routine was working for pilot teachers. This involved weekly observations of each of the four pilot teachers as well as an interview with each about their experience using the routine. This qualitative inquiry revealed that science teachers typically ran out of time for the writing routine because their in-class experiments ran longer than expected. Laura was able to use this qualitative data to iterate upon her change idea for science teachers. Instead of having teachers do an end-of-class writing routine, she developed a beginning-of-class writing routine intended to reflect on and process the learning from the prior day's activities.

Ethical Considerations When Choosing A DiP Methodology

Because practitioners frequently conduct their DiP research in the same context in which they work *and* with those they work with, it is important for scholar-practitioners to consider the ethical implications of their DiP research prior to beginning it. While we are unable to provide a holistic discussion of research ethics in this chapter, we encourage all involved in the DiP to think about the following points as they pertain to methodology.

First, scholar-practitioners should consider their positionality and be reflexive. *What is their position within their organization, and what is that position in relation to those involved in or impacted by the PoP? Does the student directly supervise or have political or organizational power over potential DiP participants? If so, how might that affect who is recruited for participation in the DiP, what they are asked to do, and the data they share? Is there the potential for research participants to feel coerced into participating? What would the ramifications be for those individuals if they opt out of the study?* There are likely power dynamics when recruiting, sampling, collecting and analyzing data, and writing up findings when working with those whom the scholar-practitioner supervises that are essential to consider before beginning the DiP.

Secondly, know whether the DiP will be published online or in a scholarly database, disseminated in a publicly-accessible platform, or shared with others within the local organization or community. *If so, how will the implications of the DiP portray the school or organization and community? How will the scholar-practitioner represent study participants and the students, parents, and community members they serve?* DiPs necessarily center on problems within the practitioner's place of practice, and many EdD programs seek to equip practitioners with tools for solving complex problems. However, scholar-practitioners have to carefully navigate organizational improvement efforts while ensuring that those efforts are not causing harm to research participants, stakeholders, and communities. One of many strategies to navigate this tension is for EdD students completing a DiP to convene a research team comprised of key stakeholders who will take part in the research from the beginning stages of the DiP process through the final analysis and write up.

Conclusion

Because it drives the DiP process, selecting a methodology should be done early, intentionally, and in conversation with the DiP chair and committee members as well as other key organizational stakeholders. We recommend students choose a methodology that best suits the:

- Inquiry question and purpose of the study;

- Research design;

- Available data or data to be collected;

- Student's data collection and analysis capabilities; and

- Implications of conducting the study in the student's place of practice.

Although we have highlighted the three major educational research methodologies in this chapter, we do want to join with others who are extending the conversation beyond quantitative, qualitative, and mixed methodological distinctions in practitioner-oriented EdD programs. Practitioners' work is frequently complex and messy, so it may be best to be pragmatic and consider what is feasible for the student to accomplish in their context given their knowledge, skills, resources, and access to data along with the ethical implications of their DiP work. Furthermore, if practitioners want to effect change in their context, we believe that change should involve people within their organization from the start, which may result in a shift to conducting research "on" to research "with" community members. Finally, we encourage program faculty and administrators to rethink traditional dissertation norms and challenge them to be open to the possibilities of the DiP as an opportunity to develop scholar-practitioners, extend their knowledge and skill set, bridge research and practice, and effect change in local schools and communities.

References

Allen, J., Chirichello, M., Wasicsko, M. (2016). The practitioner-scholar doctorate: Not a PhD lite. In J. Perry (Ed.), *The EdD and the scholarly practitioner: The CPED path* (pp. 105-130). Information Age Publishing.

Belzer, A., & Ryan, S. (2013). Defining the problem of practice: Where's the practice, What's the problem?. *Planning and Changing, 44*(3-4), 195-207.

Bengtson, E., Lasater, K., Murphy-Lee, M. M., & Jones, S. J. (2016). The role of research courses. In J. Perry (Ed.), *The EdD and the scholarly practitioner: The CPED path* (pp. 79-101). Information Age Publishing.

Bryk, A. S., Gomez, L. M., Grunow, A., & LeMahieu, P. G. (2015). *Learning to improve: How America's schools can get better at getting better.* Harvard Education Press.

Capello, S. A., Yurkofsky, M., & Bonney, E. N. (2023). Part one of the themed issue on reimagining research methods coursework for the preparation of scholar-practitioners. *Impacting Education: Journal on Transforming Professional Practice, 8*(2), 1-3. https://doi.org/10.5195/ie.2023.368

Firestone, W. A., Perry, J. A., Leland, A. S., & McKeon, R. T. (2021). Teaching research and data use in the education doctorate. *Journal of Research on Leadership Education, 16*(1), 81-102. https://doi.org/10.1177/1942775119872231

Hinnant-Crawford, B. N. (2020). *Improvement science in education: A primer.* Myers Education Press.

Hochbein, C., & Perry, J. A. (2013). The role of research in the professional doctorate. *Planning and Changing, 44*(3-4), 181-195.

Johnson, R. B., & Onwuegbuzie, A. J. (2004). Mixed methods research: A research paradigm whose time has come. *Educational Researcher, 33*(7), 14-26. https://doi.org/10.3102/0013189X033007014

Perry, J. A. (2012). To Ed.D. or not to Ed.D.. *Phi Delta Kappan, 94*(1), 41–44. https://doi.org/10.1177/003172171209400108

Perry, J. A., & Imig, D. G. (2008). A stewardship of practice in education. *Change, The Magazine of Higher Learning, 40*(6), 42–49. https://doi.org/10.3200/chng.40.6.42-49

Perry, J. A., Zambo, D., & Crow, R. (2020). *The improvement science dissertation in practice: A guide for faculty, committee members, and their students.* Myers Education Press.

Schön, D. A. (1995). Knowing-in-action: The new scholarship requires a new epistemology. *Change: The Magazine of Higher Learning, 27*(6), 27-34. https://doi.org/10.1080/00091383.1995.10544673

Shulman, L. S., Golde, C. M., Bueschel, A. C., & Garabedian, K. J. (2006). Reclaiming education's doctorates: A critique and a proposal. *Educational Researcher, 35*(3), 25-32. https://doi.org/10.3102/0013189X035003025

Tamim, S. R., & Torres, K. M. (2022). Evolution of the dissertation in practice. *Impacting Education: Journal on Transforming Professional Practice, 7*(1), 1-3. https://doi.org/10.5195/ie.2022.267

CHAPTER 10

The Impact of the DiP:

Intentionality and Application of Andragogy to Reduce Anxiety and Increase Relevancy

KELLY M. TORRES, PHD; KATHERINE GREEN, PHD; JESSICA DOWNIE-SIEPSIAK, MA

Research plays a crucial role in schools, organizations, and communities. By providing a systematic and evidence-based approach to understanding complex problems and issues, research helps to inform decision-making, advance knowledge, and improve professional practices. Dissertations in Practice (DiP), in particular, provide in-depth analyses of specific topics and can be used as tools for advocacy and change. The findings and recommendations from these types of dissertations can inform policy, regulations, and practices, and have a positive impact on professional communities and society (Green & Newcombe, 2020; Joyce & Cartwright, 2022). Particularly, through continuous learning and improvement, research helps to promote progress and ensure that the needs of professionals, students, and communities are met.

DiPs are characterized by their focus on practical applications and are frequently structured differently from traditional dissertation approaches (Frugo et al, 2016; Hendron et al., 2014). For example, some DiPs may have fewer or more chapters, or they may have different headings or sections that are more tailored to the specific study and its goals. Additionally, DiPs often include appendices, case studies, and other materials that provide practical examples and evidence of the impact of the study in real-world settings. However, regardless of the DiP approach, importance should be placed on the research effectively communicating the practical implications and impact of the study, rather than adhering to a specific format. Notably, EdD research has the potential to impact educational and organizational settings by informing policies, improving practices, and advancing knowledge. Although traditional research approaches have provided sufficient theoretical frameworks outlining the issues at hand, DiPs have provided researchers with more accessibility and focused opportunities to understand the problem(s) at hand and how these should be undertaken, with a specific focus on social justice (Carnegie Project on the Education Doctorate, 2020). Further, DiPs have resulted in the creation of products that influence all stakeholders (e.g., educators, learners, policymakers), impacting the education system, organizations, and policies on local and national levels which demonstrate the value and positive effect of this research approach.

DiP Impacts

Applied and practice-oriented research allows for addressing areas of professional practice and the creation of knowledge generation resulting in impactful change. The findings and recommendations from DiPs can inform policy makers and educational leaders in making decisions about what interventions or practices to implement in schools and classrooms. For example, DiPs tend to highlight the importance of various factors that include instructional approaches, parental involvement, and student achievement and well-being. Generally, DiPs showcase ways to promote social justice and equity by examining and addressing disparities in educational outcomes and opportunities (Stewart, 2019: Smith, 2019). This research approach further provides evidence-based insights into the impact of different interventions and factors related to problems of practice and how scholarly practitioners evolve as agents of change.

Changes to Workplace Practices

DiPs are effective research approaches that inform policies and programs that aim to reduce disparities and promote equity in education and organizations. For example, Stewart (2019) conducted a DiP that explored the best ways to support teachers for improving cultural competence to help them as they taught students who differ from their own cultural background. The study recognized that teachers need training and support to become culturally competent and able to help all students achieve at the highest level. Stewart (2019) emphasized this need in order to bridge the gap between home, school, and community. The study was aimed to specifically identify ways to challenge mindsets and then provide training to help with strategies to aid competence for teachers who were currently teaching in diverse settings. The study was a qualitative study with teachers who were able to help answer the applied research goals.

The findings revealed three themes, including building relationships and effective classroom management, using culturally relevant teaching strategies, and use of collaborative strategies. The participants also shared their own stories of culture and background thus becoming more aware of their own self. From the data provided by the participants, Stewart (2019) crafted trainings and material to use for future professional development work and this was included in the DiP. The findings of this dissertation can be applied in several ways to promote social justice and equity in education. For example, the study provides evidence-based insights into the benefits of the ways teachers can learn cultural competence in the classroom and can inform teacher professional development programs that aim to promote culturally responsive teaching and cultural competence. The study can also informs policies and programs that aim to promote diversity, equity, and inclusion in education, and can contribute to a better understanding of the ways in which diversity can impact teacher practices and student learning. As this study demonstrates, DiPs provide valuable contributions to the field of education through evidence-based insights into the impact of cultural competence and diversity in the classroom on teacher practices; and student learning and can inform policies and programs that aim to promote equity and inclusion in education.

DiPs also have the potential to significantly impact workplace practices through a focus on topics related to leadership, organizational development, and curriculum design. The research conducted in DiPs can further offer insights into best practices and provide evidence-based strategies for improving workplace performance. For example, Frugo et al. (2016) examined leadership frameworks, characteristics, and effective education practices to help improve student growth. They used a mixed methods approach with three members focusing on specific leadership variables and the fourth looking at educational practices. From this collaborative research study, they were able to propose a new model of effective school leadership and propose applied and specific findings. However, some DiPs may provide practical insights that can be directly applied in the workplace, while others may contribute to a broader understanding of a particular issue and inform future research. For instance, Summers (2019) conducted a study which helped to address the problem of teacher attrition by examining the induction program for one Texas school district. The DiP used a developmental research design in order to work towards improvement of the existing teacher induction program. The district had higher teacher attrition than the state average and this DiP uncovered challenges that included: high levels of leadership turnover, curriculum problems, low levels of teacher support and development, and a weak comprehensive teacher induction program. Through the DiP, these gaps were able to not only be identified, but a framework was developed and put into place for improved systemic teacher induction which was scalable and beneficial to other districts in a much wider area (Summers, 2019).

Another DiP study to improve day-to-day workplace practices was that of Irish (2021), who examined how educators that serve students with significant learning problems described their participation in a leadership development program. The study explored how this program impacted the educators' work and leadership experiences using the theories of positive leadership and appreciative inquiry via interpretative phenomenology. Through the initial research, various themes were identified which led to the development of The Positive Leadership Development Framework Tool. This tool allows practitioners to integrate positive leadership practices that support professional growth while incorporating individual (human capital) and collective (social capital) foci (Irish, 2021). As with Summers' (2019) DiP, this type of framework and tool are hoped to prove beneficial to other districts and organizations.

These examples demonstrate the significant impacts that EdD dissertations can have on workplace practices. By providing evidence-based strategies for improving performance and advancing our understanding of education's role in the workforce, these dissertations can help organizations stay competitive and effective in today's rapidly changing educational landscape.

Advancements of Knowledge

Scholarly practitioners also have a critical role in advancing knowledge and understanding in the field of education. Researchers in education explore a wide range of topics that include areas such as teaching and learning to organizational structures and policy changes. By conducting rigorous studies, analyzing data, and drawing conclusions, education researchers generate new insights that advance knowledge in their respective fields. One example is a DiP conducted by Smith (2019) which focused on better understanding the ways in which mindfulness practices can impact student outcomes. The study was conducted in a diverse urban high school and used a randomized controlled design to compare the outcomes of students who participated in a mindfulness-based stress reduction program to those who did not. The findings of the study showed that the mindfulness-based stress reduction program had a positive impact on both academic performance and well-being. Specifically, the study found that students who participated in the program showed improved grades, increased motivation, and reduced symptoms of stress, compared to students who did not participate.

The findings of this DiP can be applied in several ways to promote social justice and equity in education and the workplace, and advance the field of education. For instance, the study provides evidence-based insights into the benefits of mindfulness-based stress reduction programs and can inform school-based programs that aim to reduce stress and promote well-being among students. The study can also inform workplace wellness programs that aim to improve employee well-being and productivity. In general, DiPs contribute to the professional development of the researcher. Writing a dissertation requires a significant amount of time and effort and it involves developing a range of skills such as critical thinking, research design, and data analysis. By developing these skills, researchers can become better equipped to conduct future research and contribute to the field of education resulting in an advancement of knowledge creation.

Creation of Change Agents

Although there are many important outcomes of educational research, one of the most effective products that the DiP establishes are scholar-practitioners. Particularly, the processes and work involved within the DiP encourages and provides an opportunity for learners to transform into agents of change and into valuable leaders within their organizations and communities (Dana et al., 2021; Tamim & Torres, 2022). DiP methodologies provide frameworks for meaningful research on a personal and professional level. Further, these methodologies promote and enhance the critical thinking and analytical skills required to view issues from all angles, develop required skills associated with change management, conflict resolution, and communication blending of practical knowledge and professional skills to define, outline, and solve problems at hand (CPED, 2021; Dana et al., 2021). Most notably, EdD programs are committed to guiding students to become agents of change in the field of education. EdD programs are designed to develop the skills and knowledge needed to address complex educational challenges and make positive changes in educational institutions and systems. Therefore, DiPs can further serve as a means for individuals to become change agents in the field of education by providing students opportunities to focus on a specific program, apply research to practice, and engage stakeholders in their findings. Ultimately, the DiP allows practitioners to become the products of change. It creates active change agents and leaders in which the skills developed through their doctoral programs cascade into professional settings by applying an analytical and scholarly scope to challenges they discover.

Creation of and Improvements to Programs, Policies, and Products

As the DiP results in agents of change, scholarly practitioners have the opportunity to focus on defining current issues, establishing processes, and examining policies within academic and organizational settings. Through DiP research, scholar-practitioners create more innovative, sustainable, and equitable products for their schools or organizations. For example, various DiPs have outlined the problems regarding equity among minorities in academic institutions and how these problems must be addressed. Richardson and Harrington (2022) identified the limitations single parents encounter within higher education institutions due to the lack of equitable policies and inclusive services. With inequitable policies, the success of many students (i.e., those who fall outside the traditional scope of a university/college student) can be negatively affected. More specifically, Richardson and Harrington's (2022) study demonstrated how there needs to be more institutional support and engagement for single parents and the difficulties they experience due to a lack of reliable childcare within higher education. These immense challenges for single-parent students have resulted in unique difficulties in completing their formal education. Subsequently, it was further established that universities and external services must adapt to such social changes, in which they provide more accessibility, opportunities, and support services, to create an equitable educational experience thus resulting in new policies within education (Richardson & Harrington, 2022).

Similarly, Jeter and Melendez (2022) demonstrated the gaps within the formal education system and processes, specifically toward potential Black male educators. They found a significant lack of financial resources and opportunities, both from an individual and an institutional level, which affected enrollment rates (Jeter & Melendez, 2022). Additionally, there was a substantial feeling of displacement and, thus, an increase in imposter syndrome among Black male students in higher education (Jeter & Melendez, 2022). A significant product of their research was the need to establish and reinforce more mentoring support and intervention programs (e.g., African American Male Initiative) to enhance Black male academic achievement (Jeter & Melendez, 2022). Further, it was noted that institutions needed to provide more opportunities for financial backing and, more importantly, policies and opportunities to improve the campus racial climate to help create a sense of belonging for students (Jeter & Melendez, 2022).

Among the various equitable progressions within academic policies, the DiP has produced procedural and professional development changes in academic and corporate organizations. For example, on a corporate level, Franz et al. (2022) outlined how companies contributed to the issue of ageism, which many job seekers find to be an obstacle. Such inequality is typically found in the language used in job advertisements or a lack of diverse and equitable workplaces (Franz et al., 2022). Subsequently, their research concluded that for companies to avoid ageism, they should use age-inclusive language as well as avoid language that plays to a youth stereotype and implement an anti-ageist recruitment strategy and practices, while also offering appropriate training, career planning, and mentoring for older workers (Franz et al., 2022). This study demonstrated the need for organizations to readjust processes and policies to be more equitable amongst older applicants and employees.

Professional Improvements

Educational research has the potential to result in professional improvements in a variety of ways. Specifically, educational research can help identify effective teaching practices and instructional strategies that can improve student learning outcomes. By studying best practices and implementing evidence-based teaching methods, educators can improve their teaching and help their students succeed at higher rates (Hollinger, (2021). Particularly, Hollinger (2021) used responsive evaluation to try and improve student math scores in developmental math courses at a community college after identifying the critically high numbers of failure in these courses, not only at the research site but across the United States in similar institutions. Hollinger (2021) was able to develop a 12-step implementation plan for the math lab program to help more students be successful in these classes. This study resulted in the dissemination of an implementation plan that has been shared with community colleges across the U.S. with the goal of improving student outcomes and incorporating more effective teaching practices.

Alsen and Buss (2022) demonstrated the necessity of developing appropriate linguistic and equitable skills and pedagogies to be culturally responsive within teaching a diverse set of students. A positive response and increased self-efficacy in teaching culturally responsive practices were established by creating a multi-faceted intervention of theoretical and pedagogical theories for a culturally diverse classroom that is utilizing community practice-based and service-learning approaches (Alsen & Buss, 2022). The authors described the applied research, but in each section of the dissertation, they included "interludes" that focused on the thought process as well as the research which allows readers to follow the unfolding of the work. Seeing this explanation of the thought process provides a deeper understanding of how the work changed the authors and led to this deeper professional development experience.

Correspondingly, Hankins and Harrington (2022) emphasized that although many professors in higher education institutions provide the expertise needed to create active members of society, they lack the appropriate pedagogical skills to facilitate their competencies fully. In other words, there is an imbalance between the knowledge being transferred to the students and effective methods, including, but not limited to, formative and summative assessment and feedback. Studies based on these types of topics provide evidence-based research necessary for justifying professional improvements. Precisely, educational research can provide opportunities for educators to engage in ongoing professional development focused on the pedagogical skills and best practices needed to effectively promote student academic growth and professional skill development. Using applied, evidence-based strategies also increases the need to remain knowledgeable in the most current research and thus helps ensure educators provide the most up-to-date information to students.

Researchers can disseminate their findings through professional development workshops and training sessions that gives educators the opportunity to learn about new research and best practices which they can then incorporate into their teaching. In summary, educational research can result in professional improvements by improving teaching practices, developing new programs and interventions, informing policy and decision-making, and promoting ongoing professional development. By incorporating evidence-based practices and strategies into their teaching and decision-making, educators can improve student outcomes and make a positive impact on the field of education, and serve as leaders within their respective disciplines.

Plans for Advocacy

The Carnegie Project on the Education Doctorate (CPED) has positioned itself as a leader in defining and improving practitioner-based research. Perry et al. (2020) highlighted that the education field contains strong advocates who are dedicated to transitioning the way that practitioners learn and conduct research. Particularly, EdD programs incorporate applied research approaches that focus on problems of practice within workplace settings. By conducting DiPs, scholarly practitioners have the unique opportunity to consider advocacy actions and initiate change within their places of work.

Improvements to Communities and Societies

DiPs support advocacy efforts to address topics that include social justice and equity (Pape et al., 2022). For example, DiPs may center on research topics that are inclusive of social justice leadership, including advocating for students who are currently and historically marginalized (Coaxum et al., 2022). Thus, DiPs provide students a voice in extending their social justice efforts to impact their communities. This focus is imperative given that researchers have contended that greater efforts to promote social justice initiatives have persisted and there is a further need for educational practitioners who are committed to equity, justice, and positive change (George, 2017; Guerra et al., 2013). Essentially, EdD programs are structured to both improve practice and result in community advocacy and impact (Archbald, 2008; Blevins, 2022), and to influence the discipline of study. Thus, the student practitioner's ability to develop and articulate a rigorous research design is crucial in furthering these goals (Pape et al., 2022).

The guiding principles for EdD program design developed by the CPED provides institutions of higher education a framework for preparing students to become agents of change. These principles focus on equipping doctoral students with the expertise to frame research around questions of equity, ethics, and social justice; and to work collaboratively with their communities and organizations, becoming impactful educational leaders who can promote positive differences (CPED, 2021). Alignment with these principles help students to critically consider the advocacy efforts integrated within their research and the impact on their own organization, community, and professional practices. Perry and Zambo (2018) discussed the guiding principles in relation to graduate outcomes as resulting in change through "awareness, advocacy, action, stewardship, and leadership aimed at equitable/change improvement" (p. 21). Acquisition of these skill areas result in EdD graduates becoming effective change agents in various leadership positions. Particularly, students engaging in research that is grounded in these principles and the scholar-practitioner framework allows students to become educational leaders with the knowledge of how to use research as a form of activism (Harrington & Melendez, 2020).

Empowerment Through Mentorship

Guiding students in the development of these skills is essential given that they may not initially view themselves as activists. Throughout the EdD curriculum and the dissertation process, faculty should mentor students to develop advocacy skills and model how to use research to create effective change. Through effective mentoring approaches, students experience the benefits of advocacy further empowering them to advocate for others (Statti & Torres, 2021). Indeed, Dodd and Mizrahi (2017) discovered students who are committed to activism will most likely engage in future advocacy activities. Scholar activists are considered community driven, social justice-oriented, and action-oriented with the long-term goal of challenging the status quo (Ramasubramanian & Sousa, 2021).

However, engagement of scholarly activism needs to be sustainable, malleable, and aligned with the community goals and desired outcomes (Howard & Baker, 2021).

By conducting DiPs, practitioners are provided evidence to justify their claims expressed in writing (Leach et al, 2021), allowing for further justification for advocacy and change. Addressing current and pressing issues in problems of practice allow for intentional change to occur within organizations. Shulman (2010) encouraged institutions of higher education to recognize collaborative practices to support doctoral students who seek to improve their trades. EdD students are afforded a remarkable opportunity to embrace issues found within their organizations to conduct actionable research that can positively impact the community and bring forth change. Storey and Maughan (2016) contended that "professional practitioners are intrinsically motivated toward action, a desire to improve practice (i.e., policies, procedure, and productivity), and are guided by authentic problems, or noted opportunities for improvements (p. 2014).

EdD programs position graduates to become leaders with the expertise necessary for successful advocacy when faced with topics that are complex and challenging, further allowing for activist movements in educational reform and leadership within the community. Thus, practitioner researchers engage in professional practices that result in long-lasting change. For example, DiPs have focused on topics including employment discrimination (Baker, 2021), maintenance of cultural identity and heritage language (Choi, 2022), and use of counter-spaces for support and knowledge creation (Streets, 2022). Through EdD program completion, graduates acquire skills that empower them to better serve and support students, colleagues, and community leaders. Specifically, by conducting DiPs, students develop expertise in utilizing their research findings to provide a voice and advocate for others. Indeed, conducting research studies that integrate solving real-world problems requires attention to underlying social and educational injustices (Miller et al., 2021). Moreover, scholar-practitioners engage in critical consciousness using evidence to support professional practices, policies, and procedures; and use their research findings to support recommendations for change. Hesbol et al. (2020) highlighted that "inquiry as practice pushes our capacity to innovate, dismantling oppressive systems and leading improvement" (p. 33). Essentially, students become empowered to become advocates upon graduation with the skill sets to take action and create positive change and systemic transformation. Advocacy approaches are moved beyond paradigmatic lines (e.g., race, gender, sexual orientation inclusivity) to focus on diversity and equitable educational practices and knowledge production in educational practices through differences in approach, attitude, and perspectives (Noel et al., 2020). Integrating these focuses within EdD curriculum results in students conducting DiP research that prioritizes social justice and advocacy.

Concluding Remarks

DiPs play a crucial role in professional practices and communities as they serve as a source of new knowledge and innovations. They provide an in-depth analysis of a specific topic and contribute to the advancement of the relevant field. Also, DiPs help to expand the existing body of knowledge and provide new insights and perspectives that can be used to improve professional practices. Additionally, they provide a platform for professionals to demonstrate their expertise and contribute to the development of best practices in their respective fields. Shulman (2005) proclaimed that EdD doctoral graduates are trained "to think, to perform, and to act with integrity" (p. 52). Additionally, George (2017) voiced that doctoral EdD programs of study are vital in providing students access to doctoral preparation centered on establishing practitioners who are socially just and equity-minded leaders. The findings and recommendations in dissertations can also have a significant impact on the wider community which lead to changes in policies, regulations, and practices that benefit society as a whole. Therefore, DiPs are an important tool for promoting continuous learning, improvement, and progress in professional practices and communities.

Dissertations can also be used as a tool for advocacy. Particularly, the findings and recommendations from dissertations can be used to bring attention to important issues and to promote change by highlighting the need for improvement in certain areas. Developing this mindset results in educational practitioners who understand the value of advocacy and imparting positive change. Advocacy and activism are considered long-term goals of EdD programs and should encompass a lasting commitment from graduates (Howard & Baker, 2021). Dissertations can also be used to support evidence-based decision making and to inform policy and practice. As agents of change, EdD graduates possess leadership skills to advocate for just practices, policies, and procedures within their professions and communities (Puckett & Lewis, 2022). By presenting a well-researched and thorough analysis of a particular issue, DiPs can provide valuable information and insights that can be used to support advocacy efforts. They also help to raise awareness, build consensus, and mobilize resources for positive change. Overall, DiPs provide a key role in advancing the interests of professional communities and promoting the common good.

References

Alsen, E., & Buss, R.R. (2022). Developing pre-service teachers: A social justice approach for educating culturally and linguistically diverse students. *Impacting Education: Journal on Transforming Professional Practice, 7*(2). 61-73. doi.org/10.5195/ie.2022.213

Archbald, D. (2008). Research versus problem solving for the education leadership doctoral thesis: Implications for form and function. *Educational Administration Quarterly, 44*(5), 704-739. https://doi.org/10.1177/0013161X07313288

Baker, V. (2021). *Employment discrimination: An efficacy study of African American inequalities in the California utility sector* [Doctoral Dissertation]. (Publication No. 85), University of Missouri, St. Louis. ProQuest Dissertations & Theses Global.

Blevins, B. E., Papadakis, L. K. C., Howell, L., Meehan, J., Pratt, S., Talbert, S., Cooper, S., Earl, J., Lively, C., Murray, E. A., Sanguras, L., Talbert, T. L., & Werse, N. R. (2022). Reframing the problem of practice: Transitions in Baylor University's Ed.D. in learning and organizational change program. *Impacting Education: Journal on Transforming Professional Practice, 7*(1), 32-41. https://doi.org/10.5195/ie.2022.230

Carnegie Project of the Education Doctorate (2021). *The CPED framework.* https://www.cpedinitiative.org/the-framework

Choi, Y. (2022). *Understanding the perspectives, practices, and expectations of Korean American parents toward the heritage language education of their children* [Doctoral Dissertation]. University of San Francisco; Publication number: 603. ProQuest Dissertations & Theses Global.

Coaxum, J., Farrow, M., & Manning, J. (2022). Education leadership programs responding to current American crises. *Impacting Education: Journal on Transforming Professional Practice, 7*(3), 347-39. https://doi.org/10.5195/ie.2022.223

Dana, N.F., Rigney, J., Vesico, V., & Ma, W.M. (2021). Project-based learning and doctoral student research skill development: A case study. *Impacting Education: Journal on Transforming Professional Practice, 6*(4), 27-35. https://www.doi.org/10.5195/ie.2021.148

Dodd, S. J., & Mizrahi, T. (2017). Activism before and after graduate education: Perspectives from three cohorts of MSW students. *Journal of Social Work, 53*(3), 503-519. https://doi.org/10.1080/10437797.2016.1272514

Franz, N.E., Werse, N. R., & Talbert, T. L. (2022). Ageism-induced anxiety of job seekers aged 50-83: Preliminary findings from a phenomenological case study problem of practice dissertation. *Impacting Education: Journal on Transforming Professional Practice, 7*(2). 11-18. https://www.doi.org/10.5195/ie.2022.199

Frugo, J. A., Johnston, A. E., McCauley, B. J., & Navarro, K. C. (2016). *Leading character: An investigation into the characteristics and effective practices of character education leaders.* [Doctoral Dissertation]. (Publication No. 566), The University of San Francisco. ProQuest Dissertations & Theses Global.

George, P. (2017). Toward a social justice model for an EdD program in higher education. *Impacting Education: Journal on Transforming Professional Practice, 2*(1). https://doi.org/10.5195/ie.2017.29

Green, C. S., & Newcombe, N. S. (2020). Cognitive training: How evidence, controversies, and challenges inform education policy. *Policy Insights from the Behavioral and Brian Sciences, 7*(1), 80-86. https://journals.sagepub.com/doi/pdf/10.1177/2372732219870202

Guerra, P. L., Nelson, S. W., Jacobs, J., & Yamamura, E. (2013). Developing educational leaders for social justice: Programmatic elements that work or need improvement. *Education Research and Perspectives: An International Journal, 40*(1). 124-129.

Hankins, A., & Harrington, C. (2022). Lack of high-quality, frequent feedback contributes to low success rates for community college students. *Impacting Education: Journal on Transforming Professional Practice, 7*(4), 2-7. https://www.doi.org/10.5195/ie.2022.201

Harrington, C., & Melendez, J. (2020). Launching an EdD in community college leadership program with activism in mind. *Impacting Education: Journal on Transforming Professional Practice, 5*(2), 11-19. https://doi.org/10.5195/ie.2020.114

Hendron, J., Kim, A., Tolliver, S., & Deloatch, D. (2014). *Ubiquitous computing in schools: A multi-case study of 1:1 districts.* CPED. https://www.cpedinitiative.org/dissertation-in-practice#dissertation-in-practice/award-winner

Hesbol, K. A., Bartee, J. S., & Amiri, F. (2020). Activism in practice: The influence of a rural school leader's beliefs and practices in disrupting historical patterns and underachievement in traditionally marginalized students. *Impacting Education: Journal on Transforming Professional Practice, 5*(2), 33-43. https://doi.org/10.5195/ie.2020.134

Hollinger, L. S. N. (2021). *Responsive evaluation of a community college mathematics laboratory: A dissertation in practice* (Publication No. 2555322950), University of West Florida. ProQuest Dissertations & Theses Global.

Howard, J., & Baker, T. (2021). Activating activism within the EdD: Connecting DiP research and the community. *Impacting Education: Journal on Transforming Professional Practice, 6*(1), 37-44. https://doi.org/10.5195/ie.2021.162

Irish, M. (2021). *Skillfully learning and leading: Educators describe the impact of their participation in an appreciative leadership development program on their work* (Publication No. 28545311), Southern New Hampshire University. ProQuest Dissertations & Theses Global.

Jeter, F. & Melendez, J. (2022). Too few Black male educators. *Impacting Education: Journal on Transforming Professional Practice, 7*(2), 19-25. https://www.doi.org/10.5195/ie.2022.200

Joyce, K. E., & Cartwright, N. (2022). How should evidence inform education policy? In R. Curren (Ed), *Handbook of philosophy of education* (pp. 86-99). Routledge.

Leach, L. F., Baker, C., Leamons, C. G., Bunch, P., & Brock, J. (2021). Using evidence to frame problems of practice. *Impacting Education: Journal on Transforming Professional Practice, 6*(4), 1-7.

Miller, B., Bogiages, C., Yow, J., & Lotter, C. (2021). Embedding activism in a STEM EdD program. *Impacting Education: Journal on Transforming Professional Practice, 6*(1), 3-10. https://doi.org/10.5195/ie.2021.172

Noel, T. K., Gorlewski, J., & Kearney, E. (2020). SMACKtivism: A program redesign so good, you won't know what hit you. *Impacting Education: Journal on Transforming Professional Practice, 5*(2), 3-10. https://doi.

org/10.5195/ie.2020.112

Pape, S. J., Bryant, C. L., JohnBull, R. M., & Karp, K. S. (2022). Improvement science as a frame for the dissertation in practice: The John Hopkins experience. *Impacting Education Journal on Transforming Professional Practice, 7*(1), 59-66. https://doi.org/10.5195/ie.2022.241

Perry, J., & Zambo, D. (2018). Themed section of impacting education focused on CPED's principle. *Impacting Education: Journal on Transforming Professional Practice, 3*(2), 17-23. https://doi.org/10.5195/ie.2018.89

Perry, J., Zambo, D., & Crow, R. (2020). *The improvement science dissertation in practice: A guide for faculty, committee members, and their students.* Myers Education Press.

Puckett, H., & Lewis, T. (2022). Do I really belong here? EdD student perceptions of a poster gallery walk to mitigate imposter syndrome and match with a dissertation chair. *International Journal of Educational Leadership Preparation, 17*(1), 101-116.

Ramasubramanian, S., & Sousa, A. N. (2021). Communication scholar-activism: Conceptualizing key dimensions and practices based on interviews with scholar-activists. *Journal of Applied Communication Research, 49*(5), 477-496. https://doi.org/10.1080/00909882.2021.1964573

Richardson, F. & Harrington, C. (2022). Single mother students are lacking sufficient support to persist to graduation in community colleges. *Impacting Education: Journal on Transforming Professional Practice, 7*(2), 26-31. https://www.doi.org/10.1595/ie.2022.202

Shulman, L. S. (2010). Doctoral education shouldn't be a marathon. *Chronicle of Higher Education, 56*(30), B9-B12. https://www.chronicle.com/article/doctoral-education-shouldnt-be-a-marathon/

Shulman, L. S., Golde, C. M., Bueschel, A. C., & Garabedian, K. J. (2006). Reclaiming education's doctorates: A critique and a proposal. *Educational Researcher, 35*(3), 25–32. https://doi.org/10.3102/0013189X035003025

Smith, M. A. (2019). *The effect of a mindfulness-based stress reduction program on high school students' academic performance and well-being.* [Doctoral Dissertation]. (Publication No. 609), University of San Francisco. ProQuest Dissertations & Theses Global.

Statti, A., & Torres, K. M. (2021). Creating agents of change through doctoral learning. *Impacting Education: Journal on Transforming Professional Practice, 6*(1), 17-21. https://doi.org/10.5195/ie.2021.115

Stewart, M. G. (2019). *A dissertation in-practice: Building culturally competent professional development for teachers.* [Doctoral Dissertation]. (Publication No. 2407577646), Lamar University. ProQuest Dissertations & Theses Global.

Storey, V. A., & Maughan, B. D. (2016). Dissertation in practice: Reconceptualizing the nature and role of the practitioner-scholar. In V. A. Storey (Ed), *International perspectives on designing professional practice doctorates* (pp. 213-232.). Palgave Macmillan.

Streets, H. M. (2022). *The Collegiate Black Space: Black College Students' Use of New Counter-Spaces for Support, Knowledge Production, and Organizing for Activism.* University of San Francisco. https://repository. usfca.edu/diss/609

Summers, C. (2019). *A design study to improve a teacher induction program in a south Texas school district,* (Publication No. 13811905), Texas A&M University Corpus Christi. ProQuest Dissertations & Theses Global.

Tamim, S.R., & Torres, K.M. (2022). Evolution of the dissertation in practice. *Impacting Education: Journal on Transforming Professional Practice, 7*(1), 1-3. https://www.doi.org/10.5195/ie.2022.267

SECTION 3:

Some DiP
Approaches and Formats

CHAPTER 11

Improvement Science:

The Disquisition—A Dissertation in Practice Capstone for Developing Equity-Oriented Scholar-Practitioners

ROBERT CROW, PHD

Forward-thinkers in the academy have recently begun to make great strides in differentiating the nature and purpose of U.S. doctoral programs in educational leadership. As such, this differentiation intentionality creates a tension for reconsidering the role and structure of the dissertation in practice (DiP). The Carnegie Project on the Education Doctorate (CPED) has been clear in envisioning and manifesting the DiP. In past years we had very few resources for guidance, yet we now have available rubrics, books, and award-winners—all of which serve as useful models for initiating and sustaining improvement work.

This chapter illustrates how, when equipped with an arsenal of tools, programs can challenge and even begin to dismantle the systemic structures that continue to squelch our vision for creating the unique capstone exercise, the DiP. As a faculty, we asked ourselves, "How can we innovate for the production of a different, scholar-practitioner-focused output when we retain the vestigial form and function of the doctoral dissertation that have perpetuated for over 800 years?" Therefore, the purpose of this chapter is to highlight how one CPED-influenced program, the Doctor of Education at Western Carolina University, embeds CPED's Working

Principles, infuses current theories in educational leadership, and uses an improvement science methodology to identify and address a problem of practice all within our graduates' capstone exercise, the *disquisition* (DQ).

The chapter tasks readers to think beyond what is familiar and typical in the academy and to re-envision the roles and structures as functions directly related to the inherent purpose for the DiP; to effect change that leads to sustained institutional improvement. The charge here, albeit narrowly focused, calls for a critical mass of forward-thinkers who are ready and undoubtedly willingly able to explore new roles, alternative formats, and yet-to-be-conceived of structures of the doctoral dissertation-in-practice toward a collective vision be actualized. This chapter is intended for those with interest in exploring alternatives to the one-size-fits-all 5-chapter dissertation approach typical in most doctoral programs today.

What Does an EdD Degree Have to do With Improvement Science?

Over the past decade, programs in educational leadership have been influenced by reform efforts led by the Carnegie Project on the Education Doctorate (CPED) and other like-minded higher education associations. Among CPED's guiding principles is a focus on preparing graduates who can name, frame, and ultimately work to solve complex problems related to the inequities existing in our current education systems. Part of the ability to identify, address, and solve complex problems is to engage enough stakeholders closest to the problem so that one can examine an issue through multiple perspectives. In this case, a problem of practice (PoP) is defined as "a persistent, contextualized, and specific issue embedded in the work of a professional practitioner, the addressing of which has the potential to result in improved understanding, experience, and outcomes" (CPED, n.d.).

To develop skill in systematic inquiry, such as identifying root causes of persistent problems, or formulating potential solutions to complex issues, students in programs in educational leadership learn about and ultimately become proficient in the science of improvement. Improvement science is considered a signature methodology

(Shulman, 2005) that allows aspiring leaders to engage in real change. Improvement science as a signature methodology for systemic inquiry for educational leaders consists of deploying rapid tests of change to guide the development, revision, and continued fine-tuning of new tools, processes, work roles, and relationships" (Carnegie Foundation for the Advancement of Teaching, n.d.).

Like other programs nationwide, the doctoral DiP is the culminating product for the Doctorate in Education (EdD) degree. In further effort to move toward a more distinct form and format for the culminating product (i.e., the DiP), our faculty purposefully elect to change the title of the capstone product to a *disquisition* (Crow, et al., 2015). Webster defines a disquisition as a "long, formal essay and line of inquiry on a subject."

In considering CPED's guiding principles and their implications for developing the scholar-practitioner (a student learning program outcome) the disquisition fosters the development of a change agent capable of leading projects aimed at combating social and other justice inequities present in our classrooms and in our students' lives.

In reading this book, you likely have an interest in achieving a different outcome in your doctoral program. If this quest strikes a chord, then you may be at a point where you are vying alternatives to the traditional capstone product. Your developed perspective is likely due to professional engagement in associations such as the Carnegie Project on the Education Doctorate (CPED), the University Council of Educational Administrators (UCEA), and the American Educational Research Association (AERA). An openness to having an innovative perspective will allow you to see how our EdD capstone product, the DQ, is a pedagogical exercise leading to a host of benefits, such as: improving student learning outcomes, developing capacity to take on and lead improvement efforts, and most important, demonstrating the capacity to confront and (begin to) dismantle the inequities embedded in our education systems.

The Disquisition's Signature Methodology: Improvement Science

The DQ employs improvement science (IS) as the model of inquiry for identifying and addressing complex problems of practice for the development of the scholar-practitioner's skill set. Requiring doctoral students to integrate IS methodology to identify and address persistent issues present in organizations and intuitions is a major component in completing the DQ.

Why is improvement science used as a methodology for understanding equity?

How can IS be used as a mechanism to bring inefficiency, inequity, and other systemic failures to the forefront for action? Among data like school report cards, end-of-grade reports, and other archival accountability, figures can be used to pinpoint system variance in outputs. Identifying these outputs allows for the formulation of targeted improvement interventions. Prompting educational leadership program faculty discussion were many influences promoting improvement science as a signature methodology for education leaders. When first becoming inducted, we asked ourselves as the program faculty, "Could improvement science be used as a signature methodology in our educational leadership program? And if so, can it be used as a mechanism for promoting and ensuring rigor in critical praxis?"

Over the years, we have challenged ourselves to not only teach improvement science but to incorporate it into the dissertation structure. We ask ourselves, "What prior knowledge must we faculty possess (since none of us have earned a terminal degree in the field)?" We found that through a lot of professional development, mentoring of both veteran and faculty new to the program, and much discussion, we were able to construct a pedagogical capstone that produces the outcome we desired–an equity-focused scholar-practitioner.

Using improvement methodology to dismantle systemic inequities

The requirement of using improvement science as the signature methodology for all graduating EdD students is based on the notion that improvement science is currently being used as a signature methodology by educational leaders in the field. It is imperative to include this inquiry-related content in graduate leadership coursework. Upon conferral, graduates are trained in this way of disciplinary thinking (improvement inquiry). Anecdotally, in our own practitioner-oriented doctoral program, Methods in improvement science is one of the initial inquiry courses in which students enroll alongside Leading Complex Organizations that provides context.

It is important to acknowledge one's knowledge and comfort levels for employing improvement science as a blueprint to identify and dismantle inequitable systems. Given the charge, the challenge is posed to educational leaders with know-how about ways systems work, or not work, and to build that same capacity in the leadership field's future graduates.

The DQ is conceptualized to include the six principles of improvement (Bryk, 2015). For example, the doctoral disquisitioners may choose to use an organizational chart to illustrate a deficit in diversity among the institution's work force. Or the student might elect to include a fishbone diagram to illustrate root causes for the problem of practice. Better yet, students may include a diagram that was co-constructed with key stakeholders who are closest to the problem. Lastly, the student may elect to represent their own system output to illustrate that the system is not performing as intended.

Improvement Science Leads to Theories of Improvement

Although the tools of improvement science include several improvement-oriented frameworks, there is no more powerful tool for improvement than the driver diagram. The driver diagram is a graphical representation that visually illustrates a group's working theory of practice improvement and organizes information on proposed activities so the relationships between the aim of the improvement project and the changes to be tested and implemented are made clear (Carnegie Foundation for the Advancement of Teaching, carnegiefoundation.org). Conceptualized as a ubiquitous structure in improvement science, the driver diagram illustrates one's "theory of improvement" which is the crux of DQ work. Figure 11.1 depicts a localized theory that provides the aim of the overall improvement initiative: the primary and secondary drivers related to actions, leading to "ways forward" for achieving the aim, and the more granular change ideas associated with the drivers.

Figure 11.1

Driver Diagram Illustrating a Theory of Improvement

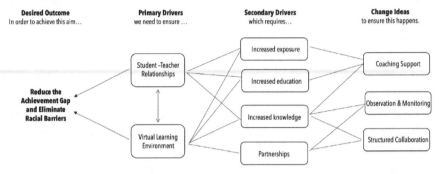

(Rasmussin, et al., 2020)

In this example, the driver diagram illustrates a set of tangible actions believed to contribute to the aim. The diagram also provides a glimpse of the four practical measures that should be used to evaluate the improvement project: outcome measures, driver measures, process measures, and balancing measures (Hinnant-Crawford, 2020). The aim depicts the outcome measure associated with the overall goal, such as a measure of campus climate on a community college. The primary drivers represent major categories where a subset of data may be collected that are related to the general outcome construct (i.e., a welcoming campus climate).

When using driver measures, data are collected in more frequent intervals, rather than only prior to and post-initiative, as is the function of the outcome measure. Even more granular are the assessments of the individual change ideas, where process measures are collected and analyzed. Process measures are used frequently, following each learning cycle, to evaluate delivery of the intervention, professional development, and other learning processes from the perspective of the DQ project's participants. Process measures answer questions such as—*Was the content delivery effective for your learning? Was the topic covered comprehensively? Were the materials and resources used adequate?*—so that these formative assessments can identify and address planning and delivery efficacy as the project unfolds.

The Disquisition in Relation to Other Professional Frameworks

At Western Carolina University, we define the disquisition as:

a formal, problem-based discourse or treatise in which a problem of practice is identified, described, analyzed, and addressed in depth, including methods and strategies used to bring about change and to assess whether the change is an improvement. A social justice framework informs this transformational exercise with a focus on equitable and ethical practice. The purpose of the DQ is to document the scholarly development of leadership expertise in organizational improvement. The DQ and the associated activities contribute a concrete good to the larger community and the dissemination of new relevant knowledge. (Lomotey, 2015, p.1-9)

There are several elements characterizing the DQ which differentiate it from a traditional dissertation. Because the nature of the DiP generates practical knowledge, aspects such as a focus on promoting systemic equity comprise the model (Table 11.1). Although many nuances distinguish the DQ, depicted in the table are seven of its more prominent features.

Table 11.1

Description of Elements Comprising the Disquisition (DQ) Model

DQ Dimension	DQ Description	CPED Principle*	IS Principle*
Social Justice & Equity Focused	From the systems level, all DQs have at their focus a specific social justice orientation as evidenced by variance in system output	Is framed around questions of equity, ethics, and social justice to bring about solutions to complex problems of practice	See the system that produces the current outcomes
Improvement Science Methodology	All DQs use improvement science principles, tools, and analyses in improvement initiatives	Provides field-based opportunities to analyze problems of practice … using multiple frames to develop meaningful solutions	Anchor practice improvement in disciplined inquiry

Collaborative Design	All DQs include the use of a design team comprised of key stakeholders for all phases in the process	Provides opportunities for collaboration and communication ... to work with diverse communities ... building partnerships	Make the work user-centered
Theory of Improvement	All DQs include a theory of improvement illustrated by aim, drivers, and change ideas	To use multiple frames to develop meaningful solutions	Anchor practice improvement in disciplined inquiry
Practical Measurement through Iterative Design	All DQs incorporate four practical measures: outcome, driver, process, and balancing through a cyclical Plan-Do-Study-Act framework	Emphasizes the generation, transformation, and use of professional knowledge and practice	We cannot improve at scale what we cannot measure
Lessons for Leaders and Leadership	All DQs include a reflective component; reflecting upon oneself as a developing leader to make recommendations for practitioners enacting similar initiatives	Is grounded in and develops a professional knowledge base ... integrating practical and research knowledge	Accelerate improvements through networked communities
Embedded Sustainability	All DQs embed new processes, procedures, and/or policies within the organizational context to ensure sustainability	Prepares leaders who can construct and apply knowledge to make positive differences in the lives of individuals, families, and communities	Accelerate improvements through networked communities

Note* The latter two columns are CPED Working Principles (https://www.cpedinitiative.org/the-framework) and Principles of Improvement Science (https://www.carnegiefoundation.org/our-ideas/six-core-principles-improvement/)

First and foremost, the DQ is an equity-focused doctoral-level capstone exercise in identifying and addressing a problem of practice (PoP) within one's laboratory of practice. PoPs are identified through various indicators, including archival/institutional data, published research findings, and through anecdotal and other experiential insights from veteran leaders. Program faculty created a DQ Idea Template that students use to describe their proposed work. The template is submitted by the student (or students, as we allow group DQs) and reviewed by the entire faculty for approval. The faculty deliberate, "Is the project equity focused? Is the work sufficient given the context?" The Idea Template is completed and approved prior to the DQ proposal defense.

Further, each DQ must base the design and analysis in improvement science. To dismantle inequitable systems, disquisitioners must articulate a theory of improvement, represented through a driver diagram, which proposes the potential tactics for dismantling the inequitable system. Once the details of the proposed theory of improvement have been worked out, the project then moves into the reiterative cyclical design framework known as the Plan-Do-Study-Act (PDSA) model. For those interested in further reading about a modified PDSA cycle specific to doctoral dissertation work, see Perry, Zambo and Crow (2020) for their discussion on a similar Study-Investigate-Analyze-Reflect (SIAR) model.

The Nature of Leadership Inquiry

As educators, we often start with the end product, or outcome, in mind. As we construct any learning experience, we ask ourselves: "What knowledge, skills and dispositions comprise X?".

Heeding Bryk et al.'s (2015) call for a New Way, and CPED's insistence for faculty development for innovations in the education doctorate, new forms and formats for academic scholarship and practical research emerged. Practitioner research is characterized as problem-oriented/user-focused as compared to the "one and done" model approach to research design that is typical in the social sciences. Those involved in practitioner research are themselves scholar-practitioners. *Who are scholar-practitioners and where did they come from?* Our program's scholar-practitioners are a relatively new breed of graduates who set themselves apart from the scientific-scholar whose focus is on empirical endeavors. In contrast, the scholar-practitioner uses and conducts improvement research to eradicate persistent and pervasive problems perpetuated by inequitably operating systems.

The scholar-practitioner does not live in isolation. Rather, today's education leader is shaped by influences and mandates of professional organizations, their professional standards, and graduate study program requirements. The DQ is conceptually built upon a solid framework of principles. For example, we do have somewhere to begin. The Professional Standards for Education Leaders [formerly ISLLC Standards] (Standard 10 - School Improvement) seeks "effective educational leaders act[ing] as agents of continuous improvement to promote each student's academic success and well-being" (PSEL, 2015, p. 33) as an outcome for doctoral graduates. Furthermore, Standard 10's sub-standards call for "develop[ing] technically appropriate systems of data collection, management, analysis, and use, connecting as needed to the district office and external partners for support in planning, implementation, monitoring, feedback, and evaluation" (PSEL, 2015, p. 24) providing exposure to the developmental stepping-stones toward proficiency. Other related sub-standards contain language representative of improvement research, such as adopting a systems perspective, promoting coherence in improvement efforts, and developing processes for improvement efforts.

The Disquisition's Building Blocks

The DQ includes the four building blocks Archbald (2015) suggests as outcomes attained through engaging in and undertaking a problem-based initiative: 1) developmental efficacy, 2) community benefit, 3) stewardship of doctoral values, and 4) distinctiveness of design. Students are exposed to opportunities to develop and hone skills in these four distinctive areas comprising doctoral capacity.

The DQ promotes developmental efficacy; students get good at leading others to think about problems faced in everyday lives. The exercise necessitates a collaborative research orientation by requiring stakeholders to have an active role in the definition of the problem at-hand, the ways to address the problem, and how to carry through a subsequent evaluation of the approaches enlisted. This cyclical reiterative design allows doctoral candidates to develop the cognitive schema for frameworks that can elicit problem deliberation and analysis, as well as the social confidence to lead others in the negotiation.

The DQ promotes community benefit; it always includes

stakeholders in the design and development and is aimed at persistent problems faced by community members (students, their parents, teachers, staff, and so on). Targeted problems can be identified through several sources, one such source being the causal analysis. A causal analysis allows participants to identify root causes for the problem at-hand and serves as an "idea hanger" upon which various stakeholders may elucidate and illustrate their viewpoints.

Stewardship of doctoral values include aspects of rigor, ethics, and positionality. The DQ process allows students to operate from a place of introspection-from conducting improvement research within one's own organization (i.e., the laboratory of practice) to involving staff and other stakeholders at the beginning of the initiative and throughout.

Our DQ model represents a distinctive design that is suited for an equity-oriented practitioner-scholar. The capstone exercise allows a synthesis of systems thinking, problem identification and address, and for the development of a cyclical predisposition for the ensuing work, characterized by reiterative evaluation and assessment.

Functional Aspects of the Disquisition Committee

Our DQ model, like most institutions, resembles the typical dissertation committee structure, at least from outward appearances. However, upon closer inspection, our model differs quite substantially from what is typical. Our doctoral dissertation model is designed to reflect the needs of educational professionals in practice.

Enlisting an External Member

As the EdD and PhD terminal degree programs have diverged with clear distinctions between them, some vestigial structures associated with the "5-Chapter Dissertation" remain. One such example is the vetting structure, the doctoral dissertation committee. The committee structure has remained relatively unchanged *despite* our revolutionary thinking on cleaving the degrees.

Program Faculty Pairing

In being intentional behind the composition, the committee structure is comprised of a DiP chair and a methodologist with expertise in improvement and/or practitioner research. This pairing arrangement is among the program (educational leadership) faculty. When it is the case that the methodologist simultaneously serves as the chair, the other program faculty member serves as a representative from educational leadership. In all committees, an educational leadership faculty member is paired with an educational research faculty (to be clear, both faculty members teach within the educational leadership program, but their doctoral backgrounds are different).

Involving an External Committee Member

As an ever-developing network of like-minded scholar-practitioners, employing an external committee member with ties to the community and its context is a strategic imperative that allows for one of multiple pathways where our work can be scaled up. As part of the committee, the external member is associated with the doctoral student's context, or the *laboratory of practice*. Like the other committee members whose function it is to provide feedback on both the proposal and final drafts of the DQ, the external member is also expected to support and assist the student in overcoming challenges faced during the project initiative. Our faculty's vision for the role of this external committee member is to function as facilitator within the student's organization and an enabler for progress to ensue during the dissertation phase. Considered a "gate-opener," the external member is one who is typically higher in the organizational structure and can therefore offer support for getting the project moving along the path of least resistance. Further, the external committee member's function (as a higher-level organizational member) is that of a liaison; scaffolding staff and other organizational stakeholders in understanding the nature of the collaborative, systematized thinking processes and procedures characterizing DiP work.

Vetting the External Member

The current practice at our Carnegie-designated regionally-comprehensive institution is that our external committee member be vetted and approved by the department head, dean, and

Graduate School. Beginning with the doctoral student suggesting potential members to their Chair, once selected, this is followed by an affirmative vote by the Graduate Council for "affiliate graduate faculty" status, and then the external member officially joins the committee. This affiliate graduate faculty designation allows for the external member to serve on the DQ committee for a limited time (in our case, three years). Once all approvals have been made, the educational leadership faculty front-load external committee members with literature and other resources related to the concept of a practice-based dissertation.

Conclusion

Ten Years After its Inception: What's Changed?

We crafted the DQ concept in 2013. Now, a decade later, we continue with a primary focus on social justice and equity; however, our efforts are now more apparent than ever. Now required in the proposal draft is a specific connection to equity, and moreover, a focus on potential ways to dismantle inequitable systems. Also evolving is the ubiquitous use of improvement science (structures, frameworks, and analyses) in the DQ. Seen in all students' work are root cause analyses, theories of improvement, Plan-Do-Study-Act cycles, and analyses and evaluations using four practical measures. Along with adopting the use of practical measurement, we have removed "formative" and "summative" language in our materials, except for the outcome measure which is typically summative in nature (the remaining three practical measures usually being formative indicators).

There is also a new section in the final DQ draft that focuses on "Lessons for Leaders." This new section contains specific recommendations for practitioners who are looking to the DQ for insight into how to address similar problems in similar contexts. Further, there is an additional focus for embedding sustainability structures so that initial improvement efforts can continue as sustained improvements with the involvement and support from institutional members.

Looking Ahead: What Remains to be Done?

For future education leaders, the behaviors of identifying and addressing persistent problems of practice are hallmark characteristics of the 21st century leader. It is of utmost importance that graduates develop into scholar-practitioners with an adequate toolkit since it is they who will be the ones to enact the improvements sought for in the local context.

Questions for Discussion

1. What aspects of using improvement science as a *signature inquiry method* were you already familiar? Which aspects were unfamiliar?

2. How do you think you could gain comfort and confidence using improvement science as a method for *combatting systemic inequities?*

3. How easily could you transfer the IS method from one pressing *problem of practice* to a different problem?

4. How could seasoned faculty and/or administrators develop new faculty capacity for incorporating an improvement science perspective in leadership work?

References

Archbald, D. (2008). Research versus problem solving for the educational leadership doctoral thesis: Implications for form and function. *Educational Administration Quarterly, 44*(5), 704-739. DOI:10.1177/0013161X07313288

Bryk, A., Gomez, L., Grunow, A., & LeMahieu, P. (2015). *Learning to improve: How America's schools can get better at getting better.* Harvard Education Press. https://doi.org/10.1002/sce.21223

Carnegie Project on the Education Doctorate. (2014). *90-Day Cycle in Improvement Science,* https://www.carnegiefoundation.org/wp-content/uploads/2014/09/90DC_Handbook_external_10_8.pdf

Crow, R., Spaulding, D., & Hinnant-Crawford, B.N. (2019). *The educational leader's guide to improvement science: Data, design and cases for reflection.* Myers Education Press.

Crow, R., Topolka-Jorrisen, K., & Lomotey, K. (2016). An adaptive model for a rigorous dissertation in practice: The disquisition. In V. Storey & K. Hesbol (Eds.), *Contemporary approaches for dissertation development and research methods* (pp.205-220). IGI Global.

DiPierro, M. (2007). Excellence in doctoral education: Defining best practices. *College Student Journal, 41*(2), 368. https://doi.org/10.2190/CS.12.4.e

Gardner, H. (2000). *The disciplined mind.* Penguin Books.

Hinnant-Crawford, B.N. (2020). *Improvement science in education: A primer.* Myers Education Press.

Kritsonis, W. A., & Green, W. R. (2008). Functions of the doctoral dissertation advisor. *Focus on Colleges, Universities and Schools, 2*(1), 1-6.

Leonard, J., & Reardon, R. M. (2017). *Exploring the community impact of research-practice partnerships in education.* Information Age.

Lewis, T., Puckett, H., & Siegel, D. (2021). Making our pitch: Supervisors in the development of the dissertation in practice. *Journal of Research on Leadership Education, 18*(2), p. 159-180. https://doi.org/10.1177/19427751211055087

Lomotey, K. (2020). *The disquisition at Western Carolina University: The capstone experience in the university's EdD program.* Unpublished manuscript. Western Carolina University, Cullowhee, NC.

National Policy Board for Educational Administration. (2015). *Professional standards for educational leaders.* https://www.npbea.org/wp-content/uploads/2017/06/Professional-Standards-for-Educational-Leaders_2015.pdf

New York City Department of Education. (2019). *NYCDOE Improvement science handbook.* https://www.weteachnyc.org/media2016/filer_public/76/97/7697a2de-ee3c-4a60-81fc-563bdf1c36d0/nycdoe_improvement_science_handbook_2018_online.pdf

Perry, J. A., Zambo, D., & Crow, R. (2020). *The improvement science dissertation in practice: A guide for faculty, committee members, and their students.* Myers Education Press.

Rasmussen, H., Hawkins, J., & Crow, R. (2022). Adaptive leadership and improvement science: Natural bedfellows. In M. Raei & H. Rasmussen (Eds.), *Adaptive leadership in a global economy: Perspectives for application and scholarship* (pp. 65-81). Routledge.

Shulman, L. (2005). Signature pedagogies in the professions. *Daedelus, 134*(3), 52-59.

Storey, V., & Hesbol, K. (2014). Can the dissertation in practice bridge the researcher-practitioner gap? The education professional practice doctorate and the impact of the Carnegie Project on the Education Doctorate consortium. *Journal of Public School Relations, 35*(3), 324-347. DOI10.3138/jspr.35.3.324

CHAPTER 12

Action Research and the Dissertation in Practice

SUHA R. TAMIM, EDD, MPH

The Carnegie Project on the Education Doctorate (CPED) is a consortium of schools and colleges that critically examines the doctor in education (EdD) and supports its members in designing or redesigning their EdD programs to prepare scholarly practitioners (CPED, 2021). The dissertation within the CPED model is identified as the dissertation in practice (DiP), "a scholarly endeavor that impacts a complex problem of practice" (CPED, 2022, Design-concepts). A typical methodology in the DiP is action research through which, a problem of practice is explored. This chapter presents an overview of action research, its origins, definitions, and goals. It also discusses its theoretical underpinnings, the different models and types, and the action research process. It ends with action research methodological considerations, a brief look at positionality, reflexivity, and ethics, and the alignment between action research and the EdD.

Origins

Action research originated from various fields. It is widely used in educational settings but also in health, social work, community planning, and business settings (Hammersley, 2004; Hersted et al., 2020). What differentiates action research from traditional research is its goal of representing the perspectives of the different stakeholders involved in the problem for which solutions are explored (Beaulieu, 2013; McKernan, 1988; Stringer, 2014). In his work against the oppression of Native peoples in North America, John Collier first described action research in 1945, calling for research that focused on real problems and action (Mertler, 2019). In the same decade and through his work in social psychology, Kurt Lewin developed action research further by advocating for research that improved professional practice with methods that identify problems and solutions through collaboration, cycles of inquiry, and fact-finding action, evaluation, and reflection (Dickens & Watkins, 1999; Kindon et al., 2007; Putman & Rock, 2018; Willis & Edwards, 2014). Although Lewin was not the first scholar to use action research, "he did construct an elaborate theory and made action research respectable inquiry for social scientists" (McKernan, 1988, p.178). Other prominent figures left their marks on action research, such as Paulo Freire in the 1970s with his work against oppression that focuses on participation and dialogue (Hersted et al., 2020) and John Dewey, with his pragmatic philosophy (Greenwood & Levin, 2011) that advocate for teachers to become reflective practitioners and play a role in educational reform (Efron & Ravid, 2013). Action research became popular in the field of education in the 1950s, following scientific methods (Hammersley, 2004) and aligning with the positivist paradigm that was mainstream at the time (Willis & Edwards, 2014). However, during the 1980s, the positivist paradigm came under harsh critique that opposed its linear causal effects and called for an interpretive perspective that focuses on the meaning of behaviors and actions and not just the behaviors and actions themselves, and stresses the importance of unveiling dominant powers in society (Gage, 1989). These paradigm wars resulted in the emergence and acceptance of alternative paradigms, which in turn paved the way for new models of action research. Gradually, interpretivism and critical theory gained stronger holds and dominance (Willis & Edwards, 2014). Hence, the nature of action research and its identity evolved according to the dominant epistemological and research paradigms of the historical phases. In the 21st century, it embodies various theories and methodologies to become multi-paradigmatic (Katsarou, 2016).

Definitions and Goals

Brydon-Miller et al. (2003) proposed that action research "is not a single academic discipline but an approach to research that has emerged over time from a broad range of fields" (p. 11). Furthermore, Reason and Bradbury (2008) considered it an orientation to inquiry rather than a methodology. Kemmis (2009) explained that "action research aims at changing three things: practitioners' *practices*, their *understandings* of their practices, and the *conditions* in which they practice" (p.463) through a critical and self-critical process. He continued, "transforming our practices means transforming what we do; transforming our understandings means transforming what we think and say; and transforming the conditions of practice means transforming the ways we relate to others and to things and circumstances around us" (Kemmis, 2009, p. 463). Although the overarching aim of action research is to address problems and propose change (Cohen et al., 2017), the diverse historical phases and epistemological viewpoints of action research generated many definitions (Herr & Anderson, 2015; Ivankova, 2015). All definitions agree that action research is a collaborative inquiry done "by and with insiders" with systematic and reflective elements (Herr & Anderson, 2015, p.3). Also, all definitions agree on the importance of taking action and creating new knowledge through research, but they diverge on the degree of balance between research and action, who conducts the research to create knowledge, and who carries out the action (McNiff, 2017).

Theoretical Foundations of Action Research

Mertler (2019b) asserted that "theory is an explanation we construct to better understand something we understand incompletely … [it] provides the basis for actions that remediate the problems requiring our attention" (p. 157). In action research, "relevant and effective theories emerge from the hermeneutic dialect—meaning-making dialogues—between stakeholders, using the concepts, terminologies, and formulations that make sense to them" (Stringer, 2014, p. 39), unlike traditional research that uses theory to drive the inquiry process and generate hypotheses. Therefore, the relationship between the researcher and the researched and between theory and practice is altered (Kemmis et al., 2014). Theory informs practice but does not mold it, because inherent to action research is the impact of local settings and the different perspectives of its stakeholders, which in turn impedes a straightforward connection between theory and practice (Stringer, 2014). Kemmis (2009) advised that action research should not aim at having practitioners conform to educational theories but at having them self-transform to become researchers and theorists of their practices. A systematic and rigorous research process allows practitioners to create their "own personal theory of practice: they can describe what they are doing and explain why they are doing it" (McNiff, 2017, p. 28), and integrate theories "implicit in the everyday life-worlds of stakeholders" (Merlter, 2019b, p. 157) with academic and professional theories. Emphasizing the critical aspect of action research, McKernan (1988) asserted that "action research is not interested in constructing grand or middle-range theories but in developing a reasoned critique grounded in social practice" (p.192). Friedman and Rogers (2009) pointed to the skepticism in the action research community regarding unified theories and contended that rather than emphasizing the predictive and causal relationships between variables present in positivist theories, action researchers should aim at creating new knowledge and new realities through the participants' understanding of their world; where the relationship between change and theory is reciprocal and where "meaningful change requires a good theory and the development of a good theory requires attempts to change the world" (p. 34).

Models and Types

Bradbury-Huang (2010) referred to action research as "an umbrella term that represents a 'family' of practices" (p. 94). Diverse views on action research exist "with different terminologies, and several breakaway groups" (McNiff, 2017, p. 13), such as action science, cooperative inquiry, participatory action research, community-based action research, and critical action research (Bradbury-Huang, 2010; Ivankova, 2015). The models and types of action research discussed in the literature are categorized based on different philosophical and epistemological perspectives. For example, Cassell and Johnson (2006) differentiated between experimental, inductive, participatory, and deconstructive. Similarly, Kemmis (2009) described three types of action research: technical action research that aims at improving outcomes in a one-way relationship with participants; practical action research that aims for long-term consequences, giving voice to participants through a reciprocal relationship; and critical action research that aims at collectively transforming "the social formation in which the practice occurs" (p. 471).

Furthermore, Reason and Torbert (2001) divided action research strategies into three types: first-person practice that revolves around self-inquiry and self-examination; second-person practice that is cooperative and engages others as co-researchers; and third-person practice that is wide-scale and aims for change at organizational or regional levels. In a more detailed classification, Willis and Edwards (2014) categorized action research based on levels of application: individual, collegial, organizational, systemic, and community. Additionally, they categorized them based on purpose (positivist, interpretive, critical, etc.) and process (participatory, cooperative inquiry, design-based, etc.).

This overview of types is not comprehensive but shows the different directions action research can take (Bradbury-Huang, 2010). Their fluidity and continuous unfolding can sometimes be confusing, especially for beginning action researchers (McNiff, 2017). In essence, action research can be categorized either by operational levels or philosophical orientations. It can be practical/pragmatic, addressing a specific problem and aiming to improve practice, often experimental and cooperative with less emphasis on theory. It can also be critical/participatory, aiming at empowerment, emancipation, and liberation (Johansson & Lindhult, 2008; Merlter, 2019a; Mills, 2017). These two categories are discussed below with an emphasis on participatory action research because it subsumes several variations.

Practical Action Research

Practical educational action research aims at short-term improvement through reflection on practice (Franklin et al., 2012), where teachers are the decision-makers in the research design (Mills, 2018). The goal here is to address a specific problem with specific actions, with little emphasis on the philosophical underpinnings (Merlter, 2019a). While still cyclical and reflective, the research process begins with identifying a problem of practice that can be addressed by trying a new practice, improving a tried practice, or examining the problem further (Ivankova, 2015; Merlter, 2019a; Putman & Rock, 2018; Schmuck, 2006). For example, Smith et al. (2020) addressed the problem of unsuccessful interactions between college students and peer tutors in an APA-style writing workshop through action research. Data from the pilot phase guided an intervention that strengthened the collaboration between students and tutors. Assignments were restructured, expectations were clarified to students, and check-ins from professors and the writing center director with tutors became more frequent. Consequently, students found the collaboration with peer tutors productive and reported increased confidence in their APA skills.

Similarly, Grogan and Roiha (2022) wanted to improve their secondary students' fluency in English and motivate them to converse in it. For that, they collected preliminary data from students and teachers that informed the design of their intervention. The intervention consisted of student-created podcast discussions on movies. The choice of intervention was based on the preferences voiced by the students, such as their interest in movies, interactivity, and authenticity. As a result, students conversed in English increasingly and enjoyed the autonomy and creativity in producing the podcasts.

Participatory Action Research (PAR)

Although most forms of action research give voice to participants to some degree, participatory action research (PAR) puts the collaboration of participants in the research project center stage, focusing primarily on issues that affect marginalized populations.

The degree of participation negotiated between the researcher and participants ranges from participants playing a passive role to mobilizing and taking full initiative (Kindon et al., 2007; Pretty et al. 1995/2002). Kemmis et al. (2014) affirmed that "participatory action research and critical participatory action research share the central aspiration that the research should be the responsibility of participants alone, though participants also remain open to receiving assistance from outsiders" (p. 9). Trott et al. (2020) summed the characteristics of PAR as such: (1) the nature of research engages participants as collaborators in the research process; (2) the actors are researchers and community partners, where researchers commit to the process as much as to the product; and (3) the goals are transformative to the participants, yielding positive outcomes to them and a strengthened sense of agency. However, Stoecker (2009) cautioned that many research projects labeled as PAR do not include participatory or action elements, thus stressing the importance of showing action outcomes. PAR can take many forms, such as youth participatory action research, community-based action research, and critical participatory action research (Kindon et al., 2007).

Youth Participatory Action Research (YPAR). PAR conducted with youth is known as youth participatory action research (YPAR). In YPAR, "youth and adult researchers share power" (Anderson, 2020, p. 243), where youth researchers bring their experiences to play a significant role in the production of knowledge through inquiry-based approaches and with a critical perspective (Caraballo et al., 2017). For example, Qui et al. (2021) examined their collaboration with historically marginalized middle school students in the design of after-school program activities aimed at developing literacy skills. They chose "critical problem-solving and multimodal engagement" (p.6) to co-construct knowledge with the students to increase their confidence in expressing themselves and advocating for their needs. The process allowed students to draw from their diverse backgrounds to gain a deeper understanding of their identities and cultures through which they developed literacy skills meaningful to them. In another example, Zion (2020) conducted a YPAR project with high school students to address school equity issues. Through a systemic equity-driven reform process, students analyzed the root causes of inequities in their school and collaborated with adults to develop better school policies. At the end of the project, students presented four policies they envisioned to help address equity issues to faculty and staff. All policies were approved and implemented, leading to a shift in the school climate.

Community-based Action Research (CBAR). Banks et al. (2013) described community-based action research (CBAR) as a complex approach to research that is participatory and aims to "mobilizse the local and indigenous knowledge of people based in community of place, identity, and interest" (p. 264). Overlapping with characteristics of PAR, CBAR aims to create "participative research communities" (Banks et al., 2013, p.264). For example, Yull et al. (2018) carried out CBAR through collaboration between university researchers, school personnel, a community activist, and family members to develop a parent mentor program to engage parents of color in marginalized school settings and give them a voice in the school system. Through discussions and cycles of action and reflection, parents' concerns about educational experiences, disciplinary actions, and graduation rates were explored. This was followed by group mentorship training sessions around topics, such as cultural competency, family engagement, and school climate and culture to prepare a selected sample of four mothers to take an active role in the classroom through encouraging student engagement and facilitating teacher-student-parent communication. Involving parents as such strengthened their sense of connectedness with each other and with the school system, and reduced classroom disruptions. At the same time, teachers welcomed the opportunity to build authentic relationships with parents who were able to leverage cultural connections and advocate for their children's education.

In another example, Senekal (2022) reported on a community-based action research project aimed at developing a community education curriculum that serves the local needs of communities usually excluded from job-focused community education programs. University-based researchers and postgraduate students teamed with community volunteers, activists, and other community members to co-create a curriculum that emerged from narratives transpiring from community walks, the sharing of personal stories relating to educational experiences, and the vision of post-schooling education. Cycles of collaborative analysis and reflection on the narratives resulted in the design and implementation of community education events for additional input from community members to connect their experiences to that of the research group. The culminating product was a "curriculum-in-motion" that is adaptive to local contexts and inclusive of "different forms of knowledge" (Senekal, 2022, p.14).

Critical Participatory Action Research (CPAR). Critical participatory action research (CPAR) is grounded in critical theory, and its ultimate goal is the emancipation and empowerment of participants, often referred to as emancipatory action research, among other similar terms (Willis & Edwards, 2014). It is "a social process of collaborative learning for the sake of individual and collective self-formation, realized by groups of people who join together in changing their practices" (Kemmis et al., 2014, p. 20). There are logistical and sometimes existential challenges to CPAR, namely asking difficult questions, navigating the policy-making landscape, and balancing the power differential and different experiences among research participants (Sandwick et al., 2018). Although its ideology and goals differ from positivist and interpretive action research, its methods are similar and always include a democratic, participatory approach (Willis & Edwards, 2014). Kemmis et al. (2014) described five steps to CPAR: (1) examining practices and their surrounding conditions, (2) taking a critical stance and asking critical questions, (3) communicating with others to reach mutual understanding and consensus, (4) taking transformative actions, and (5) documenting and monitoring the process (p. 68). In this regard, Nugent (2020) used CPAR to empower French language teachers to take control of their culture teaching practices. Initial conversations clarified teachers' needs and their lack of intercultural pedagogical preparation. Then, over a nine-month period, teachers immersed themselves in collaborative professional development and revised their teaching practices and lesson design in alignment with the intercultural communicative competence framework to give their students a transformative intercultural learning experience. Not only did teachers feel empowered by the CPAR experience, but they also felt its direct connection to improving their teaching practices and their students' learning experiences. In 2016, Nixon partnered with principals and teachers to transform their technical action research practice to CPAR and to move towards morally-oriented teaching practices that replace a model where teachers plan, teach, and debrief about a teaching practice to one where they plan, teach, document, and reflect on improving students' life chances. Through a collaborative cyclical process, teachers created their professional learning practice and voiced their needs and perspectives, which empowered them to be agents of change and reflect on students' overall well-being.

The examples presented above reflect diverse action research applications and scope levels. However, they also show that the aim is always to address and improve problems of practice.

The Process of Action Research

As with the multiple definitions of action research, the action research processes proposed in the literature vary. They all stem from the iterative process suggested by Lewin in the 1940s of fact-finding, action, and evaluation (Burnes, 2020). For example, the spiral of self-reflective cycles originally proposed by Kemmis and McTaggart in 1988, included cycles of planning, acting and observing, reflecting, replanning, acting and observing, reflecting, etc. With overlapping stages, their process is fluid and responsive to what is learned and understood about the practice (Kemmis et al., 2014). Stringer (2014) referred to an action research routine of Look-Think-Act that recycles continuously. He framed these steps under phases of planning, implementing, and evaluating in a way to have each phase include the whole cycle of Look-Think-Act. Merlter (2019a) also stressed the cyclical process of action research and offered four stages of action research: planning, acting, developing, and reflecting.

Hence, the action research process has no closure, with answers that lead to new questions (McNiff, 2017), and a methodology that evolves based on the evaluation of and reflection on previous stages (Herr & Anderson, 2015). These processes suggest that practitioners must first identify what is to be explored; in other words, define the problem (Greenwood & Levin, 2007) and gather the information that helps them better understand the issue. Accordingly, they design a plan of action and implement it. Then, they observe and interpret the evidence they collected. Subsequently, they reflect on their actions to determine if the outcomes were desirable. Next, they move through another cycle to continue the improvement process based on their new understanding of the practice (Kemmis, 2009; Merlter, 2019a; Putman & Rock, 2018; Stringer, 2014).

Action Research Methodological Considerations

McKernan (1988) described action research as "a rigorous, systematic inquiry through scientific procedures [where] participants have critical-reflective ownership of the process and the results" (p. 174). However, the dominance of the positivist approaches to research challenged action research in terms of rigor and objectivity. Its quality was often undervalued because action research approaches deviated from traditional research. Unlike positivist action research that seeks objectivity, universal generalizable knowledge, guiding theory, and quantifiable measures, action research blurs the lines between the role of researcher and practitioner, collaborates with stakeholders, and produces context-specific knowledge (Bradbury-Huang, 2014; Greenwood & Levin, 2007; Kemmis et al., 2014; Merlter, 2019a). Bradbury-Huang (2014) asserts that in action research, "the motivation for knowledge creation is not so much simply to know what is true, for the sake of objective, disembodied truth, but rather to accomplish something of mutual value" (p. 667) for the purpose of helping stakeholders improve practice. For these reasons, she argues that action research combines "objective-empirical with subjective and pragmatic orientations" (p.667). While the current methodology in action research "is strongly influenced by the qualitative paradigm" (Merlter, 2019b, p. 163), data collection methods are selected for relevance to the research questions and the area of focus (Mills, 2018). Greenwood and Levin (2007) stated:

> [Action research] is multi-method research, and its validity is tested in action. In contradistinction to the conventional social sciences,

action research rejects the superiority of professional researcher knowledge over the practical knowledge of local stakeholders. It asserts the value of both kinds of knowledge and the need to bring them together. (p.53)

Therefore, a mixed method methodology is well suited for action research in providing comprehensive information from multiple sources through systematic inquiry that is reflective and dialectic (Ivankova, 2015).

In educational settings, practitioners should select a topic they are passionate about that relates to teaching and learning; one that they would like to improve and that is within their control (Mills, 2018). Ensuring the quality and rigor of action research requires articulation of objectives, partnership and participation, contribution to action research theory-practice, use of appropriate methods and processes, actionability, reflexivity, and significance (Bradbury-Huang, 2014). Cassell and Johnson (2006) argued that "embracing standards of quality criteria to apply to all action research seems a rather pointless mission" (p. 806) because of the diversity of philosophical assumptions in action research: experimental practices, inductive, participatory, or deconstructive/critical. Moreover, the criteria of validity and reliability differ based on whether quantitative or qualitative measures are used (Puttman & Rock, 2018). Nevertheless, indicators of rigor and quality are primarily derived from the qualitative research paradigm that influences it (Melrose, 2001) and relates to methodological and interpretive rigor (Lincoln et al., as cited in Merriam & Tisdell, 2016). These include *triangulation*—emphasizing multiple data sources and types to capture different perspectives; *member checking* and *participant debriefing*—involving participants in reviewing the accuracy of data and providing insights; *prolonged engagement*—deepening the understanding of the action researcher, and *repeating cycles* (Kemmis, 2009; Melrose, 2001; Merlter, 2019a; Mills, 2018). Herr and Anderson (2015) propose additional validity criteria: the generation of new knowledge (dialogic and process validity), the achievement of action-oriented outcomes (outcome validity), the education of both researcher and participants (catalytic validity), the relevance of results to the local setting (democratic validity), and sound and appropriate methodology (process validity). To that end, McKernan (1988) described the methodology of action research as "eclectic" (p.190), one that resorts to innovative strategies as needed.

Positionality, Reflexivity, and Ethics

Positionality defines the relationship between the researcher and participants. It moves across an insider-outsider continuum based on research traditions. For example, in academic research, the researcher is an outsider in relation to the setting and participants, whereas in practitioner research, the researcher is an insider. Between these extremes are positionalities of insiders collaborating with other insiders, insiders collaborating with outsiders, reciprocal collaboration (insider-outsider teams), and outsiders collaborating with insiders (Herr & Anderson, 2015). These positionalities can exist in the different models of action research, even the outsider studying insiders, based on how closely they engage with their participants. However, action researchers often alternate between insider and outsider positionalities (Greenwood & Levin, 2007). Cohen et al. (2017) referred to it as "adopt[ing] a potential schizophrenic stance ... being both in it and of it ... viewing it with ... subjectivity and objectivity" (p. 453). Similarly, Thomson and Gunter (2011) suggested fluid researcher identities that step away from the insider/outsider binary. Indeed, action researchers' positionalities are complex because they are multiple (Herr & Anderson, 2015) and multidimensional, shaped by the practitioners' identities (culture, gender, age, race, religion, etc.) and their roles (Rowe, 2023). Separating the identity and role of action researchers is another binary view of positionality that should be avoided (Day, 2012). Then, it is the researcher's obligation to "interrogate ... multiple positionalities in relationship to the question under study" (Herr & Anderson, 2015, p. 55) and to be reflexive to clarify assumptions made in the production of knowledge (Day, 2012). Through reflexivity, researchers understand their own perspectives and strengthen their voices (Patton, 2015).

On the other hand, the positionality of action researchers brings the ethical aspect of power dynamics between researchers and participants to the forefront. Action researchers must be cognizant of power asymmetries in the research setting, how they shape the interpretations of findings, and whose voices they represent (Colombo, 2003; Day, 2012; Rowe, 2023; Strumińska-Kutra & Scholl, 2022). Additionally, researchers need to use their voices for transparency about their goals, connections to the research, and methods (Rector-Aranda, 2014). Finally, action researchers must honor the authentic collaboration and reciprocal relationship with participants, responding to their needs and enabling change (Herr & Anderson, 2015; Manzo & Brightbill, 2007).

Action Research and EdD Alignment

Signature pedagogy, which refers to adopted teaching and learning practices, is one of the design concepts developed by CPED to guide professional doctoral programs (Perry, 2013). CPED does not impose one standard signature pedagogy on all member institutions, in order not to "limit the abilities of the schools of education as well as the outcomes for their graduates" (Perry, 2013, p. 119), and signature pedagogies can vary between action research, improvement science, or others. EdD programs choosing action research do so to help students lead inquiry, make evidence-based improvements to their practice (Olson & Clark, 2009), and recognize the importance of equity and social justice (Ewell et al., 2022) in their educational contexts. Conducting a content analysis of 29 dissertations, Zambo (2010) found that action research was a good fit for the CPED-guided EdD program and that "action research can be used as a signature pedagogy to create school leaders who are stewards of practice with the knowledge, skills, and dispositions they need to identify educational problems, design solutions, and lead change" (pp. 270-271). Additionally, Buss (2018) rationalized the use of action research in CPED-guided EdD programs by saying that action research is applicable to a range of contexts for a range of problems of practice, it guides students through a systematic inquiry process, and it affords sustainability of outcomes and continuity of inquiry cycles. Furthermore, Militello et al. (2021) described PAR as their single methodology that supports a collaborative, action-oriented approach to research to develop activist school leaders who prioritize equitable student outcomes. Similarly,

Howard and Baker (2021) described their use of CPAR to embed a robust social justice component in their EdD program by engaging doctoral students in equity-oriented community research to "activat[e] activism" (p. 43).

Whether action research represents the signature pedagogy, being either the sole or one of the DiP methodological approaches, it is evident that it helps CPED-guided EdD programs design student doctoral work that aligns with the professional doctorate CPED advocates for as:

> framed around questions of equity, ethics, and social justice to bring about solutions to complex problems of practice; prepares leaders who can construct and apply knowledge to make a positive difference; ... use[s] multiple frames to develop meaningful solutions; ... integrates both practical and research knowledge ... ; and emphasizes the generation, transformation, and use of professional knowledge and practice. (CPED, Guiding Principles, 2022).

Conclusion

The characteristics of action research discussed in this chapter serve as a guide for scholarly practitioners and EdD programs who choose action research as a signature pedagogy or as a methodological approach for DiPs. Action research ensures a focus on real problems and action for improvement and social justice while collaborating with stakeholders to generate new knowledge through cycles of inquiry and reflection.

References

Anderson, A. J. (2020). A qualitative systematic review of youth participatory action research implementation in U.S. High Schools. *American Journal of Community Psychology*, *65*(1/2), 242–257. https://doi.org/10.1002/ajcp.12389

Banks, S., Armstrong, A., Carter, K., Graham, H., Hayward, P., Henry, A., Holland, T., Holmes, C., Lee, A., McNulty, A., Moore, N., Nayling, N., Stokoe, A., & Strachan, A. (2013). Everyday ethics in community-based participatory research. *Contemporary Social Science*, *8*(3), 263–277.

https://doi.org/10.1080/21582041.2013.769618

Beaulieu, R. J. (2013). Action research: Trends and variations. *Canadian Journal of Action Research, 14*(3), 29–39.

Bradbury-Huang, H. (2010). What is good action research? Why the resurgent interest? *Action Research, 8*(1), 93–109. https://doi.org/10.1177/1476750310362435

Bradbury-Huang, H. (2014). Quality. In D. Coghlan, D., & M. Brydon-Miller (Eds.), *The SAGE encyclopedia of action research* (Vols. 1-2, pp. 666-669). SAGE Publications Ltd. https://dx.doi.org/10.4135/9781446294406

Brydon-Miller, M., Greenwood, D., & Maguire, P. (2003). Why action research? *Action Research, 1*(1), 9–28. https://doi.org/10.1177/14767503030011002

Burnes, B. (2020). The origins of Lewin's three-step model of change. *The Journal of Applied Behavioral Science, 56*(1), 32–59. https://doi.org/10.1177/0021886319892685

Buss, R. R. (2018). Using action research as a signature pedagogy to develop EdD students' inquiry as practice abilities. *Impacting Education: Journal on Transforming Professional Practice, 3*(1), Article 1. https://doi.org/10.5195/ie.2018.46

Caraballo, L., Lozenski, B. D., Lyiscott, J. J., & Morrell, E. (2017). YPAR and critical epistemologies: Rethinking education research. *Review of Research in Education, 41*(1), 311–336.

Carnegie Project for the Education Doctorate. (2022). *The CPED Framework.* https://cped.memberclicks.net/the-framework

Cassell, C., & Johnson, P. (2006). Action research: Explaining the diversity. *Human Relations, 59*(6), 783–814. https://doi.org/10.1177/0018726706067080

Cohen, L., Manion, L., & Morrison, K. (2017). *Research methods in education* (8th ed.). Taylor & Francis. https://bookshelf.vitalsource.com/books/9781315456515

Colombo, M. (2003). Reflexivity and narratives in action research: A discursive approach. *Forum Qualitative Sozialforschung Forum: Qualitative Social Research, 4*(2), Article 2. https://doi.org/10.17169/fqs-4.2.718

Day, S. (2012). A reflexive lens: Exploring dilemmas of qualitative methodology through the concept of reflexivity. *Qualitative Sociology Review, 8*(1), 60–85. https://doi.org/10.18778/1733-8077.8.1.04

Dickens, L., & Watkins, K. (1999). Action research: Rethinking Lewin. *Management Learning, 30*(2), 127–140. https://doi.org/10.1177/1350507699302002

Ewell, S., Childers-McKee, C., Giblin, J., McNabb, J., Nolan, K., & Parenti, M. (2022). Taking action: The dissertation in practice at Northeastern University. *Impacting Education: Journal on Transforming Professional Practice, 7*(1), Article 1. https://doi.org/10.5195/ie.2022.219

Fraenkel, J. R., Wallen, N. E., & Hyun, H. H. (2012). *How to design and evaluate research in education* (8th ed.). McGraw-Hill Humanities/ Social Sciences/Languages.

Friedman, V. J., & Rogers, T. (2009). There is nothing so theoretical as good action research. *Action Research, 7*(1), 31–47. https://doi.org/10.1177/ 1476750308099596

Greenwood, D., & Levin, M. (2007). *Introduction to action research.* SAGE Publications, Inc. https://doi.org/10.4135/9781412984614

Grogan, K., & Roiha, A. (2022). Using podcasts as a means to increase secondary English language learners' motivation to converse in the target language. *Journal of Teacher Action Research, 8*(2), 79–96.

Heikkinen, Hannu, L. T., Huttunen, R., Syrjälä, L., & Pesonen, J. (2012). Action research and narrative inquiry: Five principles for validation revisited. *Educational Action Research, 20*(1), 5–21. https://doi.org/10. 1080/09650792.2012.647635

Herr, K., & Anderson, G. L. (2015a). *The action research dissertation: A guide for students and faculty* (2nd ed.). SAGE.

Hersted, L., Ottar, N., & Frimann, S. (2020). Action research: Tradition and renewal. In L. Hersted, N. Ottar, & S. Frimann (Eds.), *Action research in a relational perspective: Dialogue, reflexivity, power, and ethics* (pp.3-16). Routledge.

Howard, J., & Baker, T. L. (2021). Activating activism within the EdD: Connecting DiP research and the community. *Impacting Education: Journal on Transforming Professional Practice, 6*(1), Article 1. https:// doi.org/10.5195/ie.2021.162

Johansson, A. W., & Lindhult, E. (2008). Emancipation or workability? Critical versus pragmatic scientific orientation in action research. *Action Research, 6*(1), 95–115. https://doi.org/10.1177/1476750307083713

Katsarou, E. (2017). The multi-paradigmatic character of contemporary educational action research: A promising perspective or an underlying threat? *Educational Action Research, 25*(5), 673–686. https://doi.org/1 0.1080/09650792.2016.1241184

Kemmis, S., McTaggart, R., & Nixon, R. (2014). *The action research planner.* Springer Singapore. https://doi.org/10.1007/978-981-4560-67-2

Kindon, S., Pain, R., & Kesby, M. (2007). Participatory action research: Origins, approaches and methods. In S. Kindon, R. Pain, & M. Kesby

(Eds.), *Participatory action research approaches and methods: Connecting people, participation and place* (pp. 9-18). Routledge.

Manzo, L.C., & Brightbill, N. (2007.). Towards a participatory ethics. In S. Kindon, R. Pain, & M. Kesby (Eds.), *Participatory action research approaches and methods: Connecting people, participation and place* (pp. 33-40). Routledge.

McKernan, J. (1988). The countenance of curriculum action research: Traditional, collaborative, and emancipatory-critical conceptions. *Journal of Curriculum & Supervision, 3*(3), 173–200.

Melrose, M. J. (2001). Maximizing the rigor of action research: Why would you want to? How could you? *Field Methods, 13*(2), 160–180. https://doi.org/10.1177/1525822X0101300203

Merriam, S. B., & Tisdell, E. J. (2016). *Qualitative research: A guide to design and implementation.* Jossey-Bass.

Mertler C. A. (2019a). *Introduction to educational research* (2nd ed.). SAGE.

Mertler, C. A. (Ed.). (2019b). *The Wiley handbook of action research in education.* John Wiley & Sons, Incorporated.

Militello, M., Tredway, L., Rosenthal, L., & Welch, J. R. (2021). A university as the center of change: Preparing educational activists and change leaders. *Impacting Education: Journal on Transforming Professional Practice, 6*(1), Article 1. https://doi.org/10.5195/ie.2021.118

Mills, G. E. (2018). *Action research.* Pearson.

Nixon, R. (2016). Principals and teachers as partners in critical, participatory action research. *Educational Action Research, 24*(3), 404–423. https://doi.org/10.1080/09650792.2016.1182041

Nugent, K. L. (2020). Exploring the teaching of culture in the foreign language classroom within the context of collaborative professional development: A critical participatory action research study. *Educational Action Research, 28*(3), 497–517. https://doi.org/10.1080/09650792.2019.1577148

Olson, K., & Clark, C. M. (2009). A signature pedagogy in doctoral education: The leader-scholar community. *Educational Researcher, 38*(3), 216–221.

Patton, M. Q. (2015). *Qualitative research & evaluation methods: Integrating theory and practice.* Sage.

Perry, J. A. (2013). Carnegie Project on the Education Doctorate: The education doctorate—A degree for our time. *Planning & Changing, 44* (3/4), 113–126.

Pretty, J. N., Guijt, I. M., Scoones, I., & Thompson, J. (2002). *Trainers' guide for participatory learning and action.* The International Institute for

Environment and Development. (Original work published 1995).

Qiu, T., Kas-Osoka, C., & Mizell, J. D. (2021). Co-constructing knowledge: Critical reflections from facilitators engaging in youth participatory action research in an after-school program. *Journal of Language & Literacy Education / Ankara Universitesi SBF Dergisi, 17*(2), 1–19.

Reason, P., & Bradbury, H. (Eds.). (2008). *The Sage handbook of action research: Participative inquiry and practice* (2nd ed.). SAGE Publications.

Reason, P., & Torbert, W. (2001). The action turn: Toward a transformational *social* science. *Concepts and Transformation, 6*(1), 1–37. https://doi.org/10.1075/cat.6.1.02rea

Rector-Aranda, A. (2014). Voice. In D. Coghlan & M. Brydon-Miller (Eds.), *The SAGE encyclopedia of action research* (Vols. 1-2, pp.807-809). SAGE Publications Ltd. https://dx.doi.org/10.4135/9781446294406

Rowe, W. (2014). Positionality. In D. Coghlan & M. Brydon-Miller (Eds.), *The SAGE encyclopedia of action research* (Vols. 1-2, p.628). SAGE Publications Ltd, https://dx.doi.org/10.4135/9781446294406

Sandwick, T., Fine, M., Greene, A. C., Stoudt, B. G., Torre, M. E., & Patel, L. (2018). Promise and provocation: Humble reflections on critical participatory action research for social policy. *Urban Education, 53*(4), 473–502. https://doi.org/10.1177/0042085918763513

Schmuck, R. A. (2006). *Practical action research for change.* Corwin Press.

Senekal, I. (2022). Curriculum-in-motion: Bringing community education to life through community-based participatory action research. *Education as Change, 26*(1), 1–29. https://doi.org/10.25159/1947-9417/11124

Smith, M., ElBassiouny, A., & Sanders, A. (2020). Partnering across disciplines: Engaging students in peer collaborations on writing assignments. *Journal of Teacher Action Research, 7*(1), 101–125.

Stoecker, R. (2009). Are we talking the walk of community-based research? *Action Research, 7*(4), 385–404. https://doi.org/10.1177/1476750309340944

Stringer, E. T. (2014). *Action research* (4th ed.). SAGE.

Strumińska-Kutra, M., & Scholl, C. (2022). Taking power seriously: Towards a power-sensitive approach for transdisciplinary action research. *Futures, 135,* Article 102881. https://doi.org/10.1016/j.futures.2021.102881

Thomson, P., & Gunter, H. (2011). Inside, outside, upside down: The fluidity of academic researcher 'identity' in working with/in school. *International Journal of Research & Method in Education, 34*(1), 17–30. https://doi.org/10.1080/1743727X.2011.552309

Trott, C. D., Sample McMeeking, L. B., & Weinberg, A. E. (2020). Participatory action research experiences for undergraduates: Forging critical connections through community engagement. *Studies in Higher Education, 45*(11), 2260–2273. https://doi.org/10.1080/03075079.2019.1602759

Willis, J. W., & Edwards, C. (Eds.). (2014). *Action research: Models, methods, and examples.* Information Age Publishing, Incorporated.

Yull, D., Wilson, M., Murray, C., & Parham, L. (2018). Reversing the dehumanization of families of color in schools: Community-based research in a race-conscious parent engagement program. *School Community Journal, 28*(1), 319–347.

Zambo, D. (2011). Action research as signature pedagogy in an education doctorate program: The reality and hope. *Innovative Higher Education, 36*(4), 261–271. https://doi.org/10.1007/s10755-010-9171-7

Zion, S. (2020). Transformative student voice: Extending the role of youth in addressing systemic marginalization in U.S. schools. *Multiple Voices for Ethnically Diverse Exceptional Learners, 20*(1), 32–43.

CHAPTER 13

The Group Dissertation:

Re-thinking the Dissertation in Practice, Utilizing Collaborative Research Teams for Innovation

REBECCA G. HARPER, PHD

Obtaining a doctoral degree in academia represents the pinnacle of achievement for many. In numerous cases, a terminal degree is a required credential for employment and advancement in many educational settings, including institutions of higher education. However, one of the leading obstacles often expressed by potential doctoral candidates and even those currently enrolled in graduate programs is that of the dissertation. For some, completing this task is one of the major deterrents to enrolling in a doctoral program and, thus, potentially limits access to this advanced degree. According to the *Chronicle of Higher Education* (2013), half of the students who enter PhD programs do not graduate. Many of these non-completers make it through all the coursework but simply do not complete the culminating assessment: the dissertation. As a result, they end up classified as ABDs: All But Dissertation.

Part of this staggering statistic is related to the complex nature and the significant demands associated with conducting research and then writing about it. Completing a dissertation requires a considerable amount of work and dedication, not to mention a strong command of the academic writing genre, which is a difficult writing genre to master. Many students are less intimidated by the coursework required in a doctoral program and instead view the dissertation as the major obstacle. As Program Director for the doctoral program at Augusta University, when speaking with prospective students, the most common questions I receive are centered around the dissertation. Rarely am I asked questions about the coursework, professors, or readings associated with the program; instead, I find myself fielding questions exclusive to the dissertation. Recognizing that the dissertation seemed to cause students the most angst, as faculty developed our EdD program almost a decade ago, they focused on making the dissertation both innovative and accessible.

Augusta University's EdD Program is based on the Carnegie Project on the Education Doctorate (CPED) framework (CPED, 2021A), with a major focus on social justice and equity, along with the investigation of problems of practice. When planning our degree program, faculty in our EdD in Educational Innovation carefully examined the structure of the traditional dissertation as they developed and designed our doctoral program. In an effort to create an innovative and responsive program, our dissertation deviated from the traditional solo format and instead focused on the utilization of research teams for dissertation completion. In doing so, we believed this would allow us to firmly connect our newly designed program to CPED principles. In particular, we focused intently on how our dissertation model would focus on the resolution of problems of practice (PoPs) by providing students with collaborative opportunities with key stakeholders, the university, individuals, and the community. The program itself was designed as a cohort model, with students in the same cohort taking all their core classes together. Classes for their concentrations, which were focused either on leadership or curriculum, were cross-cohort courses that were only offered in the summer. Keeping the students together using the cohort model helped the students develop relationships and collaborate on smaller research projects, which we believed would aid them as they formed their respective groups for their dissertations.

Our delivery model initially began as a six-weekend per semester program, with students physically attending class on Friday evenings and all day Saturday during set weekends in the semester. COVID-19 required us to move our program online for a short time; however, in doing so, when our campus returned to face-to-face instruction, we elected to keep our Friday evenings online and return to face-to-face only for Saturday classes. This structure made it easier for students who were traveling outside of our local area, as now they could take part in class on Fridays from home. Because of our delivery model, we attract a variety of educators from a number of professional settings. Many of our current students are practicing teachers, administrators, school support personnel, and higher education faculty and/or staff.

The Why Behind the Group Dissertation

Offering students opportunities to collaborate as part of an advanced degree program can be extremely beneficial. According to Kennedy et al. (2018), co-authoring a dissertation is metacognitive in nature, as this type of collaboration focuses on conflict resolution, consensus, and ongoing critical analysis. As such, this conceptualization acknowledges the recursive nature of writing and research in general. While often conceived as linear in nature, in truth researching and writing generally involve a back-and-forth process of revising and revisiting both the data and the literature, as well as theory that inform the study. Plus, beginning this academic exercise utilizing a collaborative spirit can also aid students if they choose to continue publishing in their respective fields. Co-authoring manuscripts in academia is certainly common practice, so this experience offers students additional knowledge that would prove beneficial. Having a research team investigate a problem of practice also allows students the ability to capitalize on their individual strengths and interests. When teams are structured based on these ideas, their function immediately becomes much more effective.

Another solid reason for utilizing a collaborative format for the dissertation is directly related to the nature of the work and problem-solving that occurs in educational settings. Frequently, collaborative teams are created in the workplace for a variety of reasons, including data analysis, curriculum development, and instructional planning. Therefore, it was not a stretch for our program to utilize the modalities often employed in the workforce for the culminating assessment in our doctoral program. Plus, since our doctoral degree major is Educational Innovation, it made sense for our program to utilize an innovative approach to the dissertation itself. Considering the fact that only a small percentage of CPED institutions utilize a group dissertation format, we knew that our program would stand out amongst our university system competitors with its unique format.

Despite the fact that the faculty had articulated solid reasons for incorporating a group dissertation format, not all of our faculty were supportive of it. In fact, some openly stated that this format "cheapened" the degree, meaning that it made a doctoral degree easier to get. Yet, others explained that utilizing this innovative approach opened the door to doctoral degrees for some students who otherwise would not have pursued the degree. Those faculty believed that for students who were wary of completing a doctoral degree due to the intensive nature of the dissertation, completing this culminating assessment with a team could make attaining a terminal degree more accessible. Still, some faculty argued that permitting students to divide up the work could potentially allow students with weaker academic skills entry into the program. Plus, there were questions about how to determine equal contributions in this portion of the program. Ultimately, the argument became one that was focused on making a doctoral degree too easy, with the other was on making the degree more accessible. Clearly, the conceptualization of this new degree may have made sense on paper, but it was not until we began admitting students and moving them through their programs of study that we began to see what alterations and adjustments were needed.

The Evolution of the Group Dissertation

Initially, our group dissertation format was conceptualized as a problem-solving mechanism for local school districts. Representatives and stakeholders from local school districts would pose a problem or idea that they would like studied in their respective districts. Districts presented their problems to the doctoral faculty in writing and then came to campus and conducted a presentation for the doctoral students, followed by a brief question-and-answer session. Research teams would then determine if this was a topic that they would like to take up in their dissertation work. With this model, students still had a traditional four-person committee, with two co-chairs, a third member related to the discipline, and the fourth member who automatically came from the district pitching the problem. This fourth member was coined as the *client*. Research teams then designed their study and collected data based on the problem presented by the district. Part of the final dissertation product included a poster presentation to the stakeholders and client as well. This provided another tangible artifact that districts could utilize for dissemination to their parents, educators, and other stakeholders.

In the early days of our doctoral program, students were not able to form their individual research teams without significant faculty input. Instead, students submitted names of one or two cohort members with whom they would like to work. Doctoral faculty consulted as a team and then placed the students in their respective research teams. While student requests were considered, not all students got their first choice when it came to their research partners. Part of the rationale for faculty input and final decision was that it allowed advisors to make a deliberate attempt to place students together whom they believed would form cohesive and productive teams. This was not always the case, however, the thought process behind this approach was one in which faculty attempted to address any foreseeable challenges or obstacles that may occur with certain group compositions.

Some positives to the original conceptualization of the research team approach were directly related to gatekeeping and access to research sites. By involving the districts in the problem and topic generation, students were almost always assured of access in that particular setting. This, of course, made the Institutional Review Board (IRB) process easier, as they were able to almost immediately gain access and permission for their research. After all, districts were coming to us asking for our students to conduct their research in their settings. Because our IRB process requires researchers to provide proof of site access and permission as part of the IRB package, having close contacts within our local districts made this piece of paperwork easier to acquire. Plus, since these ideas were posed by the stakeholders of the local districts, we knew that the topics studied were relevant to our local communities and schools. Having a set of specific problems of practice also allowed faculty to plan instruction that could help guide the students as they began these specific research endeavors. Additionally, for groups who had difficulty pinning down a topic, this was also helpful as it aided them in honing in on a specific focus.

While this model was certainly innovative and responsive, there were also some major concerns. For one, it greatly limited what students could study. By leaning on the client for the research topic, some groups found themselves studying topics and concepts that were somewhat outside of their areas of expertise. This could occur if the majority of a team favored one topic over another, which may result in the remaining member having to make concessions on topic selection. Another issue was that of the investment in the topic. As Program Director, one of the main pieces of advice I give to all students in the doctoral program is that they should study something that is relevant to their fields and that it should be of interest to the student. When researchers are mired down in data, disinterest in a topic is certainly not a motivator; in fact, it can become a frustrating factor and deterrent. Thus, studying something that is relevant and of interest to a student can affect their ability to complete this portion of their doctoral program successfully.

Yet another issue had to do with the language we used when describing our outside stakeholders. When individuals were labeled as the *client*, it created an unintentional consequence regarding the perception of that relationship. Some fourth committee members (clients) made requests that implied a misunderstanding of their role in the research process. These sometimes included alterations to data collection methods, research design, and the presentation of the findings. Plus, because stakeholders were choosing the topics they wanted examined, many were looking for evidence that a particular initiative they were implementing in their districts was effective. Findings not indicating this to be the case proved problematic. As such, there might have been some implicit bias in the problems of practice. For example, one large district in our area that typically does not allow research to be conducted in their schools was implementing a professional learning initiative and needed evidence of its effectiveness. Needing this evidence posed a problem for one of our cohorts. As this research team wrote up their findings, they found themselves in a precarious situation. As both researchers and educators within that district, they were concerned that their findings would not be well-received. Consequently, both members of this research team were concerned about how this conflict positioned them as employees in the respective district.

Another drawback was the creation of research groups. Since faculty had the final say in who was grouped with whom, students sometimes ended up with people who were not their first choices. While most groups had an overall positive group dynamic, some did not. In fact, one of our doctoral students wrote about that experience and his dissertation journey, which included an initially failed proposal defense and a number of team challenges (Hamilton, 2022).

These early observations helped us plan and modify our current program to do a better job of capitalizing on the positives of the group dissertation model, while doing our best to offset the potential negatives of this format. Getting through these initial growing pains helped faculty modify not only the program of study and course rotations, but the way in which we implemented the group dissertation model.

Our Current Group Dissertation Model

Based on data collected over several cohorts, program faculty began to make some adjustments to our group dissertation model. For one, faculty no longer have an active input or final say on the composition of research teams. Instead, students create their own research teams with one specific parameter: teams can be no larger than groups of three. In fact, students now also have the option of pursuing their dissertation as a solo endeavor if they so choose. Of course, faculty offer advice and input, but at the end of the day, the decision-making lies with the students regarding their individual groups. The new selection process has been well-received by students, with most forming their research teams by the end of their fifth semester. In a few cases, some students have had difficulty finding partners, but faculty have been able to step in and offer suggestions and remedies.

Because the language we used initially with the client model was problematic, we shifted to simply referring to the fourth committee member by the designation of an outside committee member. Changing the language has helped us address the unintentional perception that the former language created. By naming them simply as a fourth outside member, those individuals saw their roles shift from one in which the students conducted research on their behalf to one where they provided their expertise on the topic. Another change that has occurred is that of topic generation. No longer do we rely on district leaders to provide our students with the topics that should be studied. Instead, students utilize their knowledge of their current settings and schools to develop their own problems of practice directly related to their interests and needs. This has proven much more effective as students automatically have a more vested interest in topics that they generate on their own.

Thinking About the Group Dissertation as an Option

If your program is currently considering adopting the group dissertation model as an option, there are certainly several reasons to do so. However, there are a number of considerations and caveats that might be considered before formally adopting the group model. These observations are based on data collected over almost a decade.

Pros

One of the biggest advantages of conducting a dissertation using a team approach is the ability to divide and conquer data collection. For teams who planned to conduct multiple interviews or focus groups, or for those who planned to collect data at multiple sites, having multiple team members divide this work was a significant advantage. Because almost all of our doctoral students are currently employed in education or related sectors, taking leave time for data collection could sometimes be difficult. While many were conducting research in their own settings, data collection often was an activity that was conducted outside of their work expectations. In addition, many teams collected data in a variety of settings, so leave time was necessary. With the team approach, teams worked on developing data collection schedules so that they could divide and conquer the task, with some electing to simultaneously take specific days off and go on a data collection blitz together, while others staggered their collection having different team members collecting data on different days. For those teams who had multiple sites, having a research team allowed them some flexibility with travel as well. Teams could collect data across multiple sites on the same day due to this increase in personpower.

Another major advantage of the research team approach occurs with the IRB submission process. Many of our doctoral students indicate that this can be a major obstacle as they begin their research projects. Because our IRB approval process requires multiple consent forms along with supplemental files and the actual research narrative, some students find IRB to be one of the more frustrating components of their degree program. In addition, getting IRB approval requires solid attention to detail and a specific skill set, one that not all students have. However, when working with a research team, many students had a designated IRB representative who was responsible for responding to any amendments, modifications, or requests mandated by the IRB board. While the representative communicated and worked with their teams on any revisions, ultimately, having one responsible party helped eliminate some issues with IRB. As Program Director, I found this to be an effective way for many groups to handle this part of the research process and even suggested teams consider this option when they made it to this point in the process.

Because our EdD program runs as a cohort model, with the exception of their concentration classes, all of their core courses are taken with the same group of students. As a result, students often find they can easily assimilate into a research team after a few semesters. Through interactions in class and course assignments that are often collaborative in nature, students can begin to determine who they might want to work with on their problem of practice. These partnerships emerge in many ways, sometimes through a consensus on a research topic with others developing out of personal relationships. Considering that faculty members no longer select the research teams, students are more likely to work with individuals they are comfortable with or with whom they share commonalities, which has helped our research teams and their collaborative efforts.

Having multiple group members also allows students the ability to look at a problem through multiple lenses. For example, a team made up of a classroom teacher, administrator, and higher education faculty member could examine a problem through an adult learning lens, a leadership lens, and an instructional lens. That, in addition to the many theoretical orientations that can be examined, can allow researchers to study one problem from a variety of perspectives, thus opening the potential for multiple publications after the dissertation is completed. Many of our students have found this to be especially attractive as, upon leaving their doctoral program, they could have multiple publication opportunities. While all of our current students have written their dissertations in the traditional five-chapter format, with the admission of Cohort 7, we offered the option of a multiple-article dissertation, where each team member drafts a manuscript with a different focus. This option had a number of benefits, not only for the students but also for the faculty. A multiple-article dissertation can allow students the ability to focus on their individual interests, but from a faculty standpoint, it allows us the ability to provide individual accountability for our students since each team member assumes the role of first/lead author on one of the articles.

Yet, another benefit of the group model is directly related to the number of dissertation committees needed each semester. By utilizing a group format, the immediate need for faculty person-power on committees is drastically reduced. For example, in the traditional format, our Cohort 7 class would need 19 committee chairs along with another 57 faculty and/or outside members to fill the remaining slots. With our current model, that same cohort will require seven committee chairs and 21 additional faculty and/or outside members. This is extremely beneficial for small colleges or for those who have only a small number of tenured faculty.

Cons

One of the earliest challenges of the research team approach was that of integrity and determining equal contributions amongst research team members. Faculty quickly realized that in a group dissertation model, it was easy for students with weak writing or research skills to hide behind their teammates. While some may assert that when this occurs, team members should let their dissertation chair or advisor know, it is not as simple as it would seem. In fact, students rarely came to their advisors with complaints about team members pulling their own weight. Instead, faculty members often had to sniff these problems out on their own. For example, early on, it was apparent that certain research teams had individuals who were contributing at far differing amounts than their teammates. Some conducted all the interviews, while others did not take part in this portion of the data collection. While they all participated in the analysis of the transcripts, there was a significant amount of labor involved in the actual interview execution. Other issues arose due to missed team deadlines or team members not providing the same level of feedback on their collaborative writing as their peers.

In different instances, I have completed team meetings that have served somewhat as interventions for underperforming team members. As a result of these interventions, some team members had to submit their individual research and writing logs for review when their individual contributions were in question. However, this required additional time and commitment on the faculty member's part; as in these cases, I was now responsible for reviewing accounts and ledgers of students' research and writing activities which added to an already full plate. That, coupled with the numerous meetings that were required to get students back on track, often took a large amount of time.

Aside from this, sometimes students were not contributing to the written component of the dissertation in an equal manner. While many groups divided up parts, it quickly became apparent that in some groups, the sections written by some students did not rise to the same quality. As a result, some group members found themselves having to re-write sections that were not originally their responsibility. Some team members elected to do their team member's part in order to complete their scheduled deadline, which often resulted in frustration. As faculty advisors, we encouraged groups to lean on the university resources, including the Writing Center. In addition, many faculty met with groups individually to model academic writing or showed them sample paragraphs that were solid examples of academic writing.

Another challenge of the group dissertation is the ability of groups to write in one collective writing voice. Since teams of students were working together to create a final research product, finding a unified writing voice was a struggle for many groups. As committee member and as chair for several teams, it was often easy to determine whose writing was whose. This was present not only through writing style in general but also in basic, fundamental academic writing. Students who were stronger academic writers often, without meaning to, shone spotlights on their counterparts who maybe did not have the same skill level as their colleagues. Learning how to write with one collective voice took some skill, practice, and deliberate attention. For example, one of our groups early on was a team of two: Mario and Stan. Both of these students are excellent writers, but it was easily apparent who was writing what. As we read their initial drafts, we could clearly tell who was responsible for each section and since they had very different writing styles, their initial drafts lacked flow and rhythm. In jest, I told them they needed to find a way to merge their writing styles and become "Stario." What was meant as a joke quickly helped them achieve the difficult job of merging multiple writing styles into one cohesive writing product where the reader is unable to tell who wrote what because of its unified voice. However, not all of the students are able to merge their writing into one unified voice as easily as Stario, and this often becomes a challenge for many groups.

As a faculty member and advisor, one of the greatest challenges I have experienced with this model has to do with the social and team dynamics of each group. When working with a student one on one, it is easier to determine what approach that single student might need. Some students need more handholding, while others need you to shoot straight. Some are more sensitive; others get defensive. Sometimes students burst into tears, while others get angry. Dealing with these unique attributes on a case-by-case basis, though challenging, is certainly manageable. Now, imagine in one research team, you have a student who gets defensive over feedback, another who needs specific and succinct direction, and yet another who needs reassurance. As a faculty member, delivering feedback to that motley crew is a completely different ball of wax. When I have meetings with different research teams, it is important that I consider each team member's individual characteristics and make a solid attempt to deliver feedback that can be well-received by the entire team. This can definitely prove challenging!

Recommendations

For programs considering the group dissertation model, several items should be considered.

- Faculty support and preparation
  Because advising a research team is significantly different from working with an individual student, it is important that faculty are provided with appropriate professional learning and support. These might include training on feedback, collaborative teams, conflict resolution, and advisement.

- Faculty buy-in
  Before making the transition to the group model, it is important to make certain that faculty in the program support the delivery model. Without faculty buy-in, it is unlikely that the program will prosper. One compromise might be to offer the research team approach as an option before moving solely to a team approach. This could allow faculty who would rather work with individual students the option to continue with their preferences, but at the same time, it would allow a program to continue to evolve.

- Student Support
  Because writing a dissertation with a team can prove challenging, having professional learning for students is

imperative. Ideas for professional learning include information on collaborative topic generation, academic writing in a collaborative nature, data collection, the IRB process, group responsibilities, and conflict resolution.

Of course, individual programs may also have other items that are important for consideration due to their unique characteristics, but considering the items above can aid in the development and construction of a new dissertation model.

Conclusion

Utilizing the group dissertation format has a significant amount of potential for doctoral program growth and innovation. With collaborative projects becoming more of the norm and traditional education formats taking a back seat to more innovative inquiry methods, the group dissertation is an option that is both responsive and timely. While there are factors that should be considered before immediately moving to this unique model, the benefits for students and faculty are apparent. With this in mind, it is possible that more programs will offer this as an option for a variety of doctoral degree programs.

References

Augusta University College of Education and Human Development. (n.d.). *Doctor of Education (Ed.D.) in educational innovation.* Augusta University College of Education [AUCOE]. https://www.augusta.edu/education/research/edd-ei.php?gclid=CjwKCAiA9NGfBhBvEi wAq5vSy_GrAKjZZoEvnHjNKq0-DP5X9eOjdKBUvIjFIdT4H6KgUTH Wt3DXfhoCO0gQAvD_BwE

Carnegie Project on the Education Doctorate. (2022). *The CPED Framework©.* https://www.cpedinitiative.org/the-framework

Carnegie Project on the Education Doctorate. (2023, February 21). *#CPED20 Annual & Virtual Convening.* https://www.cpedinitiative. org/index.php?option=com_jevents&task=icalr+epeat.detail&evid =3&Itemid=115&year=2020&month=10&day=14&title=c+ped20-oc tober-convening&uid=d96bc54a8d2271576fc684660d507adc

Cassuto, L. (2020, July 22). PhD attrition: How much is too much. *The Chronicle of Higher Education.* https://www.chronicle.com/article/ph-d-attrition-how-much-is-too-much/?cid=gen_sign_in

Hamilton, W. (2022). The group-based dissertation in Practice: A journey worth taking. *Impacting Education: Journal on Transforming Professional Practice, 7*(1), 42–46. https://doi.org/10.5195/ie.2022.234

Kennedy, B. L., Altman, M., & Pizano, A. (2018). Engaging in the battle of the snails by challenging the traditional dissertation model. *Impacting Education: Journal on Transforming Professional Practice, 3*(1). https://doi.org/10.5195/ie.2018.27

CHAPTER 14

Alternative Formats:

Thinking Differently about Dissertations in Practice and Faculty Dissertation Mentoring

VACHEL MILLER, EDD; STAR BROWN, EDD

What makes an EdD different from a PhD? This question has generated passionate responses over the last 20 or more years, leading the Carnegie Project for the Educational Doctorate (CPED) to produce a distinctive program design framework for EdD programs. Within the larger conversation about EdD program design, the nature of the doctoral capstone project–the dissertation–has remained a focal point of debate and innovation.

As EdD programs have developed a distinctive approach to dissertation research, the "dissertation in practice" (DiP) has emerged as a way to distinguish the unique role of research for scholar-practitioners. The dissertation in practice centers on the practitioner's identification of a concrete, actionable problem within an institutional setting, and chronicles what the practitioner has learned about the processes and outcomes of an improvement effort (Perry et al., 2020).

While focused on practical improvement, the DiP has largely retained the familiar format of a chapter-based (whether five or more) dissertation, since that format continues to offer academic legitimacy. For graduate schools and other university authorities, a five-chapter book looks like a dissertation is supposed to look!

In some EdD programs, however, the DiP has evolved beyond the confines of traditional text-based chapters. These programs have opened space for students to include non-traditional products for professional use within the dissertation, such as: curriculum design documents, professional development presentations, and advocacy materials (Perry, 2021). These alternative DiPs typically include a set of traditional chapters along with a portfolio of products stemming from an action-oriented inquiry (Belizer et al., 2016).

In our own EdD program at Appalachian State University, our students, like their colleagues elsewhere, gravitate toward issues/ problems rooted in their professional experience. We value practitioner inquiry, as exemplified by an action-oriented DIP. In addition, we invite students to pursue emergent forms of inquiry and representations that might fall outside the typical parameters of a DiP. In recent years, we've intentionally cultivated an appreciation for "doing dissertations differently" that encourages students to reflect on their own research passions and identities as scholar-practitioners. We want them to consider multiple avenues of inquiry and expression that fit their paradigmatic leanings and professional goals. As we discuss further below, we do not always expect faculty mentors to have established expertise in a particular genre; rather, we foreground their role in supporting students' exploration and growth–and ultimately the production of good work, even as "good work" takes multiple forms!

Our engagement with CPED has challenged us to consider this question: Even as we do dissertations differently, can alternative dissertation genres and formats remain connected to problems of practice? In this chapter, we suggest that yes, an EdD program can center problems of practice (PoPs) while opening multiple ways for students to position themselves in relation to those problems and broadening the ways that they may express what they've learned about those problems. After exploring an expansive view of dissertations in practice, we will later consider the implications for faculty mentoring.

Where's the Problem? Positioning Scholar-practitioners in Relation to Their PoPs

For educational leaders, problems found in their practice settings call for improvement. Guiding improvement through applied, action-oriented research is the hallmark of scholarly inquiry in CPED-influenced EdD programs (Perry & Zambo, 2021). Besides improvement, however, there may be other possible relationships between scholar-practitioners and their problems of practice. We suggest that, when problems of practice exceed the boundaries of a student's current professional context–or spill outside their identity as an educational leader–then alternative approaches to the dissertation's genre and/or format can allow them to more fully address their chosen problems. In other words, thinking about problems of practice in an expansive, complex manner opens the door to doing DiPs differently.

To think about their problems of practice anew, we invite students to consider a relationship of critique, using theoretical tools to analyze the ways in which a problem is formulated or understood within a professional community. In this respect, the very ways in which an issue becomes and remains a "problem" can be problematized. For example, a recent student deconstructed the ways that medical and educational practitioners frame children with autism as deficient and discount parental knowledge of their child's needs (Shoaf, 2022). The problem of practice, in this dissertation, was the very "expert knowledge" of autism that centered parents as unreliable and the child as always developmentally flawed.

Sites matter. Typically, DiP's situate a problem of practice within what CPED has called a "laboratory of practice", which is understood as a particular school or college setting in which the practitioner works and can conduct improvement-oriented inquiry. We have found that our students sometimes locate their "laboratory of practice" differently—in other times or spaces—which might include a prior professional context. They might also locate the problem within their own lived experience that intersects with, and extends beyond, an institutional context. The "site" of the inquiry, in such instances, can be expansive, running across time and place.

One of our students, for example, has proposed analyzing the affective resonances and community memories connected with the loss of a small rural elementary school that they attended as a child (Kisielewski, 2021). This student is not trying to improve anything in their current school; they are more curious about how the small school down the road continues to live on, despite its closure.

The discussion above produces several questions for EdD programs to consider, regarding their approaches to dissertations in practice.

- *What is the assumed relationship between a student and their problem of practice?* On the one hand, a problem-solving relationship is central to CPED-inspired programs. While problem-solving remains vital, what other relationships might be possible? How else can students hold a problem, if they do not want to fix it?

- *Can our problems of practice be located outside our jobs?* Can students decide which subjectivities and experiences they center, as they name which problems matter to them? In other words, can students choose problems they encounter in their lives as parents, community members, or planetary citizens that may (or may not) intersect with the problems they face as educational leaders?

- *Where is the locus of change in a dissertation in practice?* Dissertations in practice–especially those employing improvement science–typically situate the locus of change as the system in which the scholar-practitioner works. In the process of improving a problematic practice in the system, the individual scholar-practitioner is likely to experience professional growth; however, the transformation of the student's subjectivity–of the person's ways-of-seeing/thinking/engaging the world–are not the center of change. In other genres, however, change can be situated more intimately, within the person undertaking the inquiry, and/or in the long-range echoes of the work.

- *What is the right size of a problem of practice?* The wisdom of improvement science teaches that a problem should be small enough to get our hands around; in other words, amenable to intervention in the short term. What about the all-too-big problems of practice located in systems? Those are problems that a dissertation cannot dent, per se, or that are amenable to plan-do-study-act (PDSA) cycles. Yet sometimes students may wish to employ their dissertation research to shine a light on the macro-levels systems that constrain marginalized populations and limit educational possibilities.

As these questions indicate, our approach to dissertation work is to honor the rich dimensionality of our students' identities and lived experiences of problems of practice. We respect our students as practitioners, and we invite them to solve local problems with a DiP. And we respect our students not just as practitioners, but as complex people with biographies, attachments, identities, and curiosities, who experience problems in ways that may not call for "improvement." We believe that seeing students both within and beyond their professional roles opens the possibility for them to pursue multiple kinds of dissertations in practice.

The table below provides a preliminary summary of the possibilities for students pursuing dissertations in practice. It does not include all possible methodological approaches, and we have intentionally avoided linking the elements in each column in a linear way, since an action research DiP may take the form of a 5-chapter text, a 3-article portfolio, or a portfolio with alternative, use-oriented products (such as a professional development training design or an advocacy presentation).

Table 14.1

Dissertation Multiplicity

Genres of Inquiry	Format	Primary Locus of Change
Possible genres may include:	Potential formats for representing the inquiry:	Potential sites of change include:
• Action Research • Improvement Science • Autoethnography • Case Study • Phenomenology • Survey • Correlational • Mixed Methods • Post-qualitative • Arts-based	• 5-chapter text • More/less than 5-chapter text • Chaptered text with arts-based, expressive elements • 3-article or publication portfolio • Chaptered text with use-oriented (textual or digital) professional products	• Within the scholar/practitioner • In the current site/problem of practice • In larger systems of practice • In the discourse of a professional community • In future sites/problems of practice • All of the above

Overview of Dissertation Multiplicity

We suggest that DIPs may take many shapes and forms, spanning both professional and personal contexts and addressing both internal and external change. Within this land of dissertation multiplicity, the lines linking genre and format become crisscrossed and blurred. Below are some descriptive examples of how different genres referenced in the table above can be shaped into various dissertation formats resulting in change directed at multiple levels.

Post-Qualitative Inquiry

Non-empirical and more conceptually-based projects are a leading alternative dissertation genre at our institution. Many of these projects fall within the realm of post-qualitative inquiry, which employs the use of theory to think differently about problems of practice (Jackson & Mazzei, 2012, 2017). Thus, these dissertations in practice utilize a critical lens to problematize the site of practice, whether it be in professional or personal contexts. Post-qualitative projects probe into problems of practice from a systemic perspective by tracing their socio-cultural evolution and troubling how and why those structures and discourses have become embedded as the status quo, constraining the possibility for new thinking and practice.

One example of a recent post-qualitative dissertation is an intricately interwoven work that critiques the dominant discourses positioning community colleges as damage-centered (Morrison, 2023). Interspersed throughout the dissertation are breaks of poetic prose in the shape of sidelight stories that serve as disruptions to the common sense thinking about community colleges and provide glimpses into how community colleges might be viewed differently. These sidelight stories provide insight into how the student was both "thinking with theory" (Jackson & Mazzei, 2012) and grappling with the multiplicity of their own subjectivity when writing the dissertation. Doing dissertations differently in the form of post-qualitative inquiry is another instance of how problems of practice can transcend the professional context and connect more deeply to how the student is seeing and engaging with the world around them in new ways, both professionally and personally.

The organization of this dissertation was also non-traditional in that it was arranged as five large sections named assemblages, borrowing from a Deleuze-Guattarian (1987)[1] vocabulary. Although there were five assemblages, this design was not intended to mirror a traditional five-chapter dissertation. Instead, employing the term "assemblages" for the sections within the dissertation was a deliberate move to push against traditional dissertation terminology, such as chapters, in order to use language that was more reflective of the unique style and genre of this dissertation project. With five assemblages plus almost two dozen sidelight stories, this dissertation is an example of what a "more than five-chapter dissertation" might look like.

Action Research and Improvement

As with improvement science, action research is a powerful genre of research for CPED-inspired EdD programs. As Buss and

---

[1] Deleuze and Guattari (1987) use the term "assemblage" to represent a collection or conglomeration of ideas, thoughts, writings, theories, encounters, and experiences; the "multiplicity" that may emerge (pp. 3-4).

Zambo (2016) have articulated, action research moves in cycles of action-reflection, enabling practitioners to enact, document, reflect upon, and refine interventions in practice-based settings. As a pragmatic, eclectic approach to inquiry, action research may involve mixed methods of inquiry and can produce both traditional dissertation texts and alternative products that inform professional practice. Many EdD programs incorporate action research and/or improvement science as a primary methodology of inquiry.

Arts-Based Research

An ever-evolving approach to inquiry, arts-based research (ABR) opens possibilities for engaging with multiple modes of creative expression, in the doing and representation of inquiry, blending the arts with the social sciences for more holistic insight (Leavy, 2018). Arts-based research emphasizes the power of creative process and emergence. It invites embodied engagement with multiple forms of expression: poetry, drawing, dance, journaling, drumming, etc. Whereas traditional forms of inquiry privilege rationality and linearity, arts-based research welcomes non-linear, intuitive, affective, evocative leaps of insight and expression (Falck, 2022). An arts-based inquiry often includes art-making activities during several phases of inquiry, resulting in images or other forms of expression embedded within (and resonating beyond) traditional texts. In his dissertation, Falck (2022) assembled drawings, images, and quotes from his students' writing about arts-informed inquiry into a "wall of data" that provided a physical artifact for him to interact with creatively, as he explored connections within and beyond the data. Generally, arts-based inquiry opens possibilities for those involved in a project–as collaborator, participant, or researcher–to express themselves aesthetically, intuitively, and non-verbally to enable more holistic engagement with a problem of practice.

Scholarly Articles (Three-Article Dissertation)

Manuscript-oriented or portfolio-based dissertations may not be new to the scene of alternative dissertation formats, but are still solidly different from a traditional five-chapter dissertation. In fact, dissertations crafted around three ready-to-publish journal articles were one of the first alternative dissertation models and led the way for future alternative formats. Research projects best suited for this genre often have an overarching research purpose that can be viewed from multiple perspectives such as: analyzing both quantitative and qualitative data sets (mixed methods), viewing the research problem through varied theoretical lenses, or presenting key insights to both professional and academic audiences in different publications (e.g., Gilbert, 2020). This format frequently appeals to students who wish to move their ideas into public circulation, whether in academic journals or professional outlets.

Writing ready-to-publish articles is a key example of what might be called "use-oriented professional products" within a dissertation document. This approach envisions the dissertation as a portfolio that can house polished, use-oriented material that other professionals can put to work in their own contexts. Our program is only beginning to support this approach; other EdD programs already offer rich opportunities to include use-oriented products as part of a dissertation. At Rutgers University, for example, students may develop products that are designed for professional use by key stakeholders, such as training materials, funding proposals, or policy briefs (Belzer et al., 2016). Such products enable students to express their learning as scholar-practitioners in ways that are immediately accessible and relevant to professional audiences, thus increasing the professional "mileage" of the dissertation.

Emerging Forms of Inquiry

As DiPs evolve, there will likely be increasing hybridization of projects, blending different genres, formats, and loci of change. For example, one recent dissertation in our program was both collaborative and presented as a series of four journal articles woven together with alternating reflective bridges created by each author to explain the methodological and conceptual directions of the project (Burry & Nava Egget, 2021). The bridges also opened the space to provide deeper insight into how the partners collaborated together to create the unique dissertation.

As an additional element outside of the dissertation process, these students chronicled their collaborative dissertation journey via a podcast as a way to navigate their academic partnership and also to narrate their methodological choices and the research design. As both authors are instructional technology practitioners in K-12 educational settings, their work is rooted in their professional practice, yet also crosses traditional research lines by investigating the problem of practice (equitable representation of women and students of color in STEM fields) through the dual lenses of feminism and critical race theory. This is one example of how new forms of inquiry can emerge within EdD programs that are open to differences in terms of dissertation genre, format, and the identification of problems of practice. Over time, especially given the profusion of expressive options found in digital media, dissertations in practice will likely evolve in exciting, unpredictable directions, fueled by scholar-practitioners' desires to solve problems and express ideas in compelling ways that energize educational change.

Building Consensus for Alternatives

Any EdD student who contemplates an alternative genre or form of inquiry—whether including a podcast in an improvement science DiP or writing poems as chapters in an autoethnography—will likely encounter skepticism or questions about the value and validity of their work. Does this "count" as a dissertation? Is it appropriate? Does it meet university expectations for a doctoral degree?

To begin addressing these questions, we offer brief advice to doctoral students and mentors. For one, we wish to reassure dissertation mentors that any boundary that an EdD student may wish to bend or break, has already been broken. The CPED annual convening has already spotlighted a dissertation written in the form of a graphic novel, for example, and a dissertation published in the form of an interactive digital magazine. Doctoral students do not need license in the larger professional community to pursue emergent forms of dissertation work. Inevitably, something even more radical has already been done!

That said, we offer a "reality check" on the challenge of building consensus for the first alternative approach within a particular program. The proposal phase of an alternative project will require overlapping layers of advocacy, starting with the dissertation chair, to the committee, to the program, and most likely, the graduate school of the university. As part of the proposal development process, the student will need to do their homework by finding models or exemplars of their envisioned dissertation genre/format at other universities. The student will need to articulate a thoughtful rationale for their envisioned approach in their dissertation proposal and make a strong case for why an alternative approach is especially productive or powerful, in terms of addressing the problem, sharing lessons learned, or reaching relevant audiences.

Once the faculty mentor is "on board," then the case needs to be made to the entire dissertation committee. A formal meeting may be needed with a Graduate Dean or other university official who has ultimate approval authority for dissertations, to seek their pre-approval for the alternative approach with as much transparency as possible about what the dissertation will look like and why it will look that way (as currently envisioned). In this process, the dissertation chair will play a key role as a champion for the alternative work, since the chair is vouching for the quality and value of the project.

The first person to pursue an alternative approach (such as including a training video or podcast in a DiP) will necessarily devote extra time and energy to building consensus and support around the project. Alternatives become "normal" over time, and may even be embraced by the program as a "signature pedagogy." Once alternatives become a bit more ordinary, students and faculty members will feel a greater confidence in pursuing them as viable options, and less advocacy will be needed to secure institutional support. In short, the third person to include a podcast in a DiP will face far fewer questions than the first.

Mentoring Dissertation Multiplicity

For students, having options for the mode of inquiry and presentation of a DiP can enable them to craft research in unique ways that meet their professional interests, intellectual curiosities, and presentation skills. More conceptual approaches may work best for students who enjoy deep reading and extensive writing. More practical products may work best for students who desire to have immediate professional impact. The diffusion of DiP options enables students to shine in doing the kind of work they do best.

For faculty advisors, mentoring alternative dissertations in practice can involve hard work, uncertainty, and concerns about legitimacy. In this section, we offer advice to faculty members who desire to engage in alternative dissertation work to "trust the process" and conclude by providing concrete ways that EdD programs may support faculty in their roles as dissertation mentors.

"Trust the Process"

One piece of advice that resonates throughout our program, borrowing from the field of expressive arts, is to "trust the process." This can play out in a multitude of ways within the faculty-student relationship. Extending these words of wisdom to students may seem commonplace, but within our program, we have identified the need to propose a similar path forward and way of thinking for faculty mentors. What does "trusting the process" look like within the work of dissertation mentoring?

First and foremost, a stance of openness and flexibility is paramount. In order to embark on the journey toward alternative DiP models, faculty members must exhibit an openness to multiple dissertation genres and flexibility around how they may guide and mentor students toward the creation of these "different" dissertations. Secondly, vulnerability is a necessity for the evolution of exploratory dissertation genres and products. As faculty members are often regarded as experts in their respective fields, this space of uncertainty can be unsettling. In this vein, we are now approaching faculty mentoring with the same advice we offer to students: "trust the process."

Seasoned or late career faculty members have the potential to experience burnout or stagnancy in their academic pursuits, both as a researcher and mentor. Having an expansive programmatic view of dissertation possibilities also enables more experienced faculty members a space to reignite their scholarly passions by supporting new genres/formats that may fall outside their typical scholarly preferences and expertise.

Encouraging faculty members to learn alongside students in

the dissertation journey contributes to the faculty-student bonding experience. Faculty must be willing to approach the dissertation as a continual learning (and negotiation) process in partnership with the student and other committee members. In this way, the faculty member can become a "student" of the dissertation mentoring process by entering or undertaking the project as a space of co-inquiry with the student.

The Need for Additional Support for Faculty Mentors/Chairs

When faculty mentors embark on a dissertation journey with a student who may have non-traditional ideas about the research process or dissertation format, the faculty member may need additional support at the program level. By asking faculty mentors to cast aside the role of expert in exchange for that of explorer may leave faculty members feeling isolated and lacking the support needed to confidently move forward as the "lead" for the dissertation project.

So, how do programs best support dissertation committee chairs/faculty mentors in the midst of dissertation multiplicity? One way this might happen is to augment current program staffing. As program enrollment has nearly doubled in the past five years in our EdD program, we recognized that there were gaps in the ways current staffing supports both students and faculty, and the new role of Dissertation Coach was created to address these gaps in support, including dissertation chair and committee support.

In my (Star Brown's) short tenure as the program's new Dissertation Coach, I have experienced both the breadth and depth of my role to support both students and faculty. I see my role as a collaborative one, whereby I provide holistic support to faculty mentors, committee members, and students. One current example involves a methodological project shift that was particularly disorienting for the committee chair. In my role as Dissertation Coach, I entered into the dissertation project with little knowledge of the project's history or how it evolved to its current state. My encounter with the project was a fresh set of eyes to help "translate" and "reorient" the committee chair to this different methodological approach and genre. In this particular situation, synergy was harnessed through the collective experiences of the faculty mentor, student, and Dissertation Coach.

In many ways, the dissertation coach not only acts as a program liaison between chair and student, chair and program, and chair and committee members, but also as a liaison that helps faculty mentors flow in and out of the different genres and formats of dissertations. In other words, as Dissertation Coach, I often find myself in the role of "dissertation" translator (providing context, language, experiences, examples, resources) about the different genres and formats. As Dissertation Coach, I often take on the role of being a sounding board to discuss new and different possibilities for dissertation genres and formats for both students and faculty. Having a staff dedicated to assisting both students and faculty members in the post-coursework phases of the program is an intentional move recognizing the need for specialized support for the dissertation process. This is yet another way that faculty members are encouraged to "trust the process" in a more safe, supportive space.

The differing experiences of faculty members, the vast range of student interests, and the wide array of dissertation genres have all contributed to the need for additional professional development for current and future faculty dissertation mentors. We recognize this as a growth area for our program. Currently as an emergent project, experienced faculty members are working collaboratively with doctoral program staff to develop guidelines and educational materials to better equip committee chairs to assist students as they navigate the diverse landscape of alternative dissertations, as well as the different phases of the dissertation process.

Conclusion

The range of possibilities for dissertations in practice has opened widely in recent years. New spaces for inquiry in EdD programs can create exciting possibilities for students to pursue their own unique projects. It might be an improvement-oriented DiP in which change happens within a local laboratory of practice. That DiP might be presented in ways that "look like a book" regardless of how many chapters the book might contain. Alternatively, the DiP might include products for immediate use by professional audiences; thus, the DiP makes a professional contribution to educational change both locally and broadly.

In this chapter, we suggest that the notion of dissertations in practice can be productively expanded by asking questions about the nature, size, and location of our problems, as well as our relationships with those problems. In doing so, we may find that a problem might be addressed through non-traditional genres of inquiry and/or represented in ways that might still look like a book, or a hybrid of scholarly text with novel forms of expression. An expansive approach to dissertations in practice still honors the professional orientation of the EdD degree, while opening new possibilities for students and faculty mentors alike.

Each project requires unique guidance, based on the location (institutional setting), dissertation topic, committee composition, student, etc. Our programmatic philosophy is to approach each project as situational and student-specific. In other words, there is not a formulaic approach to dissertation mentoring. Instead, our programmatic philosophy to dissertation mentoring is centered around openness and exploration for both the student and faculty member. Learning to embrace this uncertainty and lack of control requires vulnerability, from both the student and faculty perspectives. Finding comfort in discomfort opens up the space for possibilities versus certainties and knowns; one must embrace an ethic of "trusting of the process" and a willingness to step out into the unknown.

Related to alternative dissertation models, we believe that "trusting the process" leads to the evolution of new dissertation genres; thus, this venturing into uncharted territory is exactly what pushes the boundaries of what a dissertation should, can, or will look like in the future. When faculty members and students alike are not confined to prescriptive guidelines of what a dissertation deliverable should look like, this is where sparks are ignited toward alternative inquiry to engage problems of practice in energizing new ways.

References

Belzer, A., Axelrod, T., Benedict, C., Jakubik, T., Rosen, M., & Yavuz, O. (2016). The problem of practice dissertation: Matching program goals, practices, and outcomes. In J. Perry (Ed.), *The EdD and the scholarly practitioner* (pp. 153-175). Information Age.

Buss, R., & Zambo, D. (2016). Using action research to develop educational leaders and researchers. In J. Perry (Ed.), *The EdD and the scholarly practitioner* (pp. 137-152). Information Age.

Burry, R., & Nava Eggett, K. (Hosts). (2021-2022). *Through our lens* [Audio podcast]. https://open.spotify.com/show/2ALCJ488IIbPsblCJwWTtZ

Burry, R., & Nava Eggett, K.A. (2022). *Leveraging instructional technology and asset-based pedagogy for equitable representations in technological opportunities* [Unpublished Doctoral Dissertation]. Appalachian State University.

Deleuze, G., & Guattari, F. (1987). *A thousand plateaus: Capitalism and schizophrenia* (B.Massumi, Trans.). University of Minnesota Press.

Falck, M. (2022). *"Why Art?" Ways of responding to the world around us* [Unpublished doctoral dissertation]. Appalachian State University.

Gilbert, C. (2020). *Participatory action research with teacher activists: Walking the spiral and "Making the invisible visible"* [Unpublished doctoral dissertation]. Appalachian State University.

Jackson, A.Y., & Mazzei, L.A. (2012). *Thinking with theory in qualitative research: Viewing data across multiple perspectives.* Routledge.

Jackson, A.Y., & Mazzei, L.A. (2017). Thinking with theory: A new analytic for qualitative inquiry. In N. Denzin, & Y. Lincoln (Eds., 5th ed.), *The SAGE handbook of qualitative research* (pp. 717-737). SAGE Publications.

Kisielewski, K. (2021). *A folk lament: An exploration of the death of a school using affect theory and rememory* [Unpublished dissertation proposal]. Appalachian State University.

Leavy, P. (2018). Introduction to arts-based research. In P. Leavy (Ed.), *Handbook of arts-based research* (pp. 3-21). Guilford.

Morrison, A. (2023). *Opening doors to disruption: A poststructural deconstruction of community college discourse* [Unpublished doctoral dissertation]. Appalachian State University.

Perry, J. (2021, November 5). *Distinguishing the EdD and understanding the dissertation in practice* [Keynote presentation] the Annual Doctoral Symposium, Appalachian State University.

Perry, J., & Zambo, D. (2021). Finding problems, asking questions, and implementing solutions: Improvement science and the EdD. In D.T. Spaulding, R. Crow, and B. N. Hinnant-Crawford (Eds.), *Teaching improvement science in educational leadership: A pedagogical guide* (pp. 43-61). Myers Education Press.

Perry, J., Zambo, D., & Crow, R. (2020). *The improvement science dissertation in practice: A guide for faculty, committee members, and their students*. Myers Education Press.

Shoaf, G. (2022). *Problematizing the deficit discourses of people with autism and autism parents: A poststructural analysis of subjectivity and power/knowledge* [Unpublished doctoral dissertation]. Appalachian State University.

SECTION 4:

Concerns and Issues

CHAPTER 15

Mentoring Students

KANDY SMITH, PHD

Assuming that leaders in the department and university have bought into the Dissertation in Practice (DiP), mentoring the EdD candidate presents a practical issue that requires attention in the shift from the traditional doctorate to the Dissertation in Practice. In this chapter, we will briefly situate mentoring, note the literature that provides support in understanding the mentoring theoretical framework, proceed from there to examine identified challenges in this mentoring metamorphosis, and inquire into possible solutions or, at minimum, next steps for mentors and candidates on the EdD journey.

As a point of clarification, while the Carnegie Project in the Education Doctorate (CPED) has established the final product in the EdD process as the DiP, in 1920, Harvard University entitled this same outcome, the Professional Practice Doctorate (PPD) (Tamim & Torres, 2022). In this chapter, "Dissertation in Process" and the initialsm "DiP" will be the dominant usage, but the term "Professional Practice Doctorate" and its initialism "PPD" will be included when doing so remains faithful to the literature concerning mentoring in the EdD doctoral process.

Mentoring

Mentoring is regarded as a vital interaction between senior and junior generations in numerous and varied roles. The term "mentor" originated in the work of Homer's epic poem, *The Odyssey*. As Odysseus prepares to leave his son and wife to journey and fight in the 10-year Trojan War, he asks Mentor to guide his family and manage his belongings until he returns. While Mentor's oversight in the situation is less than exemplary, Homer's word choice in naming the character called Mentor is the genesis for the term describing this relationship that involves an overseer and guide for the less equipped (Black, 2017; Harvard University, 2020).

Mentoring Defined

Mentoring, while recognized as a vital interaction, is not easily defined. A 1991 review of the literature concerning mentoring resulted in 15 differing definitions of the process. In a later review of the mentoring literature that was published between 1990 and 2007, more than 50 definitions for mentoring were provided by researchers (National Academies of Science, 2019). For purposes of this chapter, two working definitions of academic mentoring will provide a common understanding of the term "mentoring." Welton and colleagues (2015) credited Fletcher and Mullen with a definition of mentoring that situates the mentoring relationship between faculty and candidates: "Academic mentoring, as coined by Fletcher and Mullen (2012), consists of faculty, advisors, or supervisors involved in learning relationships that provide career and personal development for undergraduates, graduates, and junior faculty alike" (p. 56). An additionally needed definition for this chapter that addresses peer mentoring is that of Brown and colleagues (2020):

> ... we define mentoring as a mutually beneficial relationship between scholar-practitioners in the field of education that does not adhere to the typical tiered approach, but rather supports readiness, self-efficacy, and progress by providing sustained support and networking opportunities to achieve the participants' desired outcomes. (p. 21)

Mentoring in the Traditional Doctorate

In the traditional doctorate, the doctoral path progression and the roles of the mentor and student are established. Deadlines, gates, and identified phases direct and project the degree requirements forward, yet there is acceptable variety in the interactions of mentors and their candidates. When in doubt, especially in doubt that arises because there is no established protocol for mentoring doctoral candidates, those with terminal degrees most likely mentor as they were mentored. Mentors and their students may develop and move forward in natural relationships, but planned mentoring involving set structures and assigned participants succeeds as well (Black, 2017).

Black (2017) wrote about mentoring time and effort that are necessary through the early-to-late stages of the traditional dissertation, outlining specifics concerning the oversight of the prospectus, the proposal, the five chapters, the IRB application, and the defense. Pifer and Baker (2016) suggested "knowledge consumption, knowledge creation, and knowledge enactment" (p. 16) as stages that support the development of a "purposeful" mentoring program for doctoral students. Kram's (1983) mentoring model that includes the four phases "initiation, cultivation, separation, and redefinition" (p. 1) is included in Black's (2017) essay concerning what traditional mentoring entails.

As shown in Figure 15.1, in the traditional doctorate, the mentor serves as an overseer, directing the mentee as they create new knowledge (Buss et al., 2017). The mentee remains dependent on the mentor throughout the process (McGrath, 2009). Like Odysseus' friend mentioned previously, the mentor in the traditional dissertation is there for guidance, mainly guidance that moves the mentee through the phases of the work.

Mentoring in the Professional Practice Doctorate

Brown and colleagues (2020) also referenced Kram's (1983) four-phased mentoring model as part of the conceptual framework for their created "Mentoring Pathways Program" (p. 22) that leads successful candidates to the completed DiP, possibly indicating that pieces of the foundational knowledge around mentoring may be brought forward from traditional doctoral work into the mentoring of students pursuing the EdD. However, research, including research concerning mentoring, around the DiP is limited (McConnell et al., 2021), so empirical revelations in research concerning the transition from the traditional doctoral program to the DiP program are scant.

The CPED framework (Carnegie Project, 2022) contains guidance for mentoring and advising in EdD programs. Mentoring in the EdD should be undergirded by a theoretical framework that serves the mentoring process, as opposed to a theoretical framework in the research of the EdD candidate, and must be saturated with efforts for the promotion of equity and social justice. Mentoring in the DiP program allows for an individualized mentoring plan. This individualization is vital for underserved populations in doctoral work. The traditional plan allows the white male researcher to "interpret the story of the 'other' without claiming responsibility for that interpretation" (Porfilio et al., 2019, p. 117). This traditional plan also favors those that have had educational experiences that provided them with "advanced academic literacy skills" (p. 117) prior to arriving at the graduate school, skills that lead to less struggles with the "privileged, elite form of language" (p. 117) that is required for success in a traditional doctoral program. It is important to continuously examine any plan, adjusting and updating goals, that move all candidates forward.

Figure 15.1 provides characteristics of the mentor and mentee in the DiP program. While those that have mentored in the traditional dissertation may need time for the transition to occur, the guidance from Buss et al. (2017) and McGrath (2009) provides goals for the role of mentor and mentee on the DiP journey. Their roles come together in collaboration around a learner-centered approach to the dissertation process. In the DiP, mentors direct both themselves and their mentees in discovering knowledge in coursework and research. Mentors exit each mentorship with better communication and facilitation skills (Buss et al.) while mentees graduate as "employment-ready and industry-ready" (Buss et al., 2017, p. 1625).

Figure 15.1

Mentor and Student Roles in the Traditional Doctorate and in the Dissertation in Practice

Mentor and Student Roles and Responsibilities in the Traditional Doctorate		Mentor and Student Roles and Responsibilities in the Dissertation in Practice	
(Buss et al., 2017)			
For the Mentor	**For the Student**	**For the Mentor**	**For the Student**
• director	• creator of new Knowledge	• facilitator • accepter and director of the learner with a need to acquire knowledge, to be able to ask relevant questions; includer of relevant requirements in course instruction • communicator; mentor as part of a group establishing "effective communication between faculty members" (p.1636)	• participant in "Redesigning internship" (p. 1632) as part of program changes • graduate that is "employment-ready and industry-ready" (p.1625)
		For Both the Mentor and the Student	
		• collaborators with each other and with colleagues • investors in others	
(McGrath, 2009)			
For the Mentor	**For the Student**	**For Both the Mentor and the Student**	
	• dependent on mentor	• viewers of the student as adult learner • participants in a learner-centered approach	

The Mentoring Theoretical Framework

The mentoring theoretical framework must be a top priority in establishing a process for the mentoring of EdD students. A theoretical framework helps to secure the program that includes the path on which mentors and candidates will walk as they work together. The framework offers stability as everyone attempts to do what, at times seems unattainable. The theoretical framework sets a foundation, providing for equity and social justice by giving all students every opportunity available in order to fulfill the work and achieve the educational doctorate.

Resembling the theory of action as described in Chapter 9 of this book, the theoretical framework provides thought and action boundaries - a lane, or lanes - to stay in, but also provides a way to respond and recalculate in times of turmoil when boundaries have been overstepped. There are so many moving parts in the doctoral process. If each moving part, especially in times of change or shifts, can be examined through a mutually adopted theoretical lens, the result should be a coherence and stability. From this, each candidate will have the opportunity to learn how equity and social justice serve all people. Doctoral candidates will disseminate this ideal into the profession while developing scholar-practitioners, scholar-researchers, and scholar-activists (Becton et al., 2020).

The theoretical framework serves not only as a guide but also as a realignment tool. It will carry a program through good days when all mentors and candidates are thriving, and it will carry a program through times of struggle and strife. Established and agreed upon initially, the theoretical framework must be included, on the agenda or represented by proxy, in every meeting. Everyone does not have to agree on all decisions, but making decisions with the theoretical framework as the base will provide a filter that may be able to bring more unity to departmental and mentoring decisions.

The mentoring theoretical framework, either a stand-alone theory or a focus in the larger theoretical framework involving the EdD, contains theories that are based on the research concerning mentoring; while limited in number, these mentoring theories can serve as powerful factors in the framework and in the real work of mentoring. The creation of the mentoring theoretical framework, resembling the theory of action as explained in Chapter 9 of this book, allows the participants to examine the components or concepts in the mentoring that occurs in an EdD program and determine how those components work together for the benefit of both the mentor and the candidate. There are more mentoring theoretical frameworks than can be examined in this chapter, but some of the more illuminating theories are featured here.

Theoretical Frameworks for Mentoring in the Literature
Presently, the research around a mentoring framework in the EdD that requires a DiP is limited, but there is empirical thinking about several theories that may prove to be worthy of being included in a framework that provides guidance to both mentors and mentees

moving through the DiP process. Kivunja (2018) defined theory, the theoretical framework, and the conceptual framework as "a structure that summarizes concepts and theories" (p. 46) and adds that a theoretical framework provides a "scholarly foundation" and for "sensemaking" (p. 47). In the absence of an abundance of theoretical frameworks concerning mentoring, mentoring theories that may serve to stand alone or combine to construct a theoretical framework for mentoring will now be presented.

Mentoring Based in Adult Learning Theory

Strong doctoral mentoring in the DiP calls for a theoretical framework, and Adult Learning Theory is needed as a required element in all theoretical frameworks for mentoring. Knowles acknowledges that "andragogy is less a theory of adult learning than a model of assumptions about learning or a conceptual framework that serves as a basis for an emergent theory" (McGrath, 2009, p. 105). If there can be anything more foundational for the mentoring process than a well-implemented theoretical framework, it would be a conceptual framework that guides the entire doctoral program while focusing on the assumptions of the andragogy model.

Assumptions about learner and learning in the andragogy model align with the goals of a DiP program. Three assumptions include the ideas that adult learners first, arrive to the learning task with a readiness to learn; second, possess self-direction for the learning; and third, have internalized factors that provide motivation for the learning. The other two assumptions are: adult learners bring their own experiences to the learning and prefer to learn in a problem-based, student-centered environment (Chinnasamy, 2013). Success in the DiP depends on relationships that show an understanding of these five assumptions and exemplify them in all stages of the process. The top-down approach to the traditional doctoral process gives way in the DiP, and the mentor and candidate as adult learners no longer simply direct and comply respectively in the process.

In an interview with Rada (1980), Knowles indicated that, because many adults have been dependent learners in prior learning experiences for most of their lives, moving adults from this dependent learner stage to that of independent learner requires guidance. In the DiP process, this mentoring toward self-directed learning is imperative in preparing the doctoral student for the independent work and thinking required in the research and writing stages, especially as those stages move beyond coursework. Knowles suggests that this transition involves "devising short, intensive learning experiences that will help adults make the transition from being dependent learners to being self-directed learners" (p. 2). Mentoring during coursework in the DiP should include oversight of the learning experiences to which Knowles refers; oversight that may strengthen the adult student's stamina during independent stages of the process and move the doctoral candidate through the dissertation journey successfully.

Mentoring Based in Adult Development Theory

Levinson's (1986) Adult Development Theory calls out as a possible North Star for the DiP process. Also referred to as Life Structure Theory, Adult Development Theory states that we are moving through life via a "sequence of eras" (p. 5). The second era, the early adulthood era, lasts from about ages 17 to 45, and, while being a time of "rich satisfaction ... there can also be crushing stresses" (p. 5). A mentor and mentee in the DiP process most often interact while at least one of them is moving through this second era of life, a period where either or both may be choosing life partners, becoming parents, and forming their professional lives. Mentors and mentees need to acknowledge and work through the difficult times brought about by the "crushing stresses", while stopping to celebrate the times of rich satisfactions that are also part of the DiP journey.

The key concept of Levinson's (1986) theory is the "life structure," which he defined as the "underlying pattern or design of a person's life at a given time" (p. 6). A person's relationships make up the primary component of this design, and Levinson suggested: "We must make certain key choices, form a structure around them, and pursue our values and goals within this structure" (p. 7). The mentor and mentee function in a relationship must include shared values and goals as they jointly work to make key choices in the difficult but rewarding doctoral trek. Levinson suggested it takes time to develop a life structure, usually between five and seven years but sometimes as long as 10 years. Mentors and mentees that keep the knowledge of the time required for creating a relationship in mind will be able to endure those times when the relationship falters and requires time to mend and strengthen the structure, rather than abandon the partnership or doctoral degree.

Mentoring Based in Social Cognitive Theory

Bandura's Social Cognitive Theory (SCT) is the third of three major theories that stand out as undergirding the DiP mentoring relationship. Pajares (2002) outlined the evolution of Bandura's SCT, a theory that also includes Self-Efficacy Theory (SET), stating:

> Social cognitive theory is rooted in a view of human agency in which individuals are agents proactively engaged in their own development and can make things happen by their actions. Key to this sense of agency is the fact that, among other personal factors, individuals possess self-beliefs that enable them to exercise a measure of control over their thoughts, feelings, and actions, that "what people think, believe, and feel affects how they behave." (Bandura, 1986, p. 25; online manuscript, paragraph 6)

Bandura's theory suggests an "agentic perspective," a stance in which "people are [seen as] producers as well as products of social systems" (Bandura, 2001, p. 1), illuminating the mentor's mental and physical path in guiding and allowing the mentee to be their own agent. Bandura's three "modes of human agency" (p. 13) provide an unimpeded model of the needs of the mentee during the development of the DiP. Times will exist when the mentee must be solely on their own in the process, a situation which requires "personal agency" (p. 13). At other times, the mentee's progress will require direct action from the mentor; Bandura refers to this need as "proxy agency" (p. 13). Additionally, according to SCT, there will be the necessity of "collective agency exercised through socially coordinative and interdependent effort" (p. 13).

The mentor and mentee that jointly label tasks in the DiP process as requiring personal, proxy, or collective agency may find this labeling brings clarity and movement through their work. A departmental understanding of the agency modes in SCT may allow for better communication and coordination in mentoring doctoral candidates. Bandura's theory provides a vital cornerstone for the unabated transition from the traditional dissertation to that of the DiP.

Mentoring Based in Additional Theories

With Adult Learning Theory, Adult Development Theory, and Social Cognitive Theory situated in this chapter as three prominent theories concerning mentoring in the DiP expedition, there remain additional theories that should be considered. A text worthy of examination as EdD programs seek to create or strengthen their mentoring theoretical frameworks is from the National Academies of Sciences, Engineering, and Medicine (2019). In Chapter Two of the 370-page document, the authors provided an overview of six theoretical models for mentorship: 1) Ecological Systems Theory (Bronfenbrenner, 2005); 2) Social Cognitive Career Theory (Lent et al., 1994); 3) Tripartite Integration Model of Social Influence (Estrada et al., 2011); 4) Social Exchange Theory (Emerson, 1976); Social Capital Theory (Bourdieu, 1977); and Social Network Theory (Barnes, 1954). A table displays each theory's core premises and approaches, followed by a discussion of the primary tenets and applications for the mode

The same writing trio that led previously mentioned research with Brown as the first author and now publishing with McConnell as the lead author in a later paper (2021), provided a brief but well-explained presentation of two specific mentoring frameworks serving as the foundation in their EdD program. Initially identifying and accepting the conceptual framework developed by Yob and Crawford in 2012, moving forward, they selected the above-mentioned Social Cognitive Career Theory (SCCT) as a complementary theory for their doctoral program. The candidate's self-efficacy and the mentor, through "affirmative interactions" (p. 91) as a source of that self-efficacy, are presented as valuable components of their mentoring model.

While it might seem ideal if all participants in an EdD program could and would adopt the same mentoring theoretical framework, the professors in most academic departments bring their own thinking to their work. The same will be true for each doctoral candidate, although their willingness to adopt the EdD's framework may occur more frequently. Having a top-heavy adoption of a theoretical framework is not ideal. The good news is that, even if people in the room are not working through an identical mentoring theoretical framework, knowing the theoretical frameworks that are in the room will be of value. With ideas around the theoretical framework, we next examine the most attention-needing barriers to quality mentoring; including with each issue, suggestions for addressing it.

Mentoring Challenges and Possible Solutions

"PPD programs are situated at the intersection of the profession, the workplace, and the university" (Buss et al., 2017, p. 1625). Challenges in mentoring that supports students in these PPD programs therefore occur and can be organized in these same three spaces, at times as individual spaces and at times in the intersection of two or all three. Because university mentoring is most familiar to us, we begin by identifying challenges and their possible solutions.

Mentoring at the University

Mentoring that occurs within the physical and institutional spaces of the university may remain somewhat like traditional mentoring methods, to which many university faculty members are accustomed and will bring the obvious challenges: time, ability, and balance of life and work. The unspoken norms around the mentor-student relationship will need to be examined, as will understanding the role of scholar-practitioner. One unspoken norm that may be situated in mentoring and difficult to abandon is the idea that the university professor in the ivory tower is the holder of knowledge around the doctoral work, and the student should situate as empty vessel and receiver.

The Challenges. Old mentoring styles may not be enough in the DiP process and yet they are engrained in us. McConnell and colleagues (2021) determined through their research that a mentor's own dissertation process can interfere with transitioning to the DiP. Because the DiP process begins in early coursework and includes additional steps before the dissertation is defended and the doctorate awarded, the traditional dyad of advisor-and-student-only expands to include multiple people, such as peer-mentors and personnel at the workplace and research site. Figure 15.1 lists identified ways in which the roles shift; shifting DiP roles will present challenges to those involved.

- Students will continue to need guidance in deadlines and university policies and procedures; but, moving to the dissertation in practice changes even administrative guidance needs. University personnel leadership and support in the Institutional Review Board application process will increase.

- Success in coursework does not always assure success in the dissertation stage; DiP stages, presented in Chapter 2 of this book, are different from traditional stages. This increase of stages may be difficult for both mentor and student.

- McConnell and colleagues (2021) interviewed mentors in an educational leadership doctoral mentoring program and found the scholar-practitioner role to be of much interest. University personnel may not hold expertise in the components and stages of development for this identified role.

Possible Solutions. A program handbook that provides guidance to mentors and those being mentored will be a necessity. The handbook should include forms or processes that will allow for more knowledge concerning each student and mentor.

- Drago-Severson and Blum-DeStefano (2016) provided guidance concerning the most common ways of knowing and receiving feedback, including "feedback-check-in strategies for adults with different ways of knowing" (p. 67) and a list of "feedback supports and challenges for adults with different ways of knowing" (p. 65).

- Knight (2016) shared "better conversations beliefs" (p. 21) and a guide for "asking better questions" (p. 91). While Knight's work is focused on conversations that make schools stronger, his work could also be adapted to be made applicable to the mentor-mentee relationship.

- The needs of adult learners must be placed ahead of all other components in the DiP process, and all participants in the doctoral process must be made knowledgeable of and allow andragogy to always drive the process. The mentor should become a facilitator rather than a director.

- Truly understanding the role of the scholar-practitioner will be vital for mentors and students. Piantanida and colleagues (2019) suggested that the term "scholar-practitioner" is much more than the title of a role; it is "a way of being, a mindset that one brings to one's professional work" (p. 3). Traditional mindsets around the process must change.

- An example: As one of the authors was completing their dissertation, they would receive edits and guidance from the dissertation committee chair. The guidance was neither debated nor questioned by the student; it was simply accomplished. Recently, a student asked the author a question concerning submitting work. The author responded by asking what the student wanted to do in the situation. The student responded that they felt empowered by being asked; they had never been asked before, having always been told what to do.

Mentoring in the Profession

Like mentoring at the university, mentoring a doctoral student in the profession may feel, to some, like traditional mentoring. The problem is, and always has been, unless the doctoral work is preparing the student for a future in higher education, the professional requirements of the university professor and the professional requirements of the scholar-practitioner are not the same.

Mentors will need a knowledge of various disciplines in the work of candidates they guide and support. For example, if a student were shaping their problem of practice to address the lack of participation of parents in the Parent-Teacher Organization (PTO) in the middle school they teach, the mentor would need to read the literature and talk extensively with the student and others, concerning the PTO in general and the PTO at the student's school specifically.

The Challenges. Professions change. Even if, for example, the doctoral student is an elementary school principal and the university professor serving as the student's mentor were an elementary school principal prior to moving into higher education, the profession of principal has changed dramatically over the years. Mentoring in an unknown profession will be challenging.

- All professions are uniquely complex, and the role of university professor is no exception. Asking the university professor to become proficient in mentoring is asking for time and effort that the professor may not have available.

- The need for graduates to be "employment ready" and "industry ready" (Buss et al., 2017, p. 1625) is vital; yet, arriving at the readiness stage may take additional mentoring for many.

Possible Solutions. Peer-to-peer mentoring, as researched and described in DiP literature (Brill et al., 2014; Brown et al., 2020; Lowery et al., 2019; McConnell et al., 2021) may be implemented. This could provide needed knowledge in the discipline and knowledge of the doctoral process for mentoring candidates.

- Brill et al. (2014) cite the lack of research concerning the effectiveness of peer mentoring with doctoral candidates; yet also cite literature that reports better coping through discussions around confusion in the doctoral process.

- Brown et al. (2020) provide a detailed description of their Mentoring Pathways Program conceptual framework that includes a year-by-year narrative of the transitions and changes to their model, reporting that "continual evaluation and redesign of the mentoring programs is imperative" (p. 32). During the described process, the model transitioned from one-to-one mentoring to group-mentoring and then returned to one-to-one mentoring for third-year students and beyond. Throughout the changes, peers remained in the role of mentors.

- Lowery et al. (2019) researched the experiences of first-year doctoral-student mentees and their peer mentors and found that one-to-one peer mentoring benefitted goal setting, allowed for more meaningful conversations as mentees revealed needs and concerns, transferred reflection skills from mentor to mentee, and increased the self-efficacy of mentees.

- McConnell et al. (2021) describe mentor presentations delivered to groups of mentees; mentors were doctoral students or alumni of the doctoral program. Presentations were made to first and second year EdD students in the program and one-to-one partnerships were formed. Research questions for this study concerned mentor experiences. Mentors felt that their experiences were positive and included helping them make professional connections, seeing the changes in mentoring that need to occur as candidates progress, and recognizing that mentees need to connect and communicate often with their mentors.

- Group mentoring, a specific type of peer-to-peer mentoring, could be beneficial. Brill et al. (2014) cite research that reports increased "motivation to learn and succeed" (p. 32) when group mentoring occurs. The authors themselves report that they:

  experienced doctoral success by participating in a learning community cohort under the leadership of a mentor who built a sense of community among the group. In the learning community, students can benefit from an environment that provides resources and instruction, supports learning, engages students and relationship building between members of the learning community, and affords students the opportunity to build and share their experiences, lessons learned, and wisdom with one another. (p. 33)

Considerations concerning gender and identity can be made more effective as a variety of mentoring options are examined (Welton et al., 2015).

- An adaptation of using mentor texts in the DiP (Markos & Buss, 2022) may be implemented. This would include having final forms of DiPs from program graduates available for current graduate students to utilize as guides.

- Mentors and graduates could work together to study the research and graduate experiences to determine what "employment ready" and "industry ready" mean in a variety of leadership roles (Buss et al., 2017, p. 1625).

Mentoring in the Workplace

Mentoring the EdD candidate in the workplace may be challenging in several ways. Piantanida and colleagues propose that "action informs understanding and understanding informs action" (p. 3). Cosner (2011) writes of the leader becoming a "sensegiver" (p. 570). Mentoring in the workplace, as a new way of mentoring for many that are more skilled in the traditional dissertation process, will require all this thinking and more.

The Challenges. The traditional role of mentor as leader and director will need to shift to that of facilitator.

- The mentor's knowledge of the student's workplace will need to be strengthened much, as described in the profession space section previously addressed.

- The number of people that are interacting with the candidate around his research increases; more people can present more problems.

- The student may change his workplace during the study; the workplace may change during the student's study.

- There is an existing struggle in conducting traditional research; schools tire of research studies in their buildings that do not impact learning in their buildings.

- There are ethical issues the mentor must work to address with the mentee. One author had to guide a student in a different direction because a part of their proposed research gathering would have exposed very negative information concerning the school. There will be competing logics.

Possible Solutions. One of the standards for the CPED dissertation practice award is reciprocity; mentors and students must work diligently to ascertain research conducted in the building is of benefit to students in the building. The DiP situates this possible reciprocity.

- Fieldwork experiences will need to become a major focus of the work between the mentor and mentee. This focus may be developed through meetings, fieldwork experience forms, or other means.

- School personnel should be assured that the DiP is preparing "research ready" (Buss, et al., 2017, p. 1625) professionals that will have skills that benefit the school long after the research is completed.

- Clinical preparation that aligns with the DiP should be included in all coursework in the EdD.

Telementoring in All Three Spaces

Many EdD programs are available to students virtually. While some programs are completely asynchronous, others offer scheduled synchronous or hybrid options where candidates can, at times meet with their doctoral program professors via electronic means or in face-to-face settings. The mentor and mentee relationship situates in these three methods of instructional delivery as well.

Black (2017) wrote of e-mentoring in the traditional dissertation process, but the information is transferrable to the EdD process. Black (2017) discussed how e-mentoring brings additional challenges to the doctoral process. The mentor is not physically available for the mentee in times of stress where face-to-face communication seems vital. Black (2017) indicated mentoring virtually requires a "more explicit objective setting" (p. 3) than face-to-face mentoring.

In a book chapter on telementoring in an EdD program, Gordon et al. (2005) found in their research involving professors, doctoral candidates, and alumni, that high percentages of participants reported having at least one effective mentoring relationship. Effective telementoring relationships were described by participants as including: "A relationship in which a person with academic experience shares knowledge, gives effective feedback, and provides emotional and academic support" (p.40); while "personally directed support," by one alumnus described it thus:

> The faculty member I am speaking of believed in me in a way that others did not. She believed in what I could accomplish and made me know that I could finish this program. She encouraged me to the point that I believed in myself. (p.41)

Other effective qualities of mentors in the telementoring process included having "effective communication skills" (p. 41), "willing and active collaboration" (p. 42) with the mentee, occasional face-to-face contact, and "growth in the relationship" (p. 43).

Conclusion

Having educators pursuing an EdD in ivory-tower doctoral work is minimally relevant as far as student learning is concerned. Conducting the DiP as a part of the EdD process puts the doctoral candidate in the trenches and provides the candidate's workplace with an in-boots-and-on-the-ground researcher. While there are benefits to this in situating the doctoral candidate, the DiP brings new challenges to mentors. Guidance through coursework, academic gates, and the five-chapter dissertation process now becomes mentoring in spaces where actual DiP action takes place: the university, the profession, and the workplace.

There will be growing pains that come from shifts that are necessary as the traditional doctoral process gives way to the DiP;

mentoring will be part of the shifts and the pains. This chapter has identified possible pains and offered solutions to those pains. Throughout all mentoring components, there needs to be a mentoring theoretical framework that serves as the foundation of the work and an understanding of adult learning infused into every aspect of the candidate's transformation from practitioner to scholar-practitioner. Added to the role of scholar-practitioner, the scholar-researcher needs to emerge so that ongoing, effective research will be situated in real problems in real schools with real students. The scholar-activist must be graduated as well, having experienced equity and social justice in their own work so that they are able to pass that understanding forward in their role as an educational leader (Weiler & Lomotey, 2022).

References

Bandura, A. (1986). *Social foundations of thought and action: A social cognitive theory*. Prentice-Hall.

Bandura, A. (2001). Social cognitive theory: An agentic perspective. *Annual Review of Psychology, 52*, 1-26. https://doi.org/10.1146/annurev.psych.52.1.1

Barnes, J. A. (1954). Class and committees in a Norwegian island parish. *Human Relations*, (7),39-58.

Becton, Y., Bogiages, C., Currin, E., D'Amico, L., Jeffries, R., Lilly, T., & Tamim, S. (2020). An emerging framework for the EdD activist. *Journal on Transforming Professional Practice, 5*(2), 43-54, https://doi.org/10.5195/ie.2020.131

Black, R. (2017). E-mentoring the online doctoral student from the dissertation prospectus through dissertation completion. *Journal of Learning in Higher Education, 13*(1), 1-8.

Bourdieu, P. (1977). *Outline of a Theory of Practice*. Cambridge University Press.

Brill, J.L., Balcanoff, K. K., Land, D., Gogarty, M., & Turner, F. (2014). Best practices in doctoral retention: *Mentoring. Higher Learning Research Communications, 4*(2), 26-37. http://dx.doi.org/10.18870/hlrc.v2i2.66

Bronfenbrenner, U. (2005). Ecological systems theory (1992). In U. Bronfenbrenner (Ed.), *Making human beings human: Bioecological perspectives on human development* (pp. 106–173). Sage Publications

Brown, R. D., Geesa, R. L., & McConnell, K. R. (2020). Creating, implementing, and redefining a conceptual framework for mentoring pathways for education doctorate students. *Higher Learning Research Communications, 10*(2), 20–37. https://10.0.73.182/hlrc.v10i2.1188

Buss, R., Zambo, R., Zambo, D., Perry, J., & Williams, T. (2017). Faculty members' responses to implementing re-envisioned EdD programs. *Studies in Higher Education, 42*(9), 1624-1640. Carnegie Project on the Education Doctorate. (2022). *The CPED framework©.* https://www. cpedinitiative.org/the-framework

Chinnasamy, J. (2013). Mentoring and adult learning: Andragogy in action. *International Journal of Management Research and Review, 3*(5), 2835-2844.

Cosner, S. (2011). Teacher learning, instructional considerations, and principal communication: Lessons from a longitudinal study of collaborative data use by teachers. *Educational Management, 39*(5), 568-589. https://doi.org/10.1177/1741143211408453

Drago-Severson, E., & Blum-DeStefano, J. (2016). *Tell me so I can hear you: A developmental approach to feedback for educators.* Harvard Education Press.

Emerson, R. (1976). Social Exchange Theory. *Annual Review of Sociology, 2*, 335-362.

Estrada, M., Woodcock, A., Hernandez, P. R., & Schultz, P. W. (2011). Toward a model of social influence that explains minority student integration into the scientific community. *Journal of Educational Psychology, 103*(1), 206-222. https://doi.org/10.1037%2Fa0020743

Fletcher, S. J., & Mullen, C. A. (2012). *The SAGE handbook of mentoring and coaching in education.* SAGE Publications Ltd.

Gordon, S. M., Edwards, J., Brown, G., Finnigan, F. A., Yancey, V., Butler, A. Y., Davis, W. D., & Stitt, D. M. (2005). Effective mentoring at a distance: A collaborative study of an EdD program. In F. Kochan, & J. Pascarelli (Eds.), *Creating successful telementoring programs.* (pp. 29-50). Information Age Publishing.

Harvard University. (Nov.2, 2020). *"Kind like a father:" On mentors and kings in the odyssey.* The Center for Hellenic Studies. https://chs.harvard.edu/stamatia-dova-kind-like-a-father-on-mentors-and-kings-in-the-odyssey/

Kivunja, C. (2018) Distinguishing between theory, theoretical framework, and conceptual framework: A systematic review of lessons from the field. *International Journal of Higher Education, 7*(6), 44-53. https://

doi.org/10.5430/ijhe.v7n6p44

Knight, J. (2016). *Better conversations: Coaching ourselves and each other to be more credible, caring, and connected.* Corwin.

Kram, K. (1983). Phases of the mentor relationship. *The Academy of Management Journal, 26,* 608-625. https://doi.org/10.2307/255910

Lent, R. W., Brown, S. D., & Hackett, G. (1994). Toward a unifying social cognitive theory of career and academic interest, choice, and performance [Monograph]. *Journal of Vocational Behavior, 45,* 79-122. https://doi.org/10.1006/jvbe.1994.1027

Levinson, D. (1986). A conception of adult development. *American Psychological Association, 41*(1), 3-13. https://psycnet.apa.org/doi/10.1037/00 03-066X.41.1.3

Lowery, K., Geesa, R. L., & McConnell, K. R. (2019). Self-regulated learning of mentees and mentors in an education doctorate peer mentoring program. *Mid-Western Educational Researcher, 31*(2), 186-209.

Markos, A., & Buss, R. (2022). Using mentor texts to develop disciplinary literacy of scholarly practitioners through dissertations in practice. *Impacting Education: Journal on Transforming Professional Practice, 7*(1), 9-15. https://doi.org/10.5195/ie.2022.222

McConnell, K. R., Geesa, R. L., & Brown, R.D. (2021). Mentoring future education leaders: Mentor perceptions of an educational leadership doctoral mentoring program. *International Journal of Educational Leadership Preparation, 16*(1), 88-105.

McGrath, V. (2009). Reviewing the evidence on how adult student learn: An examination of Knowles' model of andragogy. *Adult Learner: The Irish Journal of Adult and Community Education,* [sic], 99-110.

National Academies of Sciences, Engineering, and Medicine. (2019). *The science of effective mentorship in STEMM.* The National Academies Press. https://doi.org/10.17226/25568

Pajares, F. (2002). *Overview of social cognitive theory and of self-efficacy.* Emory University. http://people.wku.edu/richard.miller/bandurathe ory.pdf

Piantanida, M., McMahon, P., & Llewellyn, M. (2019). *On being a scholar-practitioner: Practical wisdom in action.* Learning Moments Press.

Pifer, M. J., & Baker, V. L. (2016). Stage-based challenges and strategies for support in doctoral education: A practical guide for students, faculty members, and program administrators. *International Journal of Doctoral Studies, 11,* 15-34. http://ijds.org/Volume11/IJDSv11p015-034Pifer2155.pdf

Porfilio, B., Strom, K., & Lupinacci, J. (2019). Getting explicit about social justice in educational doctoral programs in the U.S.: Operationalizing an elusive construct in neoliberal times. *The Journal of Educational Foundations, 32*(1-4), 104-123.

Rada, H., & Knowles, M. (1980). An interview with Malcolm Knowles. *Journal of Development and Remedial Education, 4*(1), 2-4.

Tamim, S. R., & Torres, K. M. (2022). Evolution of the dissertation in practice. *Journal of Transforming Professional Practice, 7*(1), 1-3. https://doi.org/10.5195/ie.2022.267

Weiler, J., & Lomotey, K. (2022). Defining rigor in justice-oriented EdD programs: Preparing leaders to disrupt and transform schools. *Educational Administration Quarterly, 58*(1), 110-140. https://doi.org/10.1177/0013161X211050926

Welton, A. D., Mansfield, K. C., Lee, P., & Young, M. D. (2015). Mentoring educational leadership doctoral students: Using methodological diversification to examine gender and identity intersections. *NCPEA International Journal of Educational Leadership Preparation, 10*(2), 53-81. ISSN: 2155-9635

Yob, I. M., & Crawford, L. (2012). Conceptual framework for mentoring doctoral students. *Higher Learning Research Communications, 2*(2), 34-47. http://dx.doi.org/10.18870/hlrc.v2i2.66

CHAPTER 16

Process Issues

MAIDA A. FINCH, PHD; CHRISTINA G. CAMILLO, EDD;
JUDITH K. FRANZAK, PHD; MELISSA M. REID, EDD;
CHRISTINE CRADDOCK, EDD;
REBECCA L. WIVELL, EDD

Author Note

*After the first author, the order of the authors is presented
according to the order in which their section appears in the text.*

The Dissertation in Practice (DiP) is the culminating work in the pursuit of the EdD. Like all ambitious undertakings, complexities and challenges are inherent in this process. In this chapter, EdD alumni and faculty reflect on issues they encountered during the DiP process and offer suggestions for addressing them. In separate sections, each authored in different voices, the following issues are addressed: forming and working with dissertation committees, centering the problem of practice (PoP) in the local community, ensuring trustworthiness in data collection methods, and designing and implementing ethical research. In the concluding section, four additional challenges are briefly discussed along with suggestions for mitigating them. Though not an exhaustive list, attending to these matters strengthens the quality of the DiP and can be used to leverage support from stakeholders.

Assembling and Working with a Committee

The composition of a doctoral dissertation committee should offer specialized expertise to the doctoral student, benefiting them as they research and write their dissertation. Experts may have specialized knowledge about methodology, discipline, technology, or participants. Forming and working with these committees can be rewarding, but also challenging when bringing together individuals from different specialties, backgrounds, and locations.

As a Medical Laboratory Scientist pursuing a Doctor of Education, I, Christina Camillo, wanted my dissertation research project to incorporate both literacy and my profession. My research focused on discovering and defining the disciplinary literacy practices (Shanahan et al., 2011; Shanahan & Shanahan, 2012) of the Medical Laboratory Science (MLS) profession, a highly specialized and technical area in healthcare involving professionals who perform laboratory testing. The discipline's literacy practices include unique reading, writing, and oral communication practices (Fang & Coatoam, 2013) though they are often tacit and not explicitly taught to pre-professionals (Gee, 2015). Defining the disciplinary literacy practices of MLS (Camillo, 2019) offers laboratory educators resources to explicitly teach and better prepare students to become laboratory professionals.

Dissertation Committee: Harnessing Specialist Knowledge

My research focused on literacy practices in a discipline that is not well understood among the general population and others in healthcare. The classic Delphi method was used to define MLS disciplinary literacy practices because the mixed method research design asks a panel of experts to complete a series of iterative surveys to come to a consensus on a problem or question (Linstone & Turoff, 2002). The method involved the creation of a series of surveys; excepting the first, each was constructed after data had been collected from a previous survey. Knowing this, individuals who offered specialty knowledge in education research, the MLS profession, and survey instrument development, were chosen for my committee to support specific parts of the research project.

Education Research Experts. Two members of the doctoral program faculty were on my dissertation committee. My dissertation advisor was an expert in education research and quantitative data analysis, which was important when using the mixed-methods Delphi method. Careful qualitative evaluation of data from the first survey was important in finding primary themes and guiding the progression of the research. The following quantitative surveys required a different evaluative approach, and having an expert in that type of analysis was beneficial.

The other doctoral program faculty member offered an important perspective as well. While they understood the methods and challenges of education research, they were also an outsider to the MLS profession and offered good suggestions for next steps in the research process. They also asked important questions to clarify the findings and make them understandable to non-MLS experts.

MLS Profession Expert. It was very important to have a representative from the MLS profession on the committee since it is a very technical and specialized area in healthcare. The perspective from this committee member helped with contextualization and application of the findings to other laboratory professionals. This individual was also a recently retired MLS educator and provided an educator's perspective, as well.

Survey Expert. The Delphi method requires the development of several survey instruments throughout the process, and questions are constructed based on results from previous survey responses. Involving an individual with survey research expertise was important in order to evaluate the best ways to approach construction of the survey questions. Choosing the right set of individuals with appropriate and relevant expertise is critical for providing the doctoral student with specific and pertinent feedback on the research methodology, methods, and contextualization of findings. With the help of their dissertation advisor, doctoral students can consider beneficial areas of expertise to provide insights for their research topic, methodology, or writing. They can then reach out to experts in those areas and invite them to be part of the dissertation committee. Experts could be part of the university faculty, a faculty member at a different university, or they could be a representative of a discipline, profession, or research skill outside of higher education. Program administrators might want to consider offering stipends to encourage external member participation.

Committee Challenges

Having the right people on my dissertation committee was important, but not without challenges. A common difficulty for any committee includes finding times to meet, which has been made easier when using online meeting platforms. However, when working with experts with very different backgrounds, managing conflicting comments on various edits can also require discussion.

Meeting Times. My research was conducted prior to the SARS-CoV-2 pandemic, when online meeting programs were not as pervasive or well developed as they are now. These platforms have become ubiquitous, and geographic considerations are no longer a barrier for choosing committee members, though schedules remain a concern.

Conflicting Feedback. Although having committee members with different areas of expertise was valuable, one challenge was managing conflicting feedback. An important way to address different points of view was through open discussions and clarification of certain comments. Often, this led to essential changes to the dissertation to make sure the information was clear and understandable to all members of the committee. My dissertation advisor was also key in leading the conversations about conflicting feedback and they were able to guide the discussions such that the concerns could be clarified. This facilitated my understanding of next steps for the writing process. Although this dissertation research project addressed a subject that was a bit different compared to other education research topics, challenges encountered can be present with any research project. The offered suggestions related to committee member selection would benefit any student embarking on their dissertation research.

Getting Those Stories Told: Considerations for Community-Based Problems of Practice

"You should end the project with the words, 'The human story continues...'" said Velda, a participant in Melissa Reid's dissertation study.

The final words of dissertations carry rich meanings, signifying both an ending and beginning. For the reader, one hopes that the journey through the dissertation has resulted in new knowledge. For the author and advisor, the closing words are interwoven with very first thoughts of what this project could be. For the two co-authors of this section, Melissa Reid, the EdD graduate, and Judith Franzak, the advisor, reflecting on Melissa's development of the problem of practice and research design offered an opportunity to revisit tenets that are central to our work. This section will describe the considerations for developing Melissa's problem of practice.

Seeing Possibilities

As an elementary school art teacher, Melissa had a variety of possibilities for her dissertation research, but together we realized the problem Melissa was passionate about was situated in her volunteer work at the local historical museum where she knew there was a lack of historical stories focusing on Black history. The recognition that *this* was the topic Melissa should pursue reflects Herr and Anderson's (2015) observation that action research is "an intimate undertaking, consistent and congruent with the ways we see ourselves in the world and the things that are important to us" (p. 92). Embracing a lack of Black historical storytelling as the problem of practice for Melissa's dissertation, we collaboratively envisioned the shape the work might take, necessitating new explorations for both of us as a complex research question and action research design emerged.

Decentering the Researcher

As much as qualitative action research prioritizes participant perspectives, it is the author-researcher with input from the advisor who is the engine of inquiry. The CPED Framework (n.d.) calls for a Dissertation in Practice that impacts a complex problem, but it is less clear on who has agency to name the problem and shape the response. Melissa is steadfast in the belief that under-resourced communities do not need another university researcher coming into their community and doing research on them. The research must be done *with* them. That foundational idea drives the problem of practice. If the researcher has done the authentic work of building relationships with participants, as Melissa did through conducting a pilot project in which she listened to what Black community members wanted, then the problem of practice will be relevant and meaningful to those participants as well as the researcher. Not only was it crucial for Melissa to listen, but it was also essential for her to decenter her needs and positionality throughout the research. If the work is going to focus on issues of equity, ethics, and social justice then the researcher must de-center themselves from the process and results. Judi often asked Melissa whether the actions of the project would happen without the writing of the dissertation to which Melissa answered an emphatic yes. This commitment to addressing a problem of practice preceded the dissertation and extended beyond it, requiring Melissa to continually consider how shifts in relationships with participants hindered or enhanced her understanding of the issues (Papen, 2019).

The Local Matters

Melissa's research focus on telling diverse stories came at a time of racial and social reckoning in America. In the last few years, the United States has been grappling with the truth of our racial history. The killing of George Floyd and subsequent protests led by the Black Lives Matter movement have brought racial and social justice issues to the forefront of our national conversation. At times it can be hard to bring this national conversation to a local level. How can an individual begin to undo deep-seated systemic racism? But it is precisely at the local individual level that positive change can take place, in the everyday actions of people who know each other. As Melissa was inspired by the work of Larson and Moses (2018), she drew on their assertions that history is in the present and work in local communities is essential for addressing inequities. Her work is predicated on the belief that change on a local level can be powerful and manageable. In advocating for this kind of work, we suggest the process could begin with researchers in conversation with either professional or community colleagues.

These conversations represent potentially hundreds of respectful listening opportunities on local levels that could then be translated into regional and national change. The questions to ask next are: "now what?" What are the research actions that are logical extensions of the respectful listening opportunities? What problems of practice could be identified from these community conversations? Melissa's study provides an authentic example of a community working together to tell and share a full and inclusive history in a town that has historically been exclusionary and segregated. This research shows researchers and readers from other communities that change is possible through focusing on a local lived experience.

Ensuring Trustworthiness in Practitioner Data Sources

Establishing trustworthiness in practitioner research can be challenging, yet integral, to study design. Thoughtful consideration of data sources is a pivotal part of this methodology. Moreover, true to the heart of DiP, it is also nearly impossible to discuss trustworthiness, data sources, and methodology without acknowledging positionality as another component of validity in this complex process. I, Christine Craddock, was a secondary mathematics teacher who was apprenticed into literacy research perspectives at the time of my dissertation. I also have always considered myself a self-reflexive, reflective, and critical educator who engaged in doctoral research because I genuinely desired to solve daily problems I saw in practice. I embraced what Cochran-Smith and Lytle (2009) described as "inquiry as stance," positioning myself and my students as central to understanding and investigating a problem of practice.

This positionality influenced my overall methodological design and choices for data sources to preserve trustworthiness. My role as teacher-researcher uniquely gave me immediate access to "in vivo" interactions, students, and artifacts, with capacity to influence, direct, and modify them at any time. Though this position can be rightly suited to aspects of DiP and practitioner action research, its concurrent advantages and validity ironically threaten trustworthiness for the same reasons.

Initial Study Design

I conducted practitioner action research in my public high school mathematics classroom. The problem of practice was identified over several years teaching geometry, endeavoring to engage students with often challenging notions of "proving" in mathematics. I investigated the nature of multimodal literacies in mathematics as a means of facilitating student agency in perspectives and engagement with mathematical content (Craddock, 2022; Taylor, 2018). Multimodal and digital literacies were utilized in class to frame mathematics instruction through a sociocultural lens (Kress, 2010). Using purposive sampling I chose multiple, diverse participants in a qualitative case study design and collected data as teacher-researcher over multiple months teaching geometric proofs (Creswell, 2014). Data sources included videos of classroom interactions, two rounds of individual student interviews, a student group interview, work samples including classroom assignments, multimodal presentations/projects, written reflections, discussion samples from an online classroom forum, and field notes.

My choices for the dissertation's data sources evolved from a pilot project conducted in the same context incorporated into my dissertation coursework. In the pilot study, rather than focusing on prolonged instruction, I collected multimodal work samples from a week-long project when students created critical presentations to "prove" their side of a chosen court case using statements and reasons similar to those used in geometric proofs. While this first design still included qualitative analysis of multiple student participants, data sources included work samples from just one project and a single interview with each participant. Although I triangulated sources, ensuring trustworthiness was limited because the short period of data collection restricted opportunities to problematize my central role in implementing assignments and questions.

Adding and Adapting Sources in the Design

Thus, it became clear through the pilot study I would need to mitigate my role as teacher-researcher to appropriately analyze data and prioritize student voices and perspectives over mine. I wanted to ensure I was not singularly creating an assessment that intentionally led to results and also hoped to limit my position of authority in influencing participant responses to questions. At the same time, I did not want to distort or disregard my role as teacher-researcher. The initial data collection had also illuminated the benefits of rapport I had with students and personal connections to the instructional design related to research questions. These combined considerations led me to incorporate a group interview with students to encourage sharing opinions, perspectives, and ideas in a peer-to-peer format instead of solely answering questions with me. Additionally, students were interviewed before and after the study, rather than just once. With additional interviews, participants made collaborative suggestions for adaptations to instruction and assignments throughout the study. Furthermore, I recorded videos of classroom sessions as a data source to corroborate my field notes. Finally, numerous student work samples were collected over several weeks of instruction instead of a single project.

Incorporating a group interview with minors posed a concern for confidentiality in these modified choices for trustworthy data sources. Nevertheless, it was an essential source to ensure trustworthiness by promoting student agency with feedback and input throughout the action research. Similarly, my choice to incorporate video recordings and student-made digital videos with identifiable faces and voices is noteworthy; it was difficult to gain this access and permission for minors from the Institutional Review Board. However, it was vital since iterations of my study revealed the need to accurately capture social context and multiple modes of gestures, tone, symbols, signs, sounds, and images. This decision to include videos was necessary in what I foresee as an increasingly relevant aspect of trustworthiness in qualitative data sources for effectively analyzing social contexts of educational practice (and perhaps others). With growing accessibility and prevalence of diverse digital literacies, technological instruction, and social applications of media in and beyond classrooms, researchers and participants use and produce authentic, real-time photos and videos in meaningful ways.

Overall, my experiences with practitioner research reveal intricate considerations for ensuring trustworthy data collection. My data sources evolved, aiming to accurately investigate place and space while somehow dually subverting and acknowledging my dynamic role as teacher-researcher. These flexible and reflective efforts in collecting data, though at times rigorous and challenging, are also what made and continue to make my practitioner research authentic and worthwhile.

To those engaging with DiP, I offer three key considerations for trustworthiness: *position, process,* and *practicality.* Practitioner researchers need to firstly evaluate multiple aspects of their *position* and thoughtfully consider how specific data sources might mitigate or bolster these facets of exploring a context within their role. Next, practitioner researchers should be open to a *process* involving multiple iterations and adaptations of design and data collection. Finally, data collection must be *practical,* or even plausible and permissible, in the practitioner's context.

Ethical Considerations in Practitioner Research

My dissertation (Rebecca Wivell) was a practitioner research exploration of how eighth-grade students integrated social media into classroom academic writing tasks. I am a literacy coach who works with teachers and students to improve literacy in our school, and for my dissertation I used my eighth-grade writing class as a research context. The dual role of teacher and researcher brings forth several key ethical issues requiring what Schaenen et al. (2012) called "engaged ethics" (p. 82). To balance my responsibilities in both of these areas, I tried to make the research methods transparent to my participants and myself (Zeni, 2012). Furthermore, since my research involved children, I was required to have a full committee review from our IRB.

As a Researcher

As a researcher, I had to carefully consider how I would communicate with the students and families of my participants. It was important neither the students nor their parents felt in any way coerced to participate (Menter et al., 2011). First, I verbally explained my study to my students and answered their questions. Next, I sent a letter home to parents with details about the study and the consent and assent forms. All of my students' parents received a follow-up email reminding them about the study and offering to answer questions they had. I obtained informed consent and assent before proceeding with data collection. Throughout the study I reminded students they did not have to participate and could stop participating in the study at any time if they wished. Acknowledging the power dynamic, I emphasized to parents and students that their participation (or lack of) in the research study would not impact their grades (Zeni, 2012). Finally, I let my participants select their own pseudonyms to encourage feelings of agency and to protect their anonymity.

As a Teacher

As a teacher, many of my instructional activities doubled as research activities, but I also strived to separate the different responsibilities in these areas. One way I accomplished this was to separate data analysis from assessing student work. These are two distinct processes with separate purposes. First, I reviewed the intent of the standard along with the criteria given for the graded assignment and assessed students accordingly. Though coding and assessment were separate processes, grading student work helped me become familiar with the data before I began coding. Additionally, building strong rapport with all of my students was of utmost importance. The energy I put into getting to know my participants as students helped to engage them in the work and build a classroom writing community. Since my study was conducted in a school, protecting students' learning time was also important. The only data beyond what was collected in class were two brief interviews conducted during participants' lunch times, which limited loss of learning.

Working with the IRB

Going into a full review meeting with the Institutional Review Board (IRB) should not be taken lightly. I made this mistake and thought because I had completed the forms and submitted the appendices, it would be a straightforward process. Instead, it was an intense meeting and there were several instances where my design and methods decisions were met with skepticism. Understandably, members of the IRB committee take their responsibility seriously, particularly when reviewing a proposal for conducting research with vulnerable populations, in my case, adolescents. However, guidelines for an outsider conducting research are often irrelevant or problematic for insiders conducting research in their professional contexts (Zeni, 2012). If the IRB is comprised of faculty from varied fields and with different types of experiences conducting research with human subjects, it can be quite challenging to explain the nuances of practitioner research.

A first step in bridging epistemological and methodological divides between doctoral students and faculty who conduct practitioner research and representatives on the IRB is to seek opportunities for dialogue about ethical considerations appropriate for practitioner research. This can be done by having doctoral faculty and students serve on the IRB so that when proposals for a practitioner research design are up for review, there are members on the committee who can speak to its merits and relevant practices for protecting human subjects. Another way to facilitate collaboration is to arrange times for IRB members and faculty who conduct practitioner research to discuss their different approaches to inquiry and how these decisions influence appropriate safeguards for protecting participants. A third way to foster a shared understanding about practitioner research is to work with the IRB to provide workshops for doctoral students as they embark on designing inquiries and preparing documents for IRB protocols.

Practitioner research comes with familiar and unique ethical considerations. These considerations, however, can be thoughtfully approached in order to design a study that forwards an ethic of caring (Zeni, 2012). As practitioners use research to solve problems of practice, addressing potential ethical issues will safeguard participants, and help all parties, including IRB and parents, become more open and comfortable with practitioner research.

Thorny Issues and Unexpected Developments

In this chapter, we have shared first-hand accounts of how doctoral students and their advisors navigated the complexity of designing and conducting a DiP. These are by no means all of the issues a doctoral student may encounter. This chapter concludes with a brief discussion (by Maida Finch) of additional process issues that merit consideration.

The distinctions between a DiP and traditional dissertation raise two thorny issues: 1). obtaining access to the research context and 2). approval to conduct the inquiry and gaining buy-in for the

DiP from university stakeholders. The nature of the DiP, addressing a problem of practice in one's own context, locates the practitioner scholar as an insider, and so gaining access to the research site and obtaining permission to conduct a study could be less problematic than for an outsider. However, although the relationship is already established, it requires ongoing negotiation to ensure all stakeholders are satisfied with the research endeavor. Therefore, rather than assuming permission will be granted, practitioner scholars should approach this issue by thinking carefully about how to explain the study, devoting time to listening to concerns and questions, being flexible and responsive to requests, and keeping the relevant parties informed throughout the research study (Mills & Gray, 2018). Program administrators can facilitate this step by developing materials to explain the purpose of the DiP, how mentors support students, and a commitment to ethical relationships with participants. These materials should be written for practitioner audiences.

Gaining support for the DiP from university stakeholders is another potentially tricky matter because solving problems in applied settings may be viewed as a less lofty endeavor than the pursuit of generalizable knowledge, and dismantling this view requires sustained effort from program faculty. For this reason, it is imperative to make visible the methodological soundness and impact of the study; there are three possibilities for doing this. First, obtaining approval from the IRB offers an opportunity to build credibility for the DiP because thoroughly developed protocols can help educate members of the IRB about practitioner research. And, since IRBs are typically comprised of faculty from various disciplines, this can also generate interest in the DiP across the university. Second, program faculty should seek ways to share doctoral students' work. This can be done by inviting stakeholders to dissertation defenses, encouraging students to participate in university-sponsored activities such as student research conferences, and by holding events pertaining to the conduct and writing of research that are open to other faculty and graduate students (e.g., writing retreats, style and formatting workshops, reference management webinars). Finally, supporting students' efforts to publish their work and, when merited, nominating students for awards are ways to promote their endeavors in public domains.

There are also times when unexpected developments arise and threaten the dissertation study's success. The need to replace a dissertation committee member and a change in the doctoral student's professional context are two such issues. In the case of the former, this issue could arise for any number of reasons, and the faculty advisor and doctoral student should review the contributions and strengths that each member of the committee offers, to consider what expertise and skills are needed in a replacement committee member. By first ascertaining the qualities you are seeking, you can then identify potential individuals best suited to join the committee. Depending upon what point in the study a new member joins the committee, the faculty advisor should determine what is needed to get the new member up to speed and also the degree of flexibility in the design and conduct of the study that might be required.

A final issue that may cause great consternation for the doctoral student is a change in their professional context. Here again, careful mentoring by the faculty member is essential because it would be easy for the student to become too overwhelmed to continue. Some possibilities for resolving the issue include re-examining the student's interests and possibilities for a problem of practice, adjusting the timeline to allow for a period of transition as the student learns about their new context and builds relationships, and considering alternative designs that do not involve participants such as content analyses or the use of publicly available datasets. As the accounts in this chapter illustrate, the DiP is a complex process, not an undertaking for the faint-hearted. However, these accounts also, and more importantly, illuminate the possibilities for exploring meaningful problems of practice. By sharing these ideas, we hope to help doctoral students, their faculty advisors, and program administrators anticipate and prepare for some of the challenges they are likely to encounter in this process.

References

Camillo, C. G. (2019). *Defining disciplinary literacy practices and evaluating the professional identity of medical laboratory science* (Publication

No. 22617268) [Doctoral dissertation, Salisbury University]. ProQuest Dissertations & Theses Global.

Carnegie Project on the Education Doctorate©. (n. d.). *The CPED Framework.* https://www.cpedinitiative.org/the-framework

Cochran-Smith, M., & Lytle, S. L. (2009). *Inquiry as stance: Practitioner research for the next generation.* Teachers College Press.

Craddock, C. (2022). "I thought MATH was actually mental abuse to humans:" Reframing student engagement with mathematical literacies. *Journal of Teacher Action Research, 9*(1), 1-16. https://teacheractionresearch.com/index.php/JTAR/article/view/24

Creswell, J. W. (2014). *Research design: Qualitative, quantitative, and mixed methods approaches.* SAGE Publications.

Fang, Z. H., & Coatoam, S. (2013). Disciplinary literacy: What you want to know about it. *Journal of Adolescent & Adult Literacy, 56*(8), 627-632. https://doi.org/10.1002/JAAL.190

Gee, J. P. (2015). *Social linguistics and literacies: Ideology in discourses* (5th ed.). Routledge.

Herr, K., & Anderson, G. L. (2015). *The action research dissertation: A guide for students and faculty* (2nd ed.). SAGE Publications.

Kress, G. (2010). *Multimodality: A social semiotic approach to contemporary communication.* Routledge.

Larson, J., & Moses, G. H. (Eds.). (2018). *Community literacies as shared resources for transformation.* Routledge.

Linstone, H. A., & Turoff, M. (2002). *The Delphi method: Techniques and applications.* New Jersey Institute of Technology. (Original work published 1975).

Menter, I., Elliot, D., Hulme, M., Lewin, J., & Lowden, K. (2011). *A guide to practitioner research in education.* SAGE Publications.

Mills, G. E., & Gray, L. R. (2018). *Educational research* (12th ed.). Pearson.

Papen, U. (2018). Literacy research as ideological practice: Knowledge, reflexivity and the researcher. In D. Bloome, M. L. Castanheira, C. Leung, & J. Rowsell (Eds.), *Re-theorizing literacy practices* (pp. 143-153). Routledge.

Schaenen, I., Kohnen, A., Flinn, P., Saul, W., & Zeni, J. (2012). "I" is for "insider:" Practitioner research in schools. *International Journal of Action Research, 8*(1), 68–101. https://nbn-resolving.org/urn:nbn:de:0168-ssoar-412864

Shanahan, C., Shanahan, T., & Misischia, C. (2011). Analysis of expert readers in three disciplines: History, mathematics, and chemistry.

Journal of Literacy Research, 43(4), 393-429. https://doi.org/10.1177/1086296x11424071

Shanahan, T., & Shanahan, C. (2012). What is disciplinary literacy and why does it matter? *Topics in Language Disorders, 32*(1), 7-18. https://doi.org/10.1097/TLD.0b013e318244557a

Taylor, C. (2018). Proving in geometry: A sociocultural approach to constructing mathematical arguments through multimodal literacies. *Journal of Adolescent & Adult Literacy, 62*(2), 175-184. https://doi.org/10.1002/jaal.884

Zeni, J. (2012). Ethics and the "personal" in action research. In Susan E. Noffke & Bridget Smokekh (Eds.), *Sage Handbook of Educational Action Research* (pp. 254-266). Sage Publications.

CHAPTER 17

Generative Artificial Intelligence and the Dissertation in Practice

KIMBERLEE K. C. EVERSON, PHD

Public access to content generators (also known as generative AI) such as ChatGPT, Microsoft Bing, and Google Bard has created a challenge for educational institutions (Heaven, 2023). They must navigate decisions such as when and how students should be allowed to use the tools in their work, when use of the AI represents cheating, and how to recognize any cheating when it occurs. It appears that, whether permitted or not, student use of AI tools is common. One study found that 33% of students ages 12-17 have used ChatGPT for schoolwork (Impact Research, 2023), and its use in higher education is assumed to be high as well (Chaudhry et al., 2023; Cotton et al, 2023).

Doctoral students, their committees and advisors, and other university administrators may be puzzled as to how AI tools might be ethically and advantageously used as part of dissertation research and writing. The dissertation in practice (DiP) includes specific elements such as a context-embedded problem of practice and cycles of intervention or change that are not always present in a traditional dissertation. These unique elements suggest unique challenges in creation of policies surrounding and using AI in the dissertation process.

Some administrators or advisors may wish to adopt a "no AI"

policy. However, nearly all students are already using AI in the form of spelling and grammar checkers when writing their DiPs. Their instructors and advisors generally encourage, and often require, this use of AI (McKnight, 2021; Morrison, 2023). Some argue that allowing the use of content generators, such as ChatGPT is simply an extension of the philosophy that technological tools should be used that improve the final product. For example, McKnight (2021) suggested that it may not make sense for humans to continue to do what machines can do so much better, and that it might be best to think of writing as Man + Machine rather than Man *or* Machine. Others describe how content generators might increase efficiency, enhance creativity, and improve overall quality of the writing (Cotton et al., 2023). A study of secondary students and teachers found that the majority of users in both groups felt the use of ChatGPT had a positive impact on learning (Impact Research, 2023). Another study found that ChatGPT use leads to more personalized learning and quicker feedback for college students, thereby improving their academic performances (Chaudhry et al., 2023). While the literature does suggest a variety of positive outcomes when generative AI is used, there are clearly challenges that must be addressed such as avoiding plagiarism, inaccuracies of AI results, and various ethical issues (Cotton et al., 2023; Lo, 2023; Rahman & Watanobe, 2023).

While there are many arguments that can be reasonably made for and against allowing EdD students to use generative AI as part of their dissertation experiences, the focus of this chapter is on exploring the various ways that AI might be ethically used by students. In addition, it provides suggestions for maintaining academic integrity and ethical standards for when these tools are used.

Using AI in DiP Projects

Brainstorming

Generative AI tools are great brainstorming assistants (Holt, 2023), though possibly not as good as working with a human brainstorming partner (Maier et al., 2022). Using AI to help with idea generation can be useful during many parts of the DiP project. For example, the tools might be used to come up with ideas for:

- Topics and problems of practice (PoPs)

- Potential enabling conditions or root causes related to the PoP

- Theoretical frameworks or theories of action that might help frame the project

- Interventions or changes that might be implemented

- Project plans and timelines

- Metrics and instruments that might be used to measure improvement

For example, I wrote a prompt in Bing asking it for some potential reasons why teachers at a high school in the Midwest might be experiencing burnout. Bing suggested the pandemic, low salaries and recognition, political pressures and public scrutiny of teachers, the shortage of teachers and resources, and a lack of professional development and autonomy. Each of these suggestions was accompanied by several sentences of explanation, and some included a link to a reference. While this information is not an adequate study of the enabling conditions of a PoP, and may not be accurate or relevant in a particular school, it may get a student started with some ideas they can use in doing a literature review or conducting interviews or a survey within their contexts.

As part of this brainstorming process, AI tools can not only come up with lists of ideas but also evaluate those ideas, flesh them out in detail, and organize and connect various elements together. By using AI, the student may be presented with more ideas than they may generate on their own, and much more quickly. Often these generated ideas will help a student get their own creative juices flowing and lead to original ideas coming from the student as well. The student will need to critically examine the ideas for feasibility (Hung & Chen, 2023) and potential impact.

One advantage of this approach is it reduces the likelihood of the student settling for only the most obvious idea at any stage of their DiP process. AI may connect the student's PoP to a theoretical framework they had never considered, for example, or suggest design elements that might have been overlooked. One common issue found with DiPs is sometimes called *solutionitis* (Kivel, 2015); where a student decides on an intervention they want to try before they have studied their PoP or its enabling conditions thoroughly. By using AI to brainstorm intervention ideas, a student can be directed to consider ideas that are potentially much more creative, feasible, and impactful than their original solution.

Reviewing Academic Literature

Content generators such as ChatGPT can be used to locate academic literature on a topic. However, this search must be done cautiously, as the results will only be as good as the program's training database-the data it was fed by its programmers. At this point, results are often not reliable, particularly for less-common topics. ChatGPT, for example, and similar content generators, will simply make up the names of articles on topics when they do not have a relevant article in their data. This result is called *hallucination*, and it is a common occurrence (Jolly, 2023; Lo, 2023; Masters, 2023). Students will need to check to see that any suggested articles really exist and that the citation is correct.

A better use of AI with its current abilities, with respect to literature reviews, is to use it to summarize and synthesize articles. If it does have an article in its data, it can provide a good summary of the article, emphasizing whatever is requested. The student can also feed their notes relating to what they have read, and the AI will synthesize and organize the findings, or outline the review. This ability can make writing the literature review much more efficient and may help the students deepen their thinking or make connections they had not thought of.

Design

AI content generators can be very effective in designing any part of the DiP. For example, the student can ask it to design a mini study to look at the enabling conditions of a particular PoP within a context. It can also make suggestions about what data collection or data analysis processes to use. AI content generation tools can be used to design surveys, interviews, and experiments. Again, the student becomes the critical curator of the information given. Because the AI tools can make errors or misunderstand, the student needs to evaluate and refine the AI's suggestions. Alternatively, AI can be used to evaluate a design created by the student and make recommendations for improvement. The AI, of course, will only understand as much of the context of the PoP, any theoretical or conceptual frameworks used, and the unique ideas of the student as it is fed. Therefore, the student must work with the AI in an iterative process, continually revising the AI's suggestions, or asking it to revise to include more criteria. From the perspective of *man + machine* (McKnight, 2021), the student using AI well can create a higher quality product than either could do alone.

Data Collection and Analysis

There are advanced AI tools available that can distribute surveys. If used, the researcher will need to be careful of confidentiality and other ethical issues. However, the focus of this chapter is on generative AI tools, and they do not currently have that capability. Basic content generation tools such as ChatGPT can analyze both quantitative and qualitative data. This process can save time and effort, and can also lead to discovering new patterns or insights. As with all uses of AI, the results will need to be checked for accuracy. Rather than using the AI to analyze data, my preference is to use it to help write the code for the software I choose. This feature can be very helpful when I do not remember how to do something and is generally more efficient than searching with Google or through user guides or notes.

Another way that AI can be helpful is in creating simulated data for practice analysis. It can create fictional survey data, and it can act as an interviewee in order to either practice and refine the use of an interview protocol or to obtain fictional interview data for practice analysis.

AI and Writing the DiP

Planning

ChatGPT and similar content generators are great tools for outlining sections or entire dissertations (Morrison, 2023). This outlining can be done at any level of detail if the software is correctly prompted. For example, a student might ask it to outline a 10,000-word Chapter 5 that addresses specifically stated ideas and issues. It is often helpful, after an outline is generated, to either request another version, or several versions of the outline or to ask for a section of the outline in more detail. The student then can revise, adapt, and feed their final outline into the software for critique. This activity can save the student a lot of time and result in a much more organized and thorough chapter than the student would have created on their own. It is a great tool for a student experiencing writer's block or who has weak organizational skills. The risk of the student not having to think at all is quite minimal as the AI will not fully understand the student's context and project, and the student will have to work iteratively with *man + machine* to refine and create an optimal outline.

Drafting

Using AI to directly write sections of the dissertation, or all of it, is probably one of the greatest fears of advisors and administrators. However, current content generators are limited in the size of response they will provide from one prompt, generally not more than a few paragraphs. While it is possible that a student could feed the AI prompt after prompt until the entire dissertation is written, it is unlikely that it would be a quality product that readers would not catch. For example, the entire document would lack consistency as AI can currently hold only so much conversation in its memory. It would also lack the ability to really describe the context of the DiP.

It would be possible, however, for a student to use AI to write various sections of their dissertation without the knowledge of their committee. If the student is an experienced and sophisticated prompt writer, this would be difficult to catch. The student can even feed in a paragraph they wrote independently and ask the AI to match their writing style. Existing tools meant to identify the use of AI written text are known to be unreliable; original text is often mis-identified as written by AI and vice versa (Ibrahim et al., 2023; Naidoo, 2023). There is potential for the generative AI tools to incorporate a feature called *watermarking* into their responses, a process where sophisticated statistics are used to create patterns in the responses that could not be detected by human eyes, and therefore not removable by the writer unless they do considerable editing to the response. It is not currently known whether watermarking is or will ever be incorporated into generative AI, or whether it will even be effective (Lawton, 2023).

Regardless, any writing created by the AI will require some thinking and evaluation by the student. I have heard many AI thought leaders and educators suggest that students are going to do it anyway, we are not going to be able to tell unless they do it poorly, and the best option is to embrace AI and teach the responsible use of its tools.

Some benefits of student use of these tools include overcoming writer's block, increased creativity and quality, and greater efficiency. However, use of the tools with insufficient student input or editing can result in the student's voice being absent from the writing (Morrison, 2023).

Daniel et al. (2023) discussed the possibilities of using AI as part of the academic writing process from the perspective of *writing virtuously*. The authors described virtuous writing as including human growth as part of the writing process, developing relationships between the writer and readers, community building, identity development, leading in the field of study, curiosity, and having compassion for the reader. They suggested that the important result is not the written product itself but the growth of the writer and the reader. The authors explained that, while these traits can accompany the use of AI tools, the AI tools cannot produce these traits on their own. AI tools reflect common human biases from the data they were trained on rather than the development of new meaning and wisdom. They cannot adequately reflect the particular culture, context, identity, and experiences of the writer. They may not adequately walk the line between confidence and humility in the description of new ideas and conclusions the way a human might. However, AI tools can support lower-level writing skills so that the writer can focus on higher-level thinking.

Revising

As mentioned earlier, students are already using AI tools such as Grammarly or Word's grammar and spell checker. Newer AI tools such as ChatGPT allow students to go beyond this by feeding it a section of text and having the software make suggestions not only related to spelling, grammar, and writing style, but also related to the coherence, organization, and logic of their ideas (Morrison, 2023). A study conducted with predecessors to current content generators found that students who used AI to help revise their essays ended up with much more complex and sophisticated ideas in their final papers (Kim et al., 2022).

The use of these AI tools for these purposes can save time and effort for both the student and the committee. It can improve the quality of the document. However, the final results depend on the quality of the AI tool; and unsophisticated use of the tool can prevent a student from learning to revise their own work. If a student is taught to use AI as part of an iterative process of human-machine rounds of revision, the writing quality can be optimized without the student being left out of the process.

AI and Social Justice in the DiP

One goal of the Carnegie Project for the Educational Doctorate (CPED) is to emphasize social justice and equity as part of DiP projects. There are some specific challenges in making sure this issue is addressed when AI is used in conducting or writing about the DiP project.

One challenge is that AI databases themselves are often biased and generally reflect the ideas and opinions of the majority (Slimi & Carballido, 2023). This means that, when AI is used for brainstorming, designing, or making conclusions, there could be bias. One way to help overcome this weakness is by specifying the underrepresented groups or voices that the researcher wants reflected in the AI response. For example, when using AI to generate a list of ideas for interventions to improve math anxiety in middle school classrooms, the researcher might tell the AI to particularly consider interventions that would be helpful to a specific minority group.

Another solution would be to make sure to engage with stakeholders and communities throughout the research and writing process to make sure their needs, values, and interests are respected and represented.

Maintaining Academic Integrity and Ethical Standards

In order to maintain integrity, administrators and educators need to create an AI policy for the DiP that is reasonable, clear, and enforceable. These tools are going to become more sophisticated and do more with time, and both faculty and students will need to know how to use them. In considering AI use policies, it is important to remember that student use of AI cannot be easily detected, and AI detectors tend to over-identify student-written work as AI-generated (Ibrahim et al., 2023; Naidoo, 2023). A reasonable policy is one that acknowledges the benefits of AI, as well as its limitations.

One possibility is to teach students how to appropriately use AI generated content with integrity. Learning objectives might include:

- Describing why completing specified parts of the project without AI assistance is important

- Citing AI generated text correctly, whether copied or paraphrased (Hung & Chen, 2023)

- Documenting the use of AI tools in the text of the DiP (Cotton et al., 2023)

- Checking AI content for accuracy (Cotton et al., 2023)

- Identifying the differences between appropriately simulated data and fake data generated by AI

For the written DiP, programs might require the students to

include a statement regarding their use, if any, of AI tools, similar to what some academic journals are starting to require. For example, the academic journal *Biological Psychology*, requires authors who have used AI to add the following statement:

> During the preparation of this work the author(s) used [NAME TOOL/SERVICE] in order to [REASON]. After using this tool/service, the author(s) reviewed and edited the content as needed and take(s) full responsibility for the content of the publication. (Dien & Ritz, 2023, p.1).

An advantage of this approach is it both requires the student to be open about their AI use and reminds the student of the need to review and revise the generated content. It also suggests a particular element that should be part of any AI use policy—the author is to blame for any inaccuracies or ethical problems with the content, not the AI.

Conclusion

In what ways generative AI should be used as part of the DiP research or writing process, if at all, poses a challenge for an EdD program's policymakers, dissertation committee members, and students. This challenge is largely rooted in fears that students will not learn as much from the process as they did before AI was readily available. This fear may result in university, departmental, or program policies that restrict the use of AI by students. Organizations that take this approach will need to carefully consider whether their policies are enforceable and in the best interests of students. On the other hand, those that are more permissive need to make sure students know how to use AI appropriately, are engaging in enough critical thinking, and know how to let their own thoughts and voice dominate their written products.

One option for educators worried about the overuse of AI is to require DiP elements that are currently not able to be faked by AI. For example, at the current time, ChatGPT and similar content generators cannot adequately describe personal experiences or practical contexts. The DiPs emphasis on context, then, may be an advantage over traditional dissertations when AI is used. Another possibility is for dissertation committee members to shift to a more active role, participating in the research and/or intervention, rather than primarily editing DiP textual content. In this way, they can evaluate the EdD candidate directly rather than through their writing. The product becomes the person, not the paper.

Over time, the DiP project may need to evolve as AI and modern technology shift what it means to be educated. Billingsley et al. (2023) stated, "Artificial intelligence is affecting what knowledge is, how knowledge is created and what it means to be a biologist, philosopher, journalist, lawyer, theologian, artist or [feel in your profession here]" (p. 453). It may be that our real question may become what it means to have completed a DiP. Does it mean to create 100+ well-written pages or does it mean to create impact, to communicate a message, or to become something new?

References

Billingsley, B., Gale, F., & Chappell, K. (2023). What is the future of knowledge? *Journal of Biological Education, 57*, 453-454, https://doi.org/10.1080/00219266.2023.2190270

Chaudhry, I. S., Sarwary, S. A. M., El Refoe, G. A., & Chabchoub, H. (2023). Time to revisit existing student's performance evaluation approach in higher education sector in a new era of ChatGPT—A case study. *Cogent Education, 10*(1), (2023), 1-30. https://doi.org/10.1080/2331186X.2023.2210461

Cotton, D. R. E., Cotton, P. A., & Shipway, J. R, (2023). Chatting and cheating: Ensuring academic integrity in the era of ChatGPT, *Innovations in Education and Teaching International.* DOI: 10.1080/14703297.2023.2190148. https://www.tandfonline.com/doi/full/10.1080/14703297.2023.2190148

Daniel, S., Pacheco, M., Smith, B., Burriss, S., & Hundley, M. (2023). Cultivating writerly virtues: Critical human elements of multimodal writing in the age of artificial intelligence. *Journal of Adolescent & Adult Literacy, 67*, 32-38. https://doi.org/10.1002/jaal.1298

Dien, J., & Ritz, T. (2023). Generative artificial intelligence in publishing – Reflection and discussion. *Biological Psychology, 181*(Article 108595), 1-2. https://doi.org/10.1016/j.biopsycho.2023.108595

Heaven, W. D. (2023). ChatGPT is going to change education, not destroy it. *MIT Technology Review, 126*(3), 42-47. https://www.tech nologyreview.com/2023/04/06/1071059/chatgpt-change-not-destroy-education-openai/

Holt, O. (2023). Brainstorming with AI. *Talent Development*, July 2023, 24-29. https://www.td.org/magazines/td-magazine/brainstorming-with-ai

Hung, J., & Chen, J. (2023). The benefits, risks, and regulation of using ChatGPT in Chinese academia: A content analysis. *Social Sciences, 12*(380), 1-15. https://doi.org/10.3390/socsci12070380

Ibrahim, H., Liu, F., Asim, R., Battu, B., Benabderrahmane, S., Alhafni, B., Adnan, W., Alhanai, T., AlShebli, B., Baghdadi, R., Bélanger, J. J., Beretta, E., Celik, K., Chaqfeh, M., Daqaq, M.F., Bernoussi, Z. E., Fougnie, D., de Soto, B. G., Gandolfi, A., ... Zaki, Y. (2023). Perception, performance, and detectability of conversational artificial intelligence across 32 university courses. *Computers and Society*, 2023, https://arx iv.org/abs/2305.13934

Impact Research. (2023, March 1). *Teachers and students embrace Chat GPTforeducation*[Pressrelease].https://www.waltonfamilyfoundation. org/learning/teachers-and-students-embrace-chatgpt-for-education

Jolly, J. (2023, January 31). ChatGPT raises misinformation concern: Lightening fast tool can't tell fact from fiction. *USA Today*. https://www. proquest.com/newspapers/chatgptraises-misinformation-concern/ docview/2770823445/se-2?accountid=15150

Kim, M. K., Kim, N. J., & Heidari, A. (2022). Learner experience in artifi-cial intelligence-scaffolded argumentation. *Assessment & Evaluation in Higher Education, 47*, 1301-1316. https://doi.org/10.1080/0260293 8.2022.2042792

Kivel,L.(2015,May18).Theproblemwithsolutions.*CarnegieCommonsBlog*. https://www.carnegiefoundation.org/blog/the-problem-with-solu tions/

Lawton (2023, August 3). *AI watermarks are coming—But will they work?* Diginomica. https://diginomica.com/ai-watermarks-are-coming-will-they-work

Lo, C. K. (2023). What is the impact of ChatGPT on Education? A rapid review of the literature. *Education Sciences, 13*(410), 1-15. https://doi. org/10.3390/educsci13040410

Maier, T., Zurita, N. F. S., Starkey, E., Spillane, D., McComb, C., & Menold, J. (2022). Comparing human and cognitive assistant facilitated brain-storming sessions. *Journal of Engineering Design, 33*, 259-283. https:// doi.org/10.1080/09544828.2022.2032623

Masters, K. (2023). Medical teacher's first ChatGPT's referencing hallucinations: Lessons for editors, reviewers, and teachers. *Medical Teacher, 45*, 673-675. https://doi.org/10.1080/0142158X.2023.2208731

McKnight, L. (2021). Electric sheep? Humans, robots, artificial intelligence, and the future of writing. *Changing English, 28*, 442-455. https://doi.org/10.1080/1358684X.2021.1941768

Morrison, A. (2023). Meta-writing: AI and writing. *Composition Studies, 51*, 155-161. https://www.proquest.com/docview/2841559650?pq-origsite=gscholar&fromopenview=true

Naidoo, L. J. (2023, March 24). *Max. classroom capacity: ChatGPT shakes up I-O psych education.* Society for Industrial and Organizational Psychology. https://www.siop.org/Research-Publications/Items-of-Interest/ArtMID/19366/ArticleID/7457/Max-Classroom-Capacity-ChatGPT-Shakes-Up-I-O-Psych-Education%E2%80%A6

Rahman, M. M., & Watanobe, Y. (2023). ChatGPT for education and research: Opportunities, threats, and strategies. *Applied Sciences, 13*(5783), 1-21. https://doi.org/10.3390/app13095783

Slimi, Z., & Carballido, B. V. (2023). Navigating the ethical challenges of artificial intelligence in higher education: An analysis of seven global AI ethics policies. *TEM Journal, 12*, 590-602. https://doi.org/10.18421/TEM122-02

CHAPTER 18

The Future of the DiP
Both Dissertation and Practice

LYNN HEMMER, PHD;
SUHA R. TAMIM, EDD; KELLY M. TORRES, PHD;
KIMBERLEE K. C. EVERSON, PHD

Since its inception in 2007, the Carnegie Project on the Education Doctorate (CPED) members have worked to advance a unifying understanding of disciplined inquiry in the form of the dissertation in practice (DiP). In doing so, the DiP has become a viable option for a culminating product for the EdD degree. Currently, the DiP is referred to as a scholar-practitioner-oriented disciplined inquiry endeavor that is concerned with "questions of equity, ethics, and social justice to bring about solutions to complex problems of practice" (CPED, n.d.). The central objective of the collection of chapters presented in this book is to provide a resource guide for EdD students, their committee members and advisors, and departmental and university leaders involved with EdD programs, specifically relative to the DiP. This book is timely because, as of 2023, over 135 institutions are part of the CPED consortium. These institutions represent not only a global presence but also different phases of their own program design re/development. Some programs are in the early stages of program design and development, others are programs in progress with no graduates, the rest are programs that are graduating students and striving for continuous improvement (CPED, 2022).

As part of CPED's work, there has been ongoing dialogue

regarding the quality of EdD program development to include "reimagining the CPED dissertation genre" (CPED, n.d.). Chapters within this book provide ways in which this reimagination has taken shape and the DiP has been operationalized. From the preceding chapters, it is apparent that more and more EdD programs are embracing the DiP for their culminating project. For example, there has been an increase of submissions for the CPED dissertation in practice award, with each submission vying to be recognized as an exemplar DiP. Even though the DiP appears to have become more established, and this book informs programs and students with ways in which to approach the DiP, for this chapter we turn our attention to the future. To achieve this goal, we look to identify gaps, questions, and concerns that have surfaced as the DiP is used more and more. As evident from the chapters, tensions exist. It is for this reason that this chapter focuses on anticipation of the DiP's "golden years," when it is no longer a novelty and there is more evidence from the field to its use.

Decreasing the Tension/Increasing Research Pathways

Despite efforts to clarify differences between a DiP and all other dissertations, philosophical and pragmatic opinions remain. This is evident in the range of dissertations submitted for the CPED DiP award. Each year, numerous dissertations are submitted to the DiP award committee for consideration of being chosen as an exemplar of a DiP that is aligned with CPED principles and framework. It is evident from these submissions that a philosophical, if not pragmatic, diversity exists as to what is considered an exemplar DiP. As Perry reported in Chapter 2 of this book, programs are shifting to applied methodologies such as action and evaluation research; however, some are still using traditional methodologies, which the committee has noticed. While several submissions clearly portray problems of practice, changes to improve practice, and innovative products through applied methodologies, many still fit into what is typically described as a traditional dissertation that aims to fill gaps in the literature and generalize findings and recommendations. Questions arise within the committee as to understanding ways in which programs are interpreting CPED principles and framework and then translating that interpretation over to students as they lay claim to conducting a DiP. As evidenced in prior chapters, CPED has worked to provide a distinction between a DiP and a traditional dissertation. However, as the committee reconvenes each year, we also have difficulties in articulating the DiP as distinct. Our own committee conversations are like what Bredo (2009) exclaimed about the methodological debate between quantitative and qualitative. However, in our case, the DiP is juxtaposed against "competing positivist and interpretive epistemologies" (Bredo, 2009, p. 443) and not placed within its own epistemology.

Tensions exist due in part to professional conjectures, opinions, and beliefs about what makes a DiP distinct and, in some ways, more importantly, different from a traditional dissertation that is often based on binary epistemologies. Additionally, tensions seem to arise from the members' varied familiarity with program designs and program development phases, based on their own institutional experiences. Borrowing again from Bredo (2009), if we can agree that "there are as many models of good research as there are research studies that clarify the situation to which they are addressed well and open up new, fruitful lines of inquiry" (p. 447), then perhaps, the DiP will not be seen as a novelty or masked by applying positivistic and interpretive epistemologies. Perhaps, future conversations surrounding what makes a DiP a DiP will include C.S. Perice's (1898/1998) first rule of logic: "Do not block the way of inquiry" (p. 48, as shared by Bredo, 2009). Bredo contended that "standards are hints for how to do things well, not rules to follow slavishly" (p. 447). This leads to the question: what practice cues or suggestions are available that hint at DiP standards?

Continue to Engage in Conversation

St. Pierre (2002) contended that diversity in the educational research community supports building a more balanced knowledge in education. This knowledge is especially significant as the CPED membership and diversity increase. As part of CPED's *Knowledge Forum on the EdD*, several organized member groups, "who share a common interest in specific topics, contexts, or components of EdD program and who want to learn about and develop strategies for improvement best practices" have come together to "strengthen, improve, support and promote the CPED framework through continued collaboration and investigation" (CPED, n.d., para. 3). These groups are referred to as CPED Improvement Groups (CIGs). One such group is the Dissertation in Practice CIG. It is for members who "are interested in exploring, discovering, and sharing exemplar, and/or inviting heuristics which will define new modes and models of scholarship and research in practice" (CPED DiP CIG, n.d., para. 1). Points of interests for the DiP CIG include the following.

- Exploring and sharing new models, exemplars, and approaches that reimagine the dissertation in practice, helping us to consider ways of engaging research that diverges from or even dismantles traditional models, practices, and output.

- Considering actionable points or examples of how EdD programs can build in program-wide or systemic supports that allow faculty and students to engage in reimagined models of the dissertation in practice.

- Exploring and discussing new possibilities and strengths (e.g., promoting equity of opportunity, encouraging new knowledge, skills, or dispositions, etc.) that emerge from reimagined dissertation in practice models.

- Sharing potential barriers that can occur in engaging in different models of scholarship and engaging actionable approaches to breaking through or dissembling those.

Reflective of this CIG's effort to "engage in building a more diverse, creative, and comprehensive understanding of the dissertation in practice and what it might be or become," so is the case with this edited book. This edited book was conceived by current and past co-chairs of the dissertation in practice award committee as a way in which to provide tangible evidence of program practice to engage students with knowledge development necessary to then engage in discipline inquiry using a DiP. This book also provides space for graduates who sought to effect change within their respective settings and the challenges they encountered and overcame when conducting a DiP. However, we need to elevate the work of individual programs and scholar-practitioner use of the DiP. It is from their stories of implementation and application that further understanding of the alignment between CPED principles and program practice will be forthcoming.

Lastly, we present questions for future consideration and discussions. Impact within a local professional setting has been a central point for using a DiP. However, as is often the case with DiP, there is a time constraint to fully vest in measuring for impact. Currently, the DiP award rubric includes criteria for a product and recommendations, which may reflect an impact; however, the rubric is not designed to assess long-term impact. There has, however, been discussion as to the possibility of establishing an award to reflect impact three to five years after the DiP. In what ways may adding an impact award to the CPED award catalog help to advance disciplined inquiry?

There has been much attention on using artificial intelligence (AI). The development of technology and AI are increasingly changing the ways research is being conducted. Both open new avenues for scientific inquiry as research gains insight into complex problems that were once impossible to solve. Furthermore, AI could be used to brainstorm ideas for the DiP, outline it, help design the intervention or "product," etc. In what ways may the DiP be affected by AI?

Lastly, as more scholar-practitioners turn to the DiP to effect change within their settings/contexts, how are conditions surfacing that become problematic for research endeavors?

References

Bredo, E. (2009). Comments on Howe: Getting over the methodology wars. *Educational Researcher, 38*(6), 441–448. http://doi.org/10.3102/00131 89x09343607

Carnegie Project on the Education Doctorate, (n.d.). *Dissertation in Practice (DiP) CIG.* https://cped.memberclicks.net/dissertation-in-practice -cig?servId=9544

St. Pierre, E. A. (2002). Comment: "Science" rejects postmodernism. *Educational Researcher, 31*(8), 25-27. http://doi.org/10.3102/0013189x03100 8025

ABOUT THE AUTHORS

Lester A. C. Archer, PhD currently serves as an Assistant Professor at Western Kentucky University. He teaches research methodology in the School of Leadership and Professional Studies. His research includes advancing mixed methods and improvement science in EdD dissertation of practice. Also, he has an interest in understanding factors relating to mathematics achievement among minority students.

Edwin Nii Bonney, PhD is an Assistant Professor in Educational and Organizational Leadership Development at Clemson University. He studies coloniality in education in order to decolonize and reimagine it with the community, including educational leaders. He also looks at how to (re)structure education that centers and empowers minoritized, racialized, and Indigenous languages, cultures, knowledge, histories, and literacies.

Star Brown is a Dissertation Coach for the Doctoral Program in Educational Leadership at Appalachian State University, North Carolina. Her work focuses on guidance for academic writing, dissertation development, and sustaining progress through the completion of the dissertation journey. Her research interests include post-structural theory, feminist pedagogies, and community college leadership.

Christina G. Camillo, EdD is an Assistant Professor and Program Director of Medical Laboratory Science at Salisbury University, Maryland.

Sarah A. Capello, PhD is an Assistant Professor at Radford University, Virginia where she teaches practitioner inquiry and dissertation research courses in the EdD program. Her research and writing center on practitioner-oriented EdD programs and research methods coursework and instruction.

W. Wesley Cottongim, EdD is an Assistant Professor at Western

Kentucky University. He teaches Educational Administration courses in the School of Leadership and Professional Studies. Prior to this role, he served as an elementary school administrator for approximately eleven years. His research has an emphasis on exploring causes for educator burnout and perceptions of efficacy. He is also interested in discovering more about the sustainability of leadership/administrative positions within schools.

Christine Craddock, EdD is an Assistant Professor at Augusta University, Georgia.

Robert Crow, PhD is an Associate Professor of educational research in the educational leadership program at Western Carolina University. Robert serves as a Carnegie national faculty for networked improvement science, is active in the Carnegie Project on the Education Doctorate consortium, and a co-editor of: *The Educational Leader's Guide to Improvement Science and Teaching Improvement Science in Educational Leadership: A Pedagogical Guide.*

Jessica Downie-Siepsiak, MA is currently an EdD student at The Chicago School. Her research focuses on EdTech, inclusive instructional design within higher education, and practices to diversify teaching methodology.

Kimberlee K. C. Everson, PhD is an Associate Professor of research methods at Western Kentucky University where she teaches graduate-level research and statistics courses. Her methodological specialties are in improvement science, Q sorting methodology, scale development, propensity score matching, and latent variable models. She conducts research in: teacher evaluation and accountability, faculty professional development, dissertation design, artificial intelligence in education, and religious belief change processes. Her work has been featured in journals such as: *Review of Educational Research, Harvard Educational Review,* and *Pastoral Psychology.* Dr. Everson is the mother of three biological children, five adopted children, seven stepchildren, plus 11 grandchildren and counting. When she is not teaching, advising, or doing research, she enjoys hiking and creating art.

Maida A. Finch, PhD is an Associate Professor of Literacy Studies at Salisbury University, Maryland.

Judith K. Franzak, PhD is a Professor of Literacy Studies at Salisbury University, Maryland.

Katherine Green, PhD is Affiliate Faculty in the Educational Psychology and Technology program at The Chicago School. Her research focuses on international child development and educational practices to increase engagement and learning.

Rebecca G. Harper, PhD is an Associate Professor of Language and Literacy in the College of Education and Human Development at Augusta University where she teaches courses in literacy, qualitative research, and curriculum, and serves as the EdD program director. Her research focuses on writing and critical literacy, and the ways in which authentic literacy can foster engagement, agency, and empathy in students. She is Director of Augusta University's Writing Project and author of: *Content Area Writing That Rocks (and Works)!, Write Now and Write On: 37 Strategies for Authentic Daily Writing in Every Content Area,* and *Writing Workouts: Strategies to Build Students' Writing Skills, Stamina, and Success.*

Lynn Hemmer, PhD is an educator, researcher, and practitioner of educational administration and leadership and a Professor in the Department of Educational Leadership at Texas A&M University—Corpus Christi. She has a BS in geology from California Lutheran University, and a MA and PhD in Educational Administration from Texas A&M University. Her professional background includes over fifteen years of experience in the K12 public school setting as a teacher, school administrator, and district coordinator. Her work entails supporting aspiring and current administrators and leaders in the PK-20 setting as they generate and disseminate new knowledge in the field of critical/social justice perspective in problem/solution formation and research refinement. Her research explores the intersections of alternative education, policy implementation, and educational equity for special populations.

Lori Ideta, EdD is Vice Provost for Student Success at the University of Hawai'i at Mānoa. She is also a tenured faculty specialist and teaches in the College of Education's Departments of Educational Administration and Educational Foundations.

Walter Kahumoku III, PhD is an Assistant Professor in the College of Education at the University of Hawai'i at Mānoa where he also serves as Director of the Doctorate in Professional Educational Practice.

Stacy Leggett, EdD is an Associate Professor in the School of Leadership and Professional Studies at Western Kentucky University with 23 years of prior PK-12 experience. She teaches in the educational administration and educational leadership programs. Her research interests include preparing and supporting educational administrators in diverse contexts.

Kofi Lomotey, PhD is the Bardo Distinguished Professor of Educational Leadership at Western Carolina University. For half a century, he has been concerned about the limited academic, social, cultural, and spiritual success of Black children in U.S. schools. He has focused largely on the significance of Black principals for the overall success of Black children.

Vachel Miller, EdD is a Professor in the Department of Leadership and Educational Studies and Director of the Doctoral Program in Educational Leadership at Appalachian State University. He has been a Fulbright Scholar at Bahir Dar University in Ethiopia. He holds an EdD in educational policy and leadership from the University of Massachusetts, Amherst.

Jill Alexa Perry, PhD is the Executive Director of CPED and a Professor of Practice at the University of Pittsburgh. Her expertise focuses on higher education and non-profit leadership in which she is recognized for leading grand-scale change. Her research focuses on professional preparation, organizational change, and faculty leadership roles.

Veronica Ramon, EdD is the Chief of Support Services Officer for

Lyford Consolidated Independent School District, Texas where she has served in various capacities for over 20 years. Her research focuses on the Peer-to-Peer Mentoring Program in her district. She resides in Harlingen, TX with her two children, Noah and Aryanna.

Melissa M. Reid, EdD works for Worcester Public Schools, Maryland.

Leslee Schauer, EdD is the Director of Federal & Special Programs at Calallen ISD in Corpus Christi, Texas. She holds a BS in Criminal Justice and a MA in Psychology. Her passions include supporting at-risk youth and spreading social awareness for the less fortunate.

Kandy Smith, PhD is an Associate Professor of Literacy at Western Kentucky University in Bowling Green, Kentucky. Her Master's degree in supervision and administration and her years of experience as a principal allow her to also teach and serve in the areas of educational administration and educational leadership.

Chris Summers, EdD is the Assistant Superintendent of Secondary Education for Montgomery ISD in Texas. Previous administrative positions include seven years as the chief academic officer in two other districts and 12 years as campus principal. Most of his career has been in urban and rural settings. He is also an adjunct professor at Houston Christian University.

Suha R. Tamim, EdD, MPH is a Clinical Associate Professor in the University of South Carolina Curriculum Studies Program. Her publications are focused on systems thinking and the design of learning environments. She is an active member of the Association for Educational Communications and Technology and the Carnegie Project on the Education Doctorate. She currently serves as co-editor in chief for *Impacting Education: Journal of Transforming Professional Practice.*

Kelly M. Torres, PhD is Department Chair of the Educational Psychology and Technology Program at The Chicago School. Her research interests are focused on international education, preservice teachers, innovative technologies, and online learning.

Rebecca L. Wivell, EdD works for Caroline County Public Schools, Maryland.

Maxwell M. Yurkofsky, EdD is an Assistant Professor in the Doctor of Education Program at Radford University, Virginia. His research focuses on how leaders can help school systems organize for continuous improvement towards more ambitious and equitable visions of learning.

INDEX